Fields of Death

Fields of Death

Battle Scenes of the First World War

by

PETER SLOWE

and

RICHARD WOODS

ROBERT HALE · LONDON

Robert Hale Limited
Clerkenwell House
Clerkenwell Green
London ECIR OHT

British Library Cataloguing in Publication Data
Slowe, Peter
Fields of death: battle scenes of the
First World War.
1. World War, 1914–1918 – Campaigns
I. Title   II. Woods, Richard
940.4'1   D521

ISBN 0-7090-2797-4

Photoset by Rowland Phototypesetting Ltd
Bury St Edmunds, Suffolk
Printed in Great Britain by
St Edmundsbury Press Ltd, Bury St Edmunds, Suffolk
and bound by WBC

Contents

List of Illustrations

Photographs by Nigel Bowles of the *Bognor Regis Post*

Maps drawn by Diana M. Smith of the West Sussex Institute of Higher Education

Acknowledgements

The authors are grateful for assistance and advice received from very many people and institutions, too many to be listed. They offer them all their sincere thanks.

They would particularly like to thank some of their colleagues at the West Sussex Institute of Higher Education who have helped them a great deal. Michael Murphy has always been constructive and encouraging; and they also very greatly appreciate the help given by Peter Allsop, Geoff Elliott, Paul Reed and Geoff Seale.

The authors also wish to thank the library staff at the Imperial War Museum and at the West Sussex Institute of Higher Education for their most competent help, Sue Hughes for all the typing, Nigel Bowles for his excellent photography and Diana Smith for the final cartography. The authors' parents have been tremendously encouraging, and Dorothy and Jim Woods provided much-needed calm hospitality during a week of intensive map-drawing. This book is rightly dedicated to them and also to Peter's wife, Karen.

This book is dedicated to Peter Slowe's wife, Karen, and to Richard Woods' parents, Dorothy and Jim.

Chronology

British Western Front

1914
4 August: Britain declares war as a result of German invasion of Belgium.
23 August to 2 October: Battles of Mons and Le Cateau lead to British retreat and establishment of early trenches along the Western Front. The British sector was from just north of Ypres south to Lens.
19 October to 2 November: Battle of Armentières.
19 October to 11 November: First Battle of Ypres.

1915
10–12 March: Battle of Neuve Chapelle.
22 April to 25 May: Second Battle of Ypres.
25–30 September: Battle of Loos.

1916
(Battle of Verdun in French sector lasted from 21 February to 18 December; meanwhile the British front line extended south to include the Arras and Somme sectors.)
1 July to 18 November: Battle of the Somme.

1917
(Battle of Aisne in the French sector lasted from 16 April to 8 May.)
25 February to 5 April: Germans on the Somme retire to the Hindenburg Line.
9 April to 27 May: Battle of Arras.
7 June: Battle of Messines.
31 July to 10 November: Third Battle of Ypres.
20 November to 5 December: Battle of Cambrai.

1918
(In the French sector, the major German attacks were at Chemin des Dames on 27 May and on the Marne on 15 July. The offensives in the last three months of the war were supported by the Americans, who operated mainly in the French sector.)
21 March to end of April: German offensive in Picardy.
28 March: German offensive in the Arras sector.
9 April: German offensive on the Lys.
8 August: Battle of Amiens.

26–29 September: Major British and Allied offensive along the whole front.

2 November: Major British and Allied offensive along the whole front.

11 November: Armistice.

Introduction

You were part of the biggest British army before or since. You were likely to be painfully injured. No one would have been surprised (though they might have been sad) if you had been killed. Death could be quick or slow.

When you wore your gas mask, and remembered to fix the nose clamp, you could breathe. When you shouted through a megaphone, your neighbour could hear you talk. When you looked down into the valley, you could see the German Army on the move towards you.

Once you were dead, your name would eventually be inscribed on your grave – unless you were blown into such small pieces that you were unidentifiable, or just sank into the mud, in which case you would be listed on the wall of a memorial.

A few soldiers who fought in Europe in the First World War are still alive. They are very old, though they can usually still remember what it was like. The rest either died in battle, died of their injuries after the battle, died in the upheavals since 1918 or are dead of old age. Some wrote stories afterwards about the war and some kept diaries.

Of the thousands of soldiers' recollections, a few dozen have been assembled for this book to provide an anthology of the First World War from the point of view of the serving soldier.

Each recollection, each story, has been traced to a piece of ground. After the story, the reader can take the map that goes with it and find the actual place where the events in the story took place. The reader can see the fields, the woods, the ditches, the trees and all the exact features of where the story happened. The story and the land together turn history into reality.

The overall layout of the book takes into account the course of the First World War as a whole. Great Britain and Germany were imperial rivals and slithered into war in August 1914. Germany and its ally Austria soon inflicted heavy defeat on Britain's allies, Russia and France but, in the case of France, failed in the main objective of capturing Paris. From late 1914 to the summer of 1918, lines were drawn from the coast of Belgium to the Swiss frontier, with the British and French digging in on one side and the Germans on the other. The enemies fought again and again over industrial north-east France and the far north-west of Belgium; the French took the brunt early in the war, the British later. The lines of trenches going through these parts of France and Belgium are the subject of this book. They were known as the Western Front.

The Western Front has been split in this book into five major sectors of battle – which are also convenient for the modern visitor to the battlefields – in the order in which the British took over the front from the French: Ypres, Loos-Armentières, Arras, Somme, Hindenburg Line. Within these sectors, the stories are in chronological order, and a short history of each area is also provided to put the stories in context.

The emphasis is on the soldiers themselves and how the war appeared to them.

Every effort has been made to obtain permission to quote copyright material. The authors apologize in any cases where this has not been possible and they will endeavour to rectify this in future editions.

Fields of Death

KEY FOR MAPS

(Owing to the use of different scales, some maps vary slightly from this key. The variations are self-explanatory).

═══════	Motorway or other major road	⊞	Military Cemetery
▬▬▬▬	Main road	—×—×—×	Wire fence
──────	Minor road	∽∽∽∽∽	Hedgerow or line of trees
- - - - - -	Footpath	☁	Wood
⊥⊥⊥⊥⊥	Embankment	══════	River or Canal
◁▦▦▷	Sunken Road	⌣⌣	Stream
—+—+—+—	Railway	⌣⌣	Lock
▨	Built-up area	⌣	Bridge
■	Isolated building	⊜	Pond or Lake
♂	Church	⊛	Crater
†	Shrine	⥋	Viewpoint
✠	Monument	— — —	Site of Trench
☐+	Civilian Cemetery	●	Site of feature which no longer exists

NOTES

1. Capital lettering on maps indicates features which did not exist at the time of the First World War.

2. Dotted lines are used when a feature in the story is no longer visible but its location is identified (e.g. trenches).

3. Visitors to the battlefields may find these general maps useful:

   Carte Touristique 2 "Lille-Dunkerque" and
   Carte Touristique 4 "Laon-Arras".

   Both 1:100,000 maps are published by the Institut Géographique Nationale, Paris, and are available through specialist stationers and booksellers in the U.K.

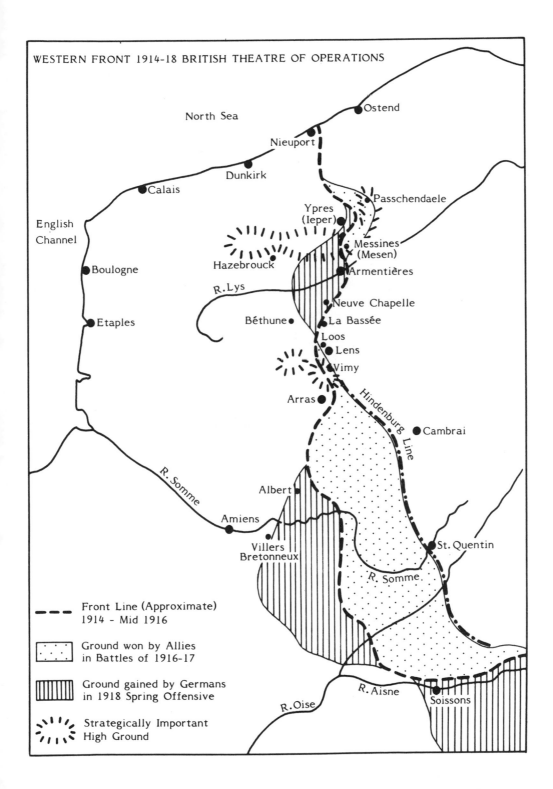

WESTERN FRONT 1914-18 BRITISH THEATRE OF OPERATIONS

North Sea

Ostend

Nieuport

Dunkirk

Calais

English
Channel

Ypres
(Ieper)

Passchendaele

Messines
(Mesen)

Boulogne

Hazebrouck

Armentières

R.Lys

Neuve Chapelle

Etaples

Béthune

La Bassée

Loos

Lens

Vimy

Arras

Hindenburg Line

Cambrai

R. Somme

Albert

Amiens

Villers
Bretonneux

St. Quentin

R. Somme

Front Line (Approximate)
1914 - Mid 1916

Ground won by Allies
in Battles of 1916-17

Ground gained by Germans
in 1918 Spring Offensive

R. Aisne

Strategically Important
High Ground

R.Oise

Soissons

YPRES

Introduction

Ypres – 'Wipers' to the Tommies – is famous mainly for war. The four great battles fought there in the First World War and the soldiers who died in them have turned Ypres into a living memorial. Its name has become an awesome symbol of the death and destruction, the heroism and patriotism and the political and military blunders of the armies which attacked and defended it.

Ypres is at sea level, and the surrounding ridges are nearly all under fifty feet high. The landscape is predominantly flat, so farming land around Ypres needs careful and expensive draining. In medieval times, Ypres had been an important centre of the cloth trade but by 1914 it had settled to the simple way of life of a minor market town on the coastal plain of Flanders.

The Ypres area became important when the opposing armies spread themselves out in a continuous line from the Channel to the Alps, Ypres being at the far northern end of the line. Further north all the land was flooded as a result of the Belgians opening the sluice gates to the sea. Ypres itself became a focus of attention, particularly as an important centre of communications, when the Germans tried to break through to get to the Channel ports, to delay British reinforcements. They nearly succeeded. They got all the higher ground to the north, south and east of Ypres in the battles of 1914, but never surrounded it. The Ypres 'Salient', a peninsula of allied land, lasted until the last few months of the war.

The decision to hold on to the Ypres Salient was political, intended to boost home civilian morale, and not military. It turned out to be a poor decision because it forced a generation of young men to fight battle after battle in a vast plain of mud almost surrounded by an enemy who could watch every move from higher ground. The political and military benefits of holding Ypres were far fewer than the terrible losses sustained in its defence.

The first fighting soldiers came to Ypres in October 1914 when the Germans were trying to break through to the Channel ports. Superior numbers of German conscripts were bravely resisted by British riflemen but eventually took the tops of the ridges.

On 22 April 1915 the Germans started another push, the Second Battle of Ypres. The style had changed. The rifle was supplemented now by gas, machine-guns and flame-throwers. The British were thrown off the ridges around Ypres altogether.

The counter-attack was prepared by the British throughout 1916 and 1917, at Messines next to the salient and also in the Ypres Salient itself. The ridge above Messines was captured first, which relieved the pressure on Ypres from the south.

The great counter-attack in the salient, the Third Battle of Ypres, started on 31 July 1917. The British fired over three million shells in the preceding bombardment, utterly destroying the drainage system and turning the whole area into a muddy morass; then heavy rain turned it into a swamp. Tanks were only occasionally effective, and men drowned trying to attack powerful German fortifications built during the year the British were preparing the counter-attack. British and Colonial forces moved slowly across the death-traps of the Ypres Salient, suffering nearly a quarter of a million casualties. The heaviest casualties on both sides were caused as usual by the artillery and occurred in the conflicts for the spurs of the ridges in October 1917, the most famous being the struggle for Passchendaele which finally fell on 6 November.

Everything gained in the Third Battle of Ypres was given up on 9 April 1918, when the German Spring Offensive was launched on the River Lys, but it was quickly captured again from an exhausted German Army in a powerful Allied counter-offensive that lasted till the Armistice. The fighting moved away from Ypres for the last time on 14 October 1918, about four years after it had begun there.

Devastation was complete around Ypres. It was to become a place of pilgrimage after the war was over; indeed, memorials and cemeteries are even now an important feature of the landscape in the few square miles of the salient.

Motorways, light industry and an expanding town are now also part of the Ypres scenery, but most of the woods, farms, roads, villages, streams and ridges that were scenes of terrible drama in the First World War are there to be seen today.

First Battle of Ypres, 1914

No Rest for Riflemen: 1–10 November 1914

They dug trenches willingly till 3 a.m. or even all night just to get down low. Experience had shown the riflemen of the 2nd Battalion of the Grenadier Guards that exposure meant death. Hundreds had been killed and wounded because they had been easily picked-off targets. These losses of trained riflemen on whom the British Army depended could not be tolerated. Lieutenant-Colonel Wilfred Smith's battalion alone lost eighty per cent of its officers and men in ten days' fighting without gaining or losing a single piece of land. They were starting to run out of professional soldiers.

The British front line was cracking at the end of October 1914. The land east of Ypres, soon to be well known as the Ypres Salient, was in imminent danger of falling. Its loss could mean the Germans reaching or cutting off the Channel ports. There was a panic. The message went out to Lieutenant-Colonel Smith, 'Our centre has been driven in: the safety of the Army depends on the Grenadier Guards holding on at all costs.'

By the end of October the front line was unclear. There were few firmly entrenched positions and some places, like Shrewsbury Wood, were at risk of being lost to the Germans simply because the British failed to establish themselves there when they were unoccupied. Smith was told to remedy the situation and to occupy Shrewsbury Wood.

He ordered his battalion up to the north-west corner of Shrewsbury Wood. They had to take off their packs and make their way through the wood, bayonets at the ready, clearing it of Germans. The first bit of the wood was not very overgrown, but the going got steadily worse. They were not however troubled by Germans. A fine avenue of beeches in the middle gave the battalion a chance to regroup before embarking on the south-eastern half of the wood. There were thorny thickets and an impenetrable plantation of young fir trees in the south-eastern half. In the end though, the clearance was completed with no casualties. It was as if the Germans had wandered into the wood without conviction; one or two were found but they lacked cohesion and offered hardly any resistance. The British were able to establish a line a few hundred yards in from the south-eastern edge.

One over-confident platoon, led by Lieutenant Hughes, ventured beyond the wood. They were cut to pieces by the Germans entrenched a few hundred yards out into the fields.

The night of 31 October was spent digging in. Light shelling made this task difficult. Sticky sap from the roots of the fir trees made it unpleasant. The soldiers who were sent back for the packs abandoned the other side of the wood found them looted, and this added to the misery. One good thing though was that, by a combination of good luck and excellent organization, they were all able to have a good hot meal of coffee and porridge. They also dug two splinter-

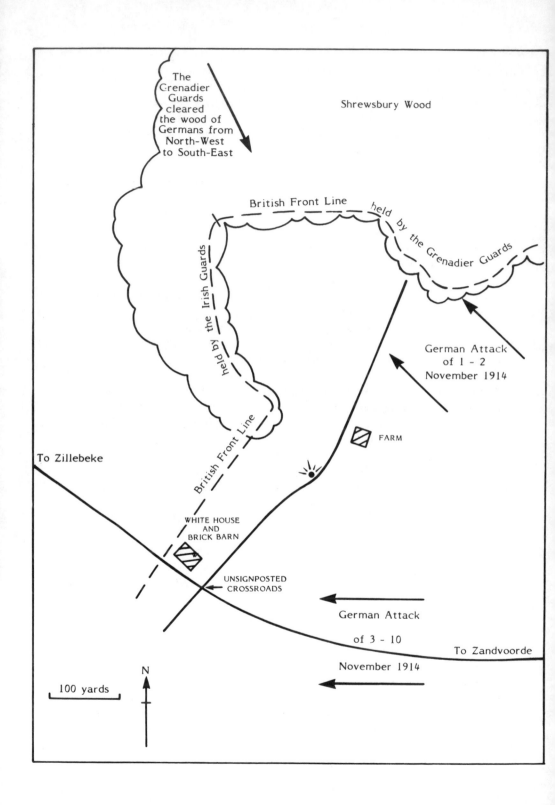

The
Grenadier
Guards
cleared
the wood of
Germans from
North-West
to South-East

Shrewsbury Wood

British Front Line

held by the Grenadier Guards

held by the Irish Guards

British Front Line

To Zillebeke

FARM

German Attack
of 1 - 2
November 1914

WHITE HOUSE
AND
BRICK BARN

UNSIGNPOSTED
CROSSROADS

German Attack

of 3 - 10

November 1914

To Zandvoorde

100 yards

N

proof dug-outs roofed with branches and covered with earth, one for the officers and one for other ranks.

In the early morning of 2 November, while it was still dark, the Germans sent out some patrols and drew rifle fire from the Grenadier Guardsmen. Then a message was passed down the front line in the Shrewsbury Wood: 'Stop firing: the Northamptons are going to charge.'

Shadowy figures passed among the trees. Northamptons? The Guardsmen ceased fire.

How the rumour started, no one ever knew, but before the Guardsmen realized there were no Northamptons but only Germans, the enemy was nearly upon them. Parts of the wood were set alight, and the horns and drums of a full-scale German attack were at full blast. 'There were fires blazing not far from us . . . the position was a nasty one and difficult to hold.'

The men could see the Germans very close now (there was a slight moon). They let rip at fifteen rounds a minute and more. The Germans came on very slowly and seemed to stagger back before the rifle fire, but always came on again a few paces. Their drummer came on with them, beating steadily all the time. Unlike the others, he never took cover. None of the Guardsmen fired at him. It seemed dishonourable to kill the drummer.

The attack gradually died away before the rifle fire, which was so fast and accurate that the Germans thought that all the Guardsmen had machine-guns. Even so, 'they got far too close to be pleasant'. The fires from the wood which had been intended to smoke the British out were eventually smothered or died down of their own accord.

This attack had been repulsed but the Guardsmen lacked the strength to advance. The most they could do was to dig in and try to hold on, no matter how unpleasant that might be. And it was unpleasant.

It was a wet, muddy and cold November. Morale was low because of the inability of the British Army to do anything effective, at least for the time being. There was no close artillery support because of the trees, although at the same time German artillery was also made less effective because the British trenches inside the wood were tricky to observe. The Germans even sent aeroplanes over from time to time but they had difficulty seeing what was going on in Shrewsbury Wood. Enemy shelling was nonetheless persistent, and enemy attacks were frequent. At one point when the Kaiser visited the front, the Germans put on a particularly impressive show. Shrewsbury Wood held with heavy casualties, while sections of the front on either side caved in.

The riflemen of the Grenadier Guards held the line in the First Battle of Ypres. It was because of this that the Ypres Salient survived.

Smith's battalion eventually lost 800 men out of 1,000 and twenty officers out of twenty-eight. The brigade of which this formed a part lost all but a few hundred of its 4,100 men. The German casualties were even higher. 'They are brave enough, jolly brave, but at night it is too much like shooting a flock of sheep, poor things. They have discipline, and do what they are told, but their attacks at night in this wood developed into the poor devils wandering rather aimlessly about under our terrific rifle fire.'

The losses exhausted both sides for a while. The front lines stabilized. The non-stop misery of static trench warfare began.

Source (referring throughout to Bibliography)
J. M. Craster, ed., *Fifteen Rounds a Minute*

Second Battle of Ypres, 1915

The First Gas Attack: 22 April 1915

'A lull in the bombardment . . . I get out my glasses . . . something threatening in the sudden silence . . . a small yellow cloud stretching along the ground.'

The Germans were the first to use gas in the war, chlorine gas. If you breathed any significant concentration of chlorine, it would acutely irritate the lungs and bronchial tubes, causing you to vomit, cough violently and gasp for breath. In a bad case, the lung tissues would deteriorate so fast that you would start to cough up blood and die in a few minutes, doubled up, fists clenched, in agony. In a less serious case, you would die much more slowly, possibly years later, and then you would avoid being classed officially as a war casualty.

The Allies' front-line trenches north of Langemarck were held by Zouaves of the 45th Algerian Division. After a long and heavy bombardment of the Zouaves, the Germans released gas from canisters just in front of their own trenches near where the Houthulst road crosses the St. Jansbeek. A thick yellow cloud of gas was carried across no man's land towards the Zouave lines by the northerly wind which was blowing that April morning.

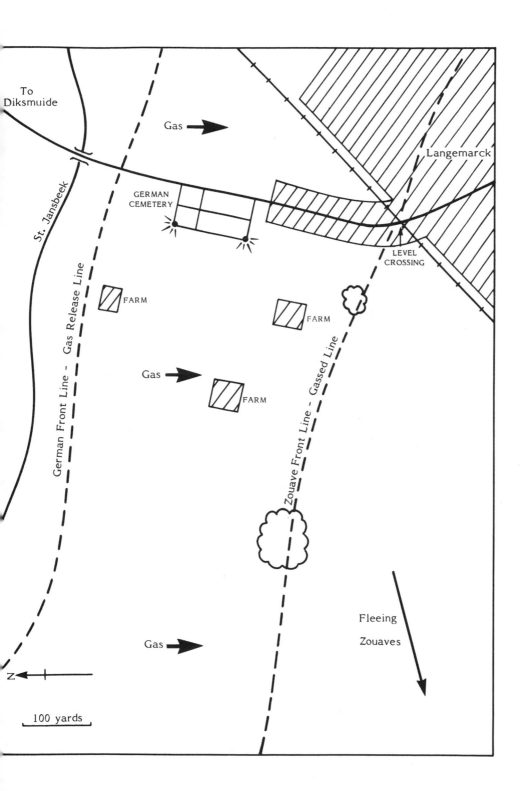

To
Diksmuide

Gas →

Langemarck

St. Jansbeek

GERMAN
CEMETERY

German Front Line – Gas Release Line

FARM

FARM

LEVEL
CROSSING

Gas →

FARM

Zouave Front Line – Gassed Line

Gas →

Fleeing

Zouaves

Z ←

100 yards

It was a terrifying sight, far beyond the most wild imaginings even of troops who had seen all the horrors of the Western Front.

Private Anthony Hossack of the Queen Victoria Rifles was watching from a distance: 'As we gazed in the direction of the bombardment, where our line joined the French, six miles away, we could see in the fading light the flash of shrapnel with here and there the light of a rocket. But more curious than anything else was a low cloud of yellow-grey smoke or vapour, and, underlying everything, a dull, confused murmuring.'

Suddenly, a galloping team of horses, charged past Hossack. The riders frantically goaded their mounts; then came another and another, till the dusty road became a seething mass. Plainly something terrible was happening. What was it? Officers, and staff officers, too, stood gazing at the scene, awestruck and dumbfounded. In the northerly breeze there came a pungent, nauseating smell that tickled the throat and made Hossack's eyes smart. Horses and men still poured down the road, two or three men on a horse; over the fields streamed mobs of infantry.

'Away went their rifles, equipment, even their tunics, that they might run faster. One man came stumbling through our lines. An officer of ours held him up with levelled revolver. "What's the matter, you bloody lot of cowards?", says he. The Zouave was frothing at the mouth, his eyes started from their sockets, and he fell writhing at the officer's feet.'

Hossack could see them streaming over the field in advance of the cloud, running, falling, being enveloped by the cloud and never rising again.

The Canadians closed the gap in the line, but the First World War would never be the same again. Gas and gas-masks were soon part of the regular war scene, and the terrible blistering mustard gas replaced chlorine. 91,000 were to die from gas.

In the meantime, the Canadians were instructed, if there were another gas attack, to protect themselves by urinating on their handkerchiefs and putting them across their mouths – and to carry on fighting.

Source
P. Purdon, ed., *Everyman at War*

Second Battle of Ypres, 1915

Attack at Dawn!: 24 April 1915

'Attack at dawn!' That was the order on 24 April 1915. The Germans had to be kept out of what was left of the Ypres Salient, an awkward few square miles of mud and low ridges which now constituted an important part of British-held territory in Belgium. The Germans threatened to swamp it. That was why, on a cold wet night, Lieutenant Bairnsfather of the Royal Warwickshires with his section of machine-gunners were making their way round Ypres and, beyond the little that was left of civilization in that part of Belgium, over the Yser-Ypres Canal to the church of St. Jean.

'On our left was a church and graveyard, both blown to a thousand pieces. Tombstones lying about and sticking out at odd angles all over the torn-up ground. I guided my section a little to one side to avoid a dead horse lying across the road. The noise of shrapnel bursting about us only ceased occasionally, making way for ghastly, ominous silences. And the rain kept pouring down. What a march! As we proceeded, the road got rougher and narrower: debris of all sorts, and horrible to look upon, lay about on either side.'

Now it was really dangerous. They were within comfortable shelling distance of the Germans in Kitchener's Wood. The rain deluged. Everyone was soaked right through their greatcoats and oilskins. There were no plans for sleep that night, but they did break for a few minutes at St. Jean and sheltered in the remains of a bar.

'And what's yours, mate?' joked a machine-gunner pulling an imaginary handle. It was to his credit that he could still attempt a joke.

Bairnsfather was exhausted. He found the only piece of furniture, a three-legged chair, and fell fast asleep for twenty minutes, balancing on it.

They marched on towards Wieltj. Ypres was burning behind them. German guns bombarded them from in front. 'As we went on we could see a faint, red glow ahead. This turned out to be Wieltj. All that was left of it, a smouldering ruin. Here and there the bodies of dead men lay about the road. At intervals I could discern the stiffened shapes of corpses in the ditches which bordered the road. We went through Wieltj without stopping.'

A slight hill lay straight ahead. On the other side there was only the battlefield itself. It was now 4 a.m. The attack was starting.

'We topped the rise . . . Now we were in it! Bullets were flying through the air in all directions. Ahead, in the semi-darkness, I could just see the forms of men running into the field on either side of the road in extended order, and beyond them a continuous heavy crackling of rifle-fire showed me the main direction of the attack. A few men had gone down already, and no wonder – the air was thick with bullets.'

Bairnsfather decided to lead his men to a large moated farm which offered some protection. Crossing the field to reach the farm was perilous. Raking machine-gun and rifle fire from the edge of Kitchener's Wood created 'a cloud of bullets flying like rice at a wedding'. Men fell all round them, but Bairnsfather's section was lucky. Only one casualty – one man with a bullet through his knee.

It was now quite light. Early dawn combined with masses of German star-shells to light up the battlefield. Infantry were rushing German positions and were keeping the enemy on the edge of Kitchener's Wood. There was little or no advance but attacks like this at least were stopping the Germans encroaching on the salient. Bairnsfather's machine-gunners waited in a gully next to the farm (which was now in the process of being blown to smithereens) and wondered where to go next.

Then they saw their chance. They spotted a disused trench halfway across the first field going from the farm towards the German front line in the wood. They ran to it, amazingly with no casualties, and set up the guns.

Meanwhile, Bairnsfather's ammunition-carriers and one of his gun teams were still trying to reach the farm. With their heavy loads they were having a terrible time. Bairnsfather started back to find them and hurry them along. Soon he got enough ammunition up to the trench for the corporal in charge to start firing. He went back for the gun team.

Bairnsfather was more exhausted from lack of sleep and non-stop tension than he had ever been in his life. On his way back for the missing gun team he tried to help carry a wounded Canadian officer to a temporary dressing-station established in one of the farm's outbuildings. Bairnsfather very nearly collapsed. 'I couldn't stand up any longer. I lay down on the side of the moat for five minutes. Twenty yards away the shells burst round and in the farm, but I didn't care, rest was all I wanted.'

He would soon get all the rest he needed.

He ran to the farm which by now was virtually destroyed. He staggered towards the field, starting back the way he had originally come. No signs of the missing gun team, and it looked as if the others he had just left were right in the worst of it now. Despair. Exhaustion.

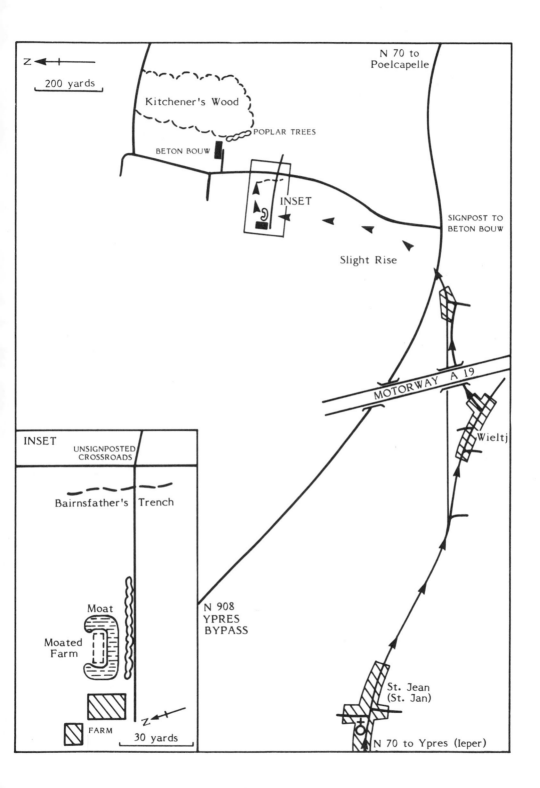

Z ← |——→
200 yards

N 70 to
Poelcapelle

Kitchener's Wood

POPLAR TREES

BETON BOUW

INSET

SIGNPOST TO
BETON BOUW

Slight Rise

MOTORWAY A 19

Wieltj

INSET

UNSIGNPOSTED
CROSSROADS

Bairnsfather's Trench

Moat

Moated
Farm

N 908
YPRES
BYPASS

FARM

Z ← |——

30 yards

St. Jean
(St. Jan)

N 70 to Ypres (Ieper)

All round him Bairnsfather heard the ponderous, gurgling, rotating sound of heavy shells. Men, buildings and rubble were being blown up. Then he heard a shell coming straight for him. But he never heard the explosion.

'All seemed dull and foggy; a sort of silence, worse than all the shelling, surrounded me. I lay in a filthy stagnant ditch covered with mud and slime from head to foot. I suddenly started to tremble all over. I couldn't grasp where I was. I lay and trembled . . . I had been blown up by a shell.'

Bairnsfather survived, with head and arm injuries, but his war was at an end. The Ypres Salient also survived the battle.

Source
B. Bairnsfather, *Bullets and Billets*

Second Battle of Ypres, *1915*

Disorganization and Death: 16 June 1915

'I am quite well, but don't feel so. On the 16th we supped full of horrors, and I feel almost competent to write another story of the descent into Hell.' Private Henry Clapham, Honourable Artillery Company.

The first officer to die was the adjutant. They had not yet reached the railway cutting on the way to Hell Fire Corner when they broke for lunch, and a burst of shrapnel during the halt finished the adjutant.

They made their way to some shallow support trenches a few yards back from the front line and waited miserably for 4.15 a.m. the next morning, 16 June, for the attack. The whistle blew the first time: front-line troops moved out and Henry Clapham and his comrades moved up to the front line. At this time the bombardment seemed to be concentrating on a building a hundred yards in the rear, so they felt relatively safe.

The whistle blew the second time: an officer in front of Clapham who was calling him to advance was struck down, but Clapham and the other men managed to clamber out of the front-line trench and into a small grassy field. With his too-heavy pack he was able only to amble down a footpath across a field to the now undefended German front line in Y Wood. He was fortunate to escape the raking German

machine-gun fire which had cut down other men and officers from
his section.

They were now faced with the task of turning the German trench
round, so it could be defended against a German counter-attack.
There was no preparation for this dangerous manœuvre. The artillery had not made any serious impact on German machine-gun
emplacements or on German artillery. Everyone who participated in
preparing that trench knew that their chance of survival was fifty-
fifty at best.

Barbed wire and sandbags had to be shifted urgently across the
trench. German machine-guns riddled many of Clapham's friends.
Among them was one youngster bowled over almost at once with a
bullet in the groin; he lay in the trench, kicking and shrieking,
ignored while all round him the feverish work went on regardless.

When all the defences had been turned, the trench had to be
deepened and improved. Clapham had just filled a sandbag:

'. . . when I happened to glance down, and saw a slight movement
in the earth between my feet. I stooped and scraped away the soil
with my fingers and found what seemed like palpitating flesh. It
proved to be a man's cheek, and a few minutes' work uncovered his
head. I poured a little water down his throat, and two or three of us
dug out the rest of him. He was undamaged except for his feet and
ankles, which were a mass of pulp, and he recovered consciousness as
we worked.' He turned out to be a German buried alive in the earlier
British bombardment. He told Clapham he was forty-five and had
been a soldier only a fortnight . . .

'We dragged him out and laid him under the hedge. There was
nothing else we could do for him. He had another drink later, but he
must have died in the course of the day. I'm afraid we forgot all about
him, but nothing could have lived there till evening.' The German
died out in the open, and Clapham's captain fell next to him with a
bullet in the lung.

The horrors were by no means over.

'When we had got our big Hun out, he left a big hole in the ground,
and we found a dead arm and hand projecting from the bottom. We
dug about but did not seem to be able to find the body, and when I
seized the sleeve and pulled, the arm came out of the ground by itself.
We had to dig deeper for our own sake, but there was nothing else
left, except messy earth, which seemed to have been driven into
the side of the trench. The man helping me turned sick, for it
wasn't pretty work, but I claimed a substitute, and between us we
carted out a barrowful in wetter sheets and dumped it under the
hedge.'

Then Clapham himself was sick. He sat down at the bottom of the trench but the shelling got worse, and a sandbag was shaken off the top of the parapet of the trench and landed squarely on his head. It nearly broke his neck and he got quite nasty concussion.

If things could hardly have been worse than in Clapham's trench in Y Wood, the experiences of the survivors of the original front line, as they ran back mumbling '. . . gas', were at least comparable. The day was burning hot. They were utterly exhausted. They had been torn to pieces in the attack. Their weapons were clogged with dust and they were gassed at a time when gas was a new and terrifying super-weapon. They had fled and rested by the hedge near Clapham's trench, but the hedge had been blown to pieces and twenty men were killed by a single shell. The survivors scrambled across the field to the original front line, bullets flying everywhere, only to be turned round by the officers of another regiment who threatened to shoot them dead with their revolvers if they continued to flee. Some finished up in despair in Clapham's trench. 'They crowded into our trench', Clapham recalled, 'until there was hardly room to move a limb.'

No sooner was the trench crammed full of men than: 'About 6 p.m. the worst moment of the day came. The Huns started to bombard us with a shell which was quite new to us. It sounded like a gigantic fire-cracker with two distinct explosions. These shells came just above the parapet, in a flood, much more quickly than we could count them. After a quarter of an hour of this sort of thing, there was a sudden crash in a trench and ten feet of the parapet, just beyond me, was blown away and everyone around blinded by dust. With my first glance I saw what looked like half a dozen bodies, mingled with sandbags, and then I smelt gas and realised that these were gas shells. Clapham and most of the men had their respirators on in no time. But a few were slower. One man was sick all over the sandbags and another was coughing his heart up. We pulled four men out of the debris unharmed. One man was unconscious, and died of gas later. Another was hopelessly smashed up and must have got it full in the chest.'

The gas attack lasted about a quarter of an hour, and then the fire-cracker shelling started again.

Yet all the time since 5.30 in the morning, when he had played his part in turning the defences of the trench, Clapham had been called upon to do absolutely nothing but be an unwilling target for everything the Germans could think of to injure him or kill him. He and his comrades had been told to look out for one enemy counter-attack which never materialized, and once a crazed major had ordered some men forward – twenty had gone and been killed but the others ignored the order. Otherwise they had just sat, hoping for a painless

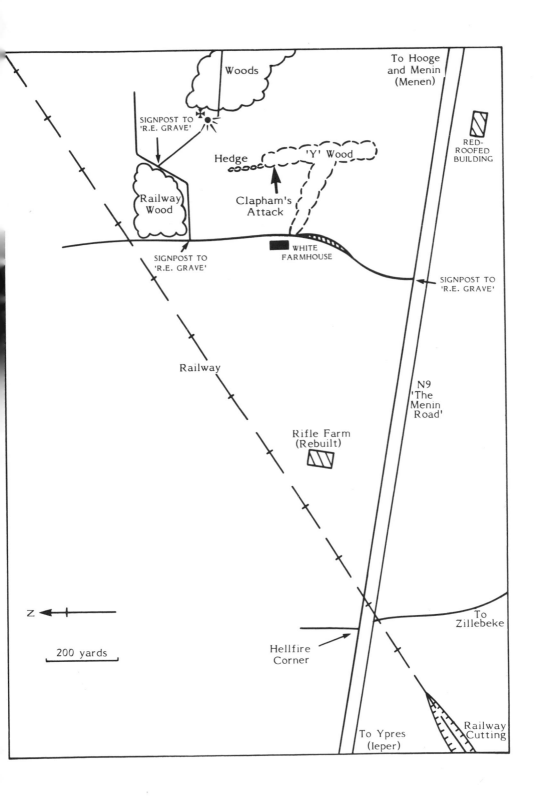

Woods

To Hooge
and Menin
(Menen)

RED-
ROOFED
BUILDING

SIGNPOST TO
'R.E. GRAVE'

Hedge   'Y' Wood

Railway
Wood

Clapham's
Attack

SIGNPOST TO
'R.E. GRAVE'

WHITE
FARMHOUSE

SIGNPOST TO
'R.E. GRAVE'

Railway

N9
'The
Menin
Road'

Rifle Farm
(Rebuilt)

Z

200 yards

To
Zillebeke

Hellfire
Corner

To Ypres
(Ieper)

Railway
Cutting

death or for a wound that would get them out of the line as soon as possible.

Clapham was lucky in the end: 'No relief turned up, and about midnight two volunteers were asked for, to carry to the dressing-station a boy prisoner whose leg was smashed. There was consider-able competition for the job, as we were told that the men selected could go on to the rear afterwards. A Fusilier and I were the lucky ones.' They managed to make a kind of splint and tied the boy's legs together, but as soon as they started moving him, he started scream-ing and screaming until he fainted.

After a struggle across gas-filled shell-holes, they hauled their pathetic burden over to a medical orderly and headed for Hell Fire Corner, where a dressing-station had been set up. Here, after a while, they were joined by others from Clapham's company and other Fusiliers, and headed back to rest-billets.

It transpired that the day's battle was seen as a success. There had been a definite advance. The Honourable Artillery Company had acquitted itself well: We were congratulated and patted on the back, and told that we had done very good work, and that next time we should have a chance on our own. What luck! . . . The regulars cannot understand that we are not soldiers and that we don't want to be soldiers, and though we shall carry on as well as we can, we don't like it, and are not in the least degree pleased at the prospect of a "brush with the Hun".'

The next day, the Brigadier turned up. 'We were all lying about, half-asleep . . . He wound up by saying that troops that could stand that shelling could not be broken, and that he was afraid that we would have to go back into the trenches almost at once.'

Source
H. S. Clapham, *Mud and Khaki*

Battle of Hooge, 1915

The First Flame Attack: 30 July 1915

Flame-throwers were used for the first time against the British at Hooge Crater. Surprise was complete and effective.

In the first few months of the war the Germans had on one or two occasions sprayed petrol over the French in their trenches and, with great difficulty, set light to it with incendiary shells. The Germans had even tested out a flame-thrower on the French but it had not been very effective.

Hooge Crater lay between the German and British front lines established after the Second Battle of Ypres. It had been created by a British mine which had blown up a German position. Once the position had been transformed into a lifeless crater – it took about ten seconds – the British occupied it and dug a narrow defensive trench on the north side of it, just fifteen yards from German lines. Heaps of rubble lay around, all that remained of Hooge Château and its outbuildings.

At one point the German and British lines actually met at the end of a former German communication trench. Only a makeshift barrier lay between the two sides, whose sentries crouched and peered at each other a few yards away through periscopes. Two British attempts to oust the Germans had ended in failure. A number of dead bodies were strewn about the disputed few yards of the trench.

On 29 July the 8th Battalion of the Rifle Brigade took over the front line at Hooge. This was their first taste of action. They crowded into the narrow trench to the north of Hooge Crater. There were no fortifications in depth there, just one tightly packed line.

At 3.15 a.m. on 30 July, the German infantry lifted the nozzles of their flame-throwers over the edge of their main front-line trench fifteen yards away and directed them towards the one thin line of British riflemen. There was a loud hiss as they were ignited. A few seconds later, four jets of liquid flame came out of no man's land. First, the young British riflemen's clothes caught fire, then their hair. Soon the flesh burnt off their writhing bodies. The ghastly shrieks of a sudden and horribly painful death mingled with the fierce shouts of charging infantry as the German infantry entered the British trench. The few survivors of the terrible incineration were bayoneted.

No one defending the north of Hooge Crater survived. The shocking effect on the morale of those who witnessed the flame attack from the trenches nearby could be imagined.

'We first heard sounds as of a splashing to our front, then there was a peculiar smoky smell just like coal-tar; next a corporal of C Company cried out that he had been hit by a shell; yet when we went to look at him we found that a huge blister as from a burn was on his forehead, while the back of his cap was smouldering. We had no time to notice anything else, for after that preliminary trial the Boches loosened their liquid fire upon us with a vengeance.'

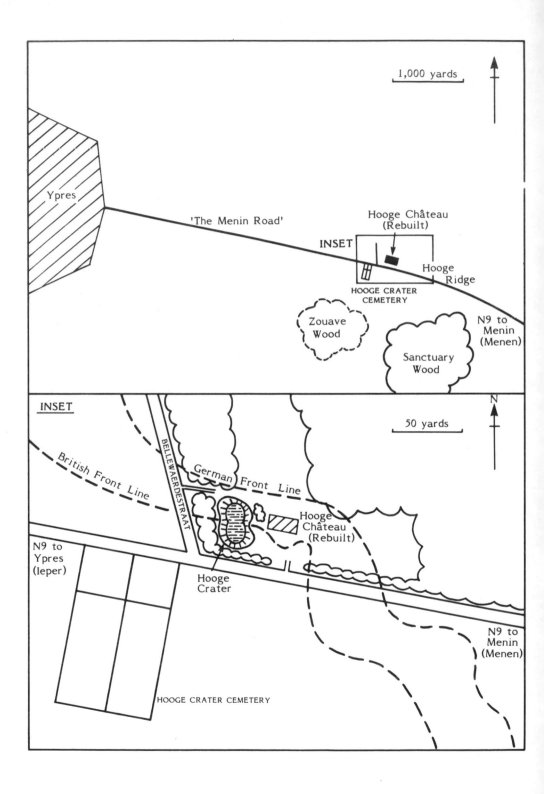

1,000 yards

Ypres

'The Menin Road'

Hooge Château
(Rebuilt)

INSET

Hooge
Ridge

HOOGE CRATER
CEMETERY

Zouave
Wood

N9 to
Menin
(Menen)

Sanctuary
Wood

INSET

N

50 yards

British Front Line

BELLEWAERDESTRAAT

German Front Line

Hooge
Château
(Rebuilt)

N9 to
Ypres
(Ieper)

Hooge
Crater

N9 to
Menin
(Menen)

HOOGE CRATER CEMETERY

Lieutenant G. V. Carey watched the whole attack – it lasted only about forty-five seconds.

'There was a sudden hissing sound, and a bright crimson glare over the crater turned the whole scene red. As I looked, I saw three or four distinct jets of flame, like a line of powerful firehoses spraying fire instead of water, shoot across my fire trench. How long this lasted it is impossible to say, probably not more than a minute, but the effect was so stupefying that I was utterly unable for some moments to think correctly . . . Those who faced the flame attack were never seen again.'

Once they were in Hooge Crater, the German infantry fanned out and bombed their way into the British trench system. The British, who had seen the flame attack from trenches either side of Hooge, fled at once. The Germans pursued them as far as Zouave and Sanctuary Woods, taking a strategically important bite of high ground out of the British line. They were unable to get near enough to the British to use their flame-throwers again.

The next day there was an attempt at a counter-attack from Zouave Wood, but it was a disaster. The men had been at Hooge and they were still badly shocked. Most were forced forward out of the wood but none got further than fifty yards. As they tried to find their way through barbed-wire entanglements, they were killed.

Source
J. Hammerton, ed., *I Was There!*

Preparations for the Battle of Messines, 1916

Construction Work Under Fire:
4 April to 12 July 1916

Lieutenant H. Russell was killed by machine-gun fire from Hollandescheschur Farm on 12 July 1916. He had been a sergeant when war broke and, after a spell as regimental sergeant-major, he had been commissioned. He always tended to be cheerful and he was an officer who got on well with the infantry working parties he commanded – after all, he had risen from the ranks and knew pretty well how they felt night after sweating night, under murderous fire. He had just finished supervising the construction of Stuart Trench (named after another officer just killed) when he was caught by a German machine-gun.

The plan was to capture the Messines Ridge in the summer of 1916. In the event, there was a whole year's delay but Lieutenant Russell and the 7th Field Company of the Royal Engineers certainly never knew about that.

The attack would need a good support trench and safe communication trenches leading up to them. In the sector opposite Grande Bois and Bois Quarante, the 7th Field Company had the responsibility of making these necessary preparations.

The whole area was overlooked by Germans on the ridge. No one had stayed out in the open for long, even before the huge mine blew a few miles north at St. Eloi on 27 March. Afterwards, the enemy got much fiercer. The St. Eloi mine had exploded under German defences and killed a great many men; it had, not surprisingly, made the Germans everywhere very suspicious of any digging activities, of which they had tended to take very little notice until that time, preferring to concentrate on their own defences. Now the machine-guns at Grande Bois, Bois Quarante and Hollandescheschur Farm let rip whenever they saw signs of activity. They certainly had reason to be suspicious, for the front line did indeed contain a deep mine which was slowly advancing towards German defences.

Lieutenant Russell and his platoon, assisted by infantry drafted in, took some four weeks to build a support line about fifty yards behind the front line, with dug-out and strong wire. Shelters more than two feet six inches high were difficult to build, so the support line would never be comfortable but would at least be reasonably safe for assault troops for the great attack envisaged.

It was the construction of the communication trenches up to the front line that was really dangerous. Casualties were in double figures every night as solid revetements were laboriously built along 'Poppy Lane' and 'Stuart Trench' extending across the wet valley of the Wijtschaatsebeek. Any stray bullet flying over the front line was liable to be stopped by a construction worker in the communication trenches, even when German artillery and machine-guns were silent.

The machine-gunning in particular was so bad by the middle of June that work had almost stopped. Two sections of field guns were brought up as special protection. From then on, whenever a machine-gun started up, a signaller with the working parties would flash a coded signal with his lamp, and the artillery would fire at the offending machine-gun. This worked well and digging resumed.

Still, the Germans knew where to aim and they took their toll. One NCO carried on working after a bullet had gone through his cap,

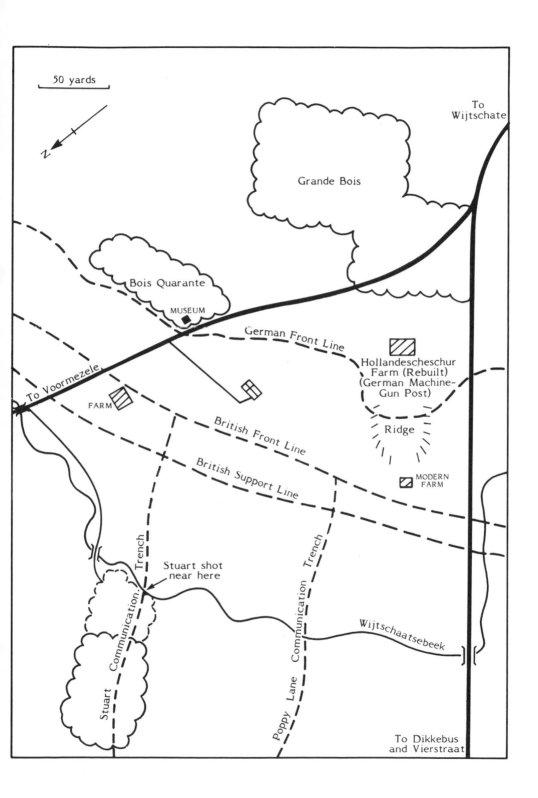

50 yards

N

To
Wijtschate

Grande Bois

Bois Quarante

MUSEUM

German Front Line

Hollandescheschur
Farm (Rebuilt)
(German Machine-
Gun Post)

To Voormezele

FARM

British Front Line

Ridge

British Support Line

MODERN
FARM

Stuart shot
near here

Stuart Communication Trench

Poppy Lane Communication Trench

Wijtschaatsebeek

To Dikkebus
and Vierstraat

parted his hair and scorched his skin. The next day, Stuart Trench was finished but Russell, who had done so much to bring it into existence, was dead.

Sources
C. L. Fox, *Narrative of the 502 (Wessex) Field Company*
W. G. Grieve and B. Newman *Tunnellers*

Battle of Messines, *1917*

The Mine that Blew up Too Late: 7 June 1917

A plan that depends on timing to within a few seconds can win a battle. At Spanbroekmolen in the Battle of Messines, the plan was to blow up a mine containing 90,000 pounds of explosive placed in a tunnel under the German fortifications at exactly 3.10 a.m. on 7 June 1917. It, and twenty other mines along the nine-mile front, would be detonated just two or three seconds before the British attack was to begin. Fifteen seconds too early, it would have been a warning. Fifteen seconds too late . . .

Miners were drafted in from all over Britain to dig tunnels for the mines at Messines. They were mostly civilians and got six shillings a week but some were soldiers and got only one shilling a week. There was deep resentment; nevertheless, they worked together in the dripping gloom of the tunnels deep in the clay of Messines.

'It was a hot spot all right. Jerry knew there was something going on there and he never left us alone. We got a lot of minenwerfers around there. "Minnies" we called them. They made a great bang and they turned over and over as they came. We feared these more than we feared heavy artillery shells. I was in D Company. We'd do 48 hours in the line and then we went into the billets, into support. The billets were in tunnels too. Larchwood saps, they called them. It was an overgrown dump of earth that had been lying there since they'd excavated a railway cutting that ran straight up through our trenches to the German line, and the Engineers had made these dug-outs in it for the miners and the troops in the line. It was only yards behind, but you felt a bit safer in there. There were two rows of beds – just timber frames with wire-netting across them, but you could lie down on them and put your overcoat on top of you and use your haversack for a pillow. There was a passage inbetween with duckboards laid along it, for it was always swimming in water. They weren't exactly billets. Just sleeping bases for the people who were in support immediately behind the front line ready to be called upon.'

The Germans were tunnelling as well to try to stop the British, and indeed from time to time work would have to stop altogether while a small 'camouflet' mine was exploded to destroy the German excavations. Still the Germans kept digging, because they were frantic to stop the mining of their positions. They knew that a big attack was in the offing, although they had no idea of the scale of the mining operation; but they had a shrewd idea that blowing up the German front-line fortifications in advance of the main attack must have been part of the plan.

Digging the tunnel at Spanbroekmolen was a problem. Blue clay from deep down appearing on the surface told enemy observers where suspicious activity was going on underground, and it attracted shelling which on one occasion made a tunnel fall in half way along. The collapse of the tunnel trapped twelve men between 1,250 and 1,500 feet from the tunnel entrance, which was in Kruisstraat Wood. All but one suffocated in the foul air and darkness. Only one sapper, an experienced miner, survived – on two army biscuits and a bottle of water, for six days until he was rescued.

Twenty-one tunnels slowly worked their way to the German lines. The method of mining was crude. 'To be a good clay-kicker you had to be long-legged, young and strong. At the age of twenty-one I was all three. You lay on a wooden cross made out of a plank with a cross-strut just behind your shoulders. The cross was wedged in the tunnel so that you were lying at an angle of 45 degrees with your feet towards the face. You worked with a sharp-pointed spade with a foot-rest on either side above the blade, and you drove the blade into the clay, kicked the clay out, and on to another section, moving forward all the time. With the old broad-bladed pick we could only get forward at best six feet on every shift, but when the clay-kicking method was introduced we were advancing as much as twelve feet, or even fourteen, on a shift.' The shifts were eight hours on and sixteen hours off, four days on and four days off. It was dangerous, exhausting and, in the end, successful, for twenty-one tunnels were built.

Bringing up the explosive for the mines was almost as bad as digging the tunnels. One infantryman had to stand at least fifty yards from the next in case a stray shell or a single bullet blew up his fifty-pound bag of ammonal, a kind of dynamite, and blew him to Kingdom Come.

When that perilous journey was over, the explosive was lowered into the narrow tunnel, wheeled gingerly along a primitive railway track laid underground and piled up at the end of the shaft directly under the German fortifications. Accidents could happen at any stage. There were continuous reports of men being blown up, being buried alive or collapsing from exhaustion. An appalling job in constant danger also took its mental toll. One Durham miner saved up all his rum tots for weeks, swallowed them all down in one go and charged out, blind drunk, into German lines before stumbling back to the tunnelling party he came from. The Germans didn't shoot him and the British didn't punish him. They both recognized the effect which the trenches and tunnels could have on ordinary men, and they were not out to get one demented individual.

By the end of April 1917 at Spanbroekmolen, the Irish 16th Division prepared to get over the top at 3.10 a.m. on 7 June. Behind them a hot-air balloon was camouflaged: the intention was that, when the attack was just starting, the balloon would be inflated, be taken to several hundred feet and be in a position to report on progress to headquarters, which was well behind the lines.

At precisely 3.10 a.m. officers pushed the plungers on twenty-one mines.

'Our plunger was in a dug-out, and the Colonel and I were actually standing outside the dug-out because we both knew what was going to happen and we wanted to see as much as we could. The earth seemed to tear apart, and there was this enormous explosion right in front of us. It was an extraordinary sight. The whole ground went up and came back down again. It was like a huge mushroom.'

Lieutenant Witherow knew that, whether his mine exploded or not, he still had to advance at 3.10 a.m.

There was no explosion.

They climbed out of the trenches and advanced. The balloon behind inflated and was exploded by a shell. To the left and to the right Witherow could see the British advancing into exploded craters. His Irish were advancing towards machine-guns and pill-boxes. They paused and advanced again. The ground they were crossing suddenly started to go up and down like an earthquake. It lasted for seconds and then, in front of them, the Spanbroekmolen mine went up.

'We'd made it through the machine-gun fire and had almost got to the German positions, when a terrible thing happened that nearly put an end to my fighting days. All of a sudden the earth seemed to open and belch forth a great mass of flame. There was a deafening noise and the whole thing went up in the air, a huge mass of earth and stone.'

Witherow survived but flying rocks and masonry sprayed down on

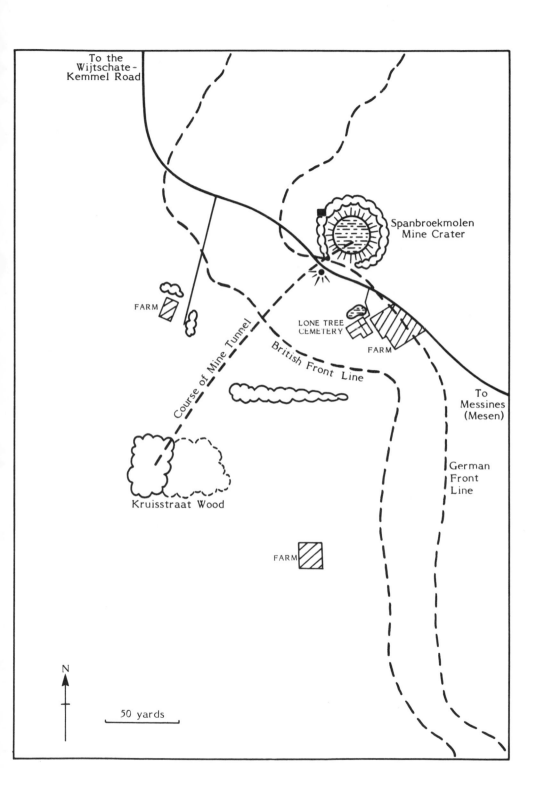

To the
Wijtschate-
Kemmel Road

Spanbroekmolen
Mine Crater

FARM

LONE TREE
CEMETERY

FARM

To
Messines
(Mesen)

British Front Line

Course of Mine Tunnel

German
Front
Line

Kruisstraat Wood

FARM

N

50 yards

the men all round him. His own battalion, the 8th Royal Irish Rifles, was obliterated. Bricks and mud poured down on the men, who had nowhere to hide. A minor fault in the wiring, a slight misunderstanding of an order, sheer bad luck, brought about the terrible irony of the destruction of a battalion by a mine men had laboured and died for weeks on end to lay.

Source
L. Macdonald, *They Called It Passchendaele*

Battle of Messines, 1917

A Medic Saves Lives at White Château: 7 June 1917

A piece of metal shrapnel cut into a young soldier's forearm, and the wound gaped wide open like a freshly cut shoulder of mutton. He cried out and danced with pain as blood poured from the cut muscle. A 'medic', Frank Dunham, saved his life by being with him up at the front, sharing all the risks, to give emergency treatment.

Frank Dunham went over the top with his battalion at 3.10 a.m. on 7 June 1917, the start of the Battle of Messines. His battalion had been waiting for zero-hour in the front line just south of the Ypres-Comines Canal. There had been a series of stupendous explosions as mines under German positions exploded and the artillery bombardment got under way. Now, in pitch darkness, the attack had started.

Clambering with heavy loads uphill over terrain heavily pock-marked with shell-holes and strewn with broken barbed wire, the 7th Londons advanced doggedly.

Several times Dunham saw men fall. He rushed to their aid only to find they had tripped on barbed wire. The British barbed wire had been cut through for the attack, and the German barbed wire had been blown to pieces, but in the darkness it still caused a lot of trouble.

The Germans meanwhile caused very little trouble. Their first and second lines had been blown up by heavy bombardments during the past week, and they were reeling from the exploded mines. A handful of defenders hardly delayed the attack and quickly surrendered. (They went willingly back down the line with no escort, clinging on to their trousers, which were falling down because the British had taken to cutting prisoners' braces to stop them running away.)

So far so good, but the real trouble began after crossing the German second-line trench. The Germans had withdrawn to the third-line trench a few hundred yards further on, but they had also held on to their position at White Château. Here they held up the 7th Londons with a fierce defence.

White Château had been an elegant three-storey mansion but now its cellars were heavily defended bunkers and contained a murderous machine-gun post. The building proper was a heap of rubble.

The first attack on White Château failed. It was driven back by relentless machine-gun fire and also intensified shelling, especially with heavy fizzling 'coal-box' shells, from the German heavy artillery.

A tiny piece of shrapnel cut Dunham's finger but preoccupied him only for a moment. He rushed to his Commanding Officer, Captain 'Nellie' Wallis, who had fallen wounded in the thigh. Dunham bound him up and suggested that, no matter how much agony it might be, he should try to drag himself back to the regimental aid post. Wallis swore he couldn't conceivably move. Hours later and with no sign of stretcher-bearers but plenty of 'coal boxes', Wallis somehow or other did get himself back off the battlefield.

'Haven't you captured this bally place yet?' asked Captain Gussy Collins of the 6th Londons.

The 6th Londons, who had just arrived, were supposed to go straight on to attack the German third line but now they would first have to help the 7th Londons capture White Château. It was, however, not to be done with infantry alone.

A British aeroplane flew over and hooted. This was the signal for the Londons to let off their flares showing their positions. A few moments later, the artillery bombarded White Château and a tank rolled up and fired some telling shells. An infantry rush finished the job. They took seventy-five prisoners.

'How you must hate us,' said a captured German to a friend of Dunham's.

'Oh no, we don't 'ate 'yer, we just looks on you like scum or vomit or some other nasty mess to be cleared up.'

The single file of prisoners disappeared back through the British lines (clinging on to their trousers).

All this happened while Dunham was out on the battlefield tending the wounded and dying. It was some hours before he himself had a chance to look at White Château. By mid-morning it had quietened down enough and the 6th Londons had advanced and taken the German third line. Dunham decided to go and have a look.

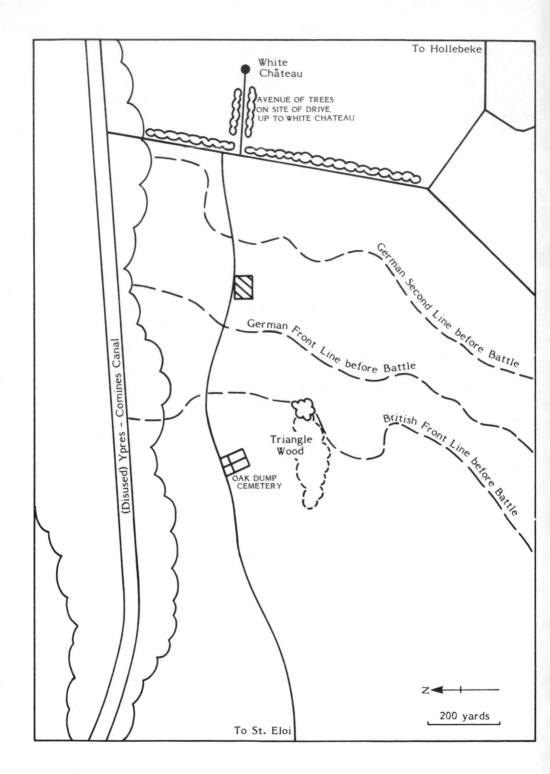

To Hollebeke

White
Château

AVENUE OF TREES
ON SITE OF DRIVE
UP TO WHITE CHATEAU

German Second Line before Battle

German Front Line before Battle

British Front Line before Battle

(Disused) Ypres – Comines Canal

Triangle
Wood

OAK DUMP
CEMETERY

Z

200 yards

To St. Eloi

The inside of White Château consisted of cellars with tiny entrances, 'So small that we had to crouch to get inside, but once inside, we had to descend several stone steps and found ourselves in a large room about sixteen feet high. The ceiling was of concrete, and supported by several large wooden beams in the centre . . . we could now understand how its garrison were safe from shell fire.' There were some dead and wounded Germans, plenty of potential souvenirs and a good deal of food. Dunham realized it would be an excellent shelter for the wounded.

In the heavy barrage preceding the inevitable German counterattack, Dunham realized that the stranded severely wounded would certainly be killed: the few stretcher-bearers were still busy elsewhere. He decided they had to improvise. He and his comrades dismantled a heavy door from the château as a makeshift stretcher: 'It was not long before we had the first case under shelter. It was very tiring work, for the door proved awkward . . . tilting violently as we lurched over the cratered ground and the poor chaps had a job to keep on it.' There were no complaints. Many lives were saved.

That night, Dunham and a good many wounded men he had brought in were protected from a terrific German bombardment by the thick concrete of White Château. The appallingly sordid conditions and even the possibility that the Germans might have mined it in anticipation of their withdrawal still made the Château a desirable place by contrast with the exposed battlefield outside.

As it turned out, the Château was not mined. Very few survived that night outside it.

Source
Haigh, R. H. and P. W. Turner, eds., *The Long Carry*

Third Battle of Ypres, 1917

Tanks Earn a Reprieve: 31 July and 16 August 1917

Field Marshal Haig never saw the map showing it was too marshy for tanks east of Kitchener's Wood. His Chief of Intelligence, Brigadier-General Charteris, not wishing to depress him, had never sent it on to him. The tanks were ordered forward to disaster.

'The tank chiefs protested vehemently; they pointed out that no tank could cross such waterlogged ground, that tanks were not submarines, and that, if they were used, it would simply be throwing away highly-trained men and wasting valuable machines.'

But the decree had gone forth . . .

High Command accepted that causeways and bridges would be needed to prepare the swamps of the Ypres Salient for tanks to attack. Everything had to be done at night. And all night the shells came, regularly, until the surviving engineers and sappers crept back to safety in the morning. The wastage of lives was terrible. True, some roads were improved and duckboards laid, but time and time again a night's work would be destroyed by a couple of shells in the day. The following night, gas would make progress dangerously slow.

The tanks themselves were provided with all sorts of luxury for the great attack of 31 July. To help the tank crews capture the ridges around Ypres, there were chocolates, biscuits, oranges and lemons, whisky and rum, various first-aid equipment and medicines and ammonia tablets to sniff when gassed. There were log-books, battle history sheets and pigeon message forms. Tank commander Lieutenant F. Mitchell observed, 'The poor pigeons were taken into action in a basket which, for lack of room, was often placed on top of the engine. In the heat and excitement of a battle they were sometimes overlooked, and when the basket was opened at last there emerged a decidedly overheated ánd semi-asphyxiated bird.'

If 31 July was successful for the infantry, who gained most of their objectives, it was awful for the Tank Corps. Tanks played a minor supporting role at first, but once it started to rain they 'bellied' in the boggy ground. They became a sitting target for artillery and aeroplanes. Many were destroyed and their crews killed.

The crews' lives were flung away. The tanks achieved nothing and sank into the mud. It was a fiasco.

Soon the driving continuous rain stopped the whole attack. Ooze overran the whole area east of Kitchener's Wood.

On 16 August, the second big attack was launched. The infantry again took their first objectives without difficulty. Indeed, this time it was easier than on 31 July because the Germans provided only token resistance in their front line. Behind the front line, however, lay the pillbox zone.

'The German artillery was drawn well back, ready to shell the attackers held up in the pillbox zone. His reserves were in the second line, waiting for an immediate counter-attack directly the advancing troops had expended their initial energy. Our infantry, toiling slowly through the mud, came to a standstill against these walls of concrete.

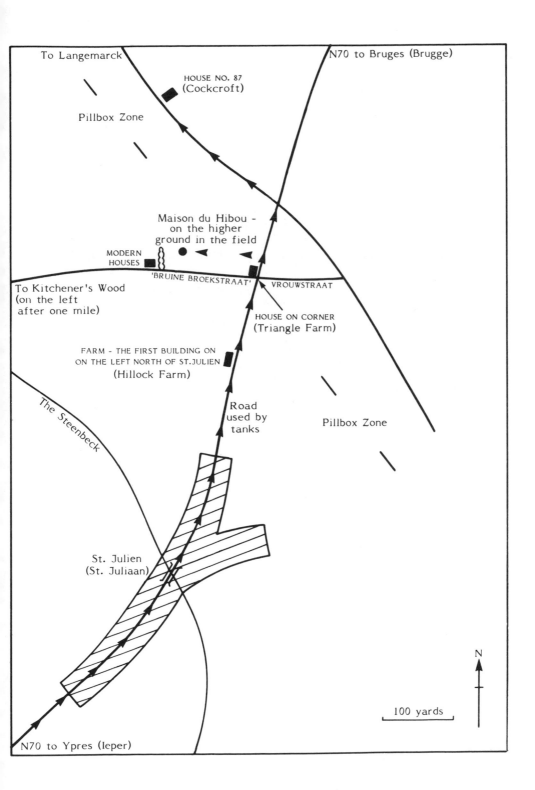

To Langemarck

N70 to Bruges (Brugge)

HOUSE NO. 87
(Cockcroft)

Pillbox Zone

Maison du Hibou -
on the higher
ground in the field

MODERN
HOUSES

'BRUINE BROEKSTRAAT'   VROUWSTRAAT

To Kitchener's Wood
(on the left
after one mile)

HOUSE ON CORNER
(Triangle Farm)

FARM - THE FIRST BUILDING ON
ON THE LEFT NORTH OF ST.JULIEN
(Hillock Farm)

The Steenbeck

Road
used by
tanks

Pillbox Zone

St. Julien
(St. Juliaan)

N

100 yards

N70 to Ypres (Ieper)

Light field guns failed to destroy them, bombs had no effect on them, and so our men fell like leaves in autumn.'

The infantry were pinned down by four pillboxes near St. Julien. There was a remnant of road which went near them. General Sir Ivor Maxse put off a proposal that a thousand men should be sacrificed to storm the pillboxes with infantry. First he would try the tanks.

A smoke screen was prepared and a batch of tanks made its way up the road from St. Julien towards the pillboxes that were causing all the trouble, Hillock Farm, Maison du Hibou, Cockcroft and Triangle Farm.

There was no warning artillery barrage.

At Hillock Farm the Germans were taken completely by surprise. They had no answer to a tank coming up the road behind them and firing through their vulnerable rear door. The few survivors fled.

Maison du Hibou was further from the road, and the tank that went for the rear door of that pillbox quickly stuck fast in the mud. As it sank deeper, it fired desperately. By chance, its six-pounder gun turned out to be pointing straight inside through the pillbox door at the garrison of sixty men. The walls of the pillbox were shellproof but the door was soon blown away. Most of the garrison was killed by the tank's fire, and few of those who got out escaped the raking machine-guns of the sinking tank.

The garrison at Cockcroft saw what had gone on at Maison du Hibou and escaped when the attacking tank was still fifty yards short and before it had fired a shell. In fact, this tank could never have done much damage since it was stuck and sinking and facing the wrong direction – but the Germans were not waiting to find out. They ran away before a clearly superior force. The tank was proving itself.

Triangle Farm had stouter defenders. They replied fiercely to the fire from the tanks but got nowhere. Eventually a gaping hole was blown in the rear of the pillbox. The infantry rushed in and gunned down and bayoneted the whole defending garrison.

Most of the tanks in this successful action returned unharmed down the St. Julien road. There were twenty-nine casualties instead of a thousand. The tank had shown its mettle.

Source
F. Mitchell, *Tank Warfare*

Third Battle of Ypres, 1917

A Drowning Army: 27 August 1917

Rotting corpses and living men were swallowed indiscriminately by liquid mud and drowned in the hopeless battle for Langemarck Ridge. The 7th and 8th Warwickshires were blown to pieces. They gained a few hundred yards – lost by the Berkshires a few days later.

Captain Edwin Campion Vaughan heard with dull horror the pronouncement of his death sentence. It was in the form of an order from General Fanshawe's headquarters: 'Move up to the Steenbeck at 1.45 p.m. and prepare to attack!'

In broad daylight!

A drying wind, it was said, had made the going much easier. The Warwickshires could see for themselves what it was really like. The Steenbeck Stream was no longer distinguishable. All the drainage had been destroyed, and the waters from the Steenbeck and from the morass between the Steenbeck and Langemarck Ridge had flooded most of the ground with a combination of water and liquid mud – the mud had the consistency of thick porridge on the surface and gradually got thicker lower down, so men who got trapped in it were sucked down and died slowly and horribly. It was just possible for men to find their way across towards the ridge by using slimy, exposed stretches of mud round the flooded shell-holes but they constantly risked falling in and drowning. The commonest death was to receive a minor shrapnel or bullet wound, to fall into the mud and to die by drowning over a period of some minutes, struggling in the full knowledge of impending death.

Vaughan's watch seemed to whirl round to 1.45 p.m. He advanced to the Steenbeck. His detailed orders were to remain for the time being in reserve at the forward command post, 'the Boiler-house', next to the St. Julien road during the initial attack. The whistles blew. Vaughan watched.

The heavy bombardment which accompanied the attack was instantaneously answered by the Germans equally heavily. Everyone realized there and then that, to make matters worse, the enemy must have known all the details of the attack in advance.

Vaughan saw with a heavy heart that the lines ahead wavered, broke and almost disappeared. A small number of the 7th Warwickshires reached their first objective, gun pits half way to the ridge. There was no question of going any further for the moment.

'Go up to the gun pits, Vaughan, and see if you can do anything. Good luck.'

Vaughan raced across the road, where a moment before a man had been killed in the barrage, and dived into the slime on the other side. He dragged himself over the corpses of his comrades and through slime made foul by decaying bodies. He dived into the flooded shell-holes to escape the raking machine-guns. He dragged himself over small exposed ridges while his friends around the gun pits were mown down ahead of him.

'I paused a moment in the shell-hole; in a few seconds I felt myself sinking, and struggle as I might I was sucked down until I was firmly gripped round the waist and still being dragged in. The leg of a corpse was sticking out of the side, and frantically I grabbed it. It wrenched off and casting it down I pulled in a couple of rifles and yelled for the troops in the gun pit to throw me more. Laying them flat I wriggled over them and dropped, half dead, into the wrecked gun position.'

The drying wind had now stopped and it started to pour with rain.

Vaughan gathered all the men he could, returned to the road and made his way up to Triangle Farm. From there he was supposed to make his way round to attack Springfield Farm from the north along Langemarck Ridge itself, but Springfield Farm had been turned by the Germans into a damaging machine-gun post, a pillbox stronghold.

Vaughan could just keep a handful of men together. The rest were dead or flatly refused. 'No fear.' 'We've done our job.' They had to be cursed and driven up the broken shelled road to Triangle Farm.

'A man stopped dead in front of me, and exasperated I cursed him and butted him with my knee. Very gently he said "I'm blind, Sir", and turned to show me his eyes and nose torn away by a piece of shell. "Oh God . . ."'

Crossing from Triangle Farm to Springfield in a continuous barrage made slightly less accurate now by the heavy rain and impending darkness, Vaughan and his men came across a mass of corpses, and hundreds of wounded men desperately clinging to the mud, trying not to drown in the now-rising liquid. They cursed and shrieked terrifyingly. They begged for stretcher-bearers.

As the rain continued to pour down, and as more and more wounded men drowned in the hell of rising foul water, the organization on both the German and British sides started to disintegrate. By sheer coincidence, Vaughan and his men happened to try to attack Springfield from the north at the same moment as another small group of Warwickshires attacked from the south after finally making their way direct across from the gun pits. Sixteen Germans surrendered at once; but they were machine-gunned by their own side as they were led back to the British lines.

The fighting died down as night fell. More Germans surrendered and shared their misery with the British. British and German officers and soldiers huddled together around Springfield pillbox waiting to die or for the horrors to end. Gradually the shrieks and groans of the wounded faded away. The water and mud were slowly consuming them.

Springfield itself was knee-deep in water and contained a few corpses along with a German officer whose left leg had been blown off by a shell. The place stank horribly. The German officer struggled in his pocket to find a small delicacy as a mark of respect for Vaughan, who staunched the remains of his leg and gave him a drink of water. At last he found his treasure. Three sugar lumps. Vaughan only pretended to eat them. They had crumbled and they were saturated with blood.

Vaughan knew that Springfield could not be defended against an attack the next day. They would all die.

Some men were approaching from Triangle Farm! They were British, the Berkshires.

'To reinforce us?'

'No, to relieve you!'

In this part of the battle for Langemarck Ridge, Vaughan's company alone had lost seventy-five out of ninety men.

Source
E. C. Vaughan, *Some Desperate Glory*

Third Battle of Ypres, 1917

The Effect on the Mind: October 1917

Living and working with heavy-duty eighteen-pounder field guns firing day and night for weeks on end broke the minds of many strong men. The pointlessness of almost inevitable death in an unwinnable battle led them to blank despair. Signaller Aubrey Wade was based for most of October 1917 in gun pits which had been dug into the bank of a sunken road. The view was of men being blown to pieces in the mud. There were no redeeming features. The Steenbeck had been shelled to a muddy river one hundred yards wide in which men

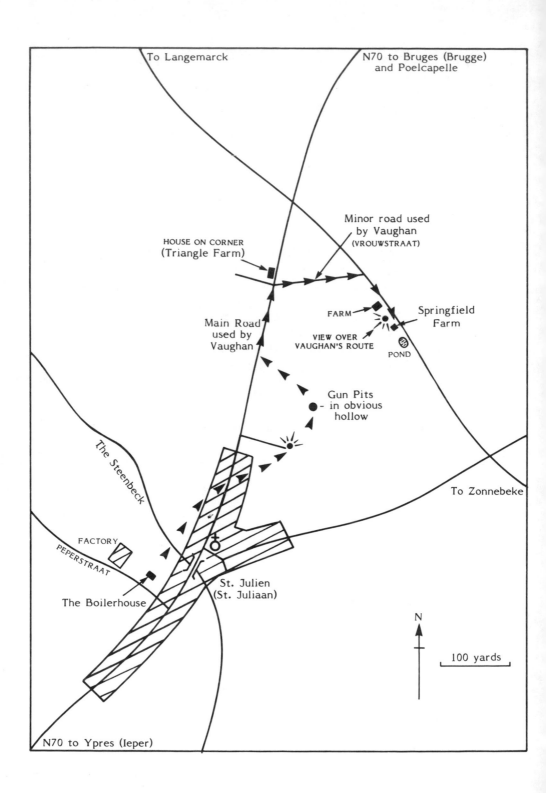

To Langemarck

N70 to Bruges (Brugge)
and Poelcapelle

Minor road used
by Vaughan
(VROUWSTRAAT)

HOUSE ON CORNER
(Triangle Farm)

FARM

Springfield
Farm

Main Road
used by
Vaughan

VIEW OVER
VAUGHAN'S ROUTE

POND

Gun Pits
- in obvious
hollow

The Steenbeck

To Zonnebeke

FACTORY

PEPERSTRAAT

The Boilerhouse

St. Julien
(St. Juliaan)

N

100 yards

N70 to Ypres (Ieper)

were drowning. Bridges over the Steenbeck were made of enemy corpses because of the lack of other building materials.

Haig had ordered the taking of Poelcapelle. It was to be one of what the newspapers called 'Haig's bites' in the German lines. The problem was that around Poelcapelle the German line was made up of a series of pillboxes with walls of concrete six feet thick. Each pillbox bristled with machine-guns which caused havoc in the ranks of the British attackers.

'Urgent messages kept coming through asking us to concentrate [our guns] on certain spots where wave after wave of infantry had been hurled back by the storm of bullets. The Fritzes must be fighting like the very demons of hell. Wounded were now coming down in a continual stream, but the number of prisoners became significantly less . . . and it seemed indeed that we were engaged in a hopeless task.'

Everyone near the front line knew the continuing attack was pointless. One by one the guns of Wade's battery were knocked out. Wagon-teams carrying ammunition and food to the batteries and to the front beyond rarely got through. The guns themselves were breaking from the strain of continuous use; they were burning hot, and their breech-blocks jammed and had to be opened with pickaxes.

'Reinforcements shambled up past the guns with dragging steps and the expressions of men who knew they were going to certain death. No words of greeting passed as they slouched along; in sullen silence they filed past one by one to the sacrifice. Now and again the flash and roar of a shell would leave a sudden gap in the procession, but they closed up with half-dazed, quickening steps. There was one less, that was all.'

The gunners were also starting to break. For Wade, a month at the front was the most he could stand. Survival was chance. Corpses were nothing to him, although the corpses of his closest comrades still made him weep. Sometimes the gunners went mad or were shell-shocked, gibbering, unable to speak or walk. Then there were the self-inflicted wounds or a desperate prayer for a 'Blighty', a wound bad enough to get them out of the gun pits and home. As they worked their guns in the battery, they drew the attention of German shells. Gunners at work were blown up with their guns. Pieces of blown-up bodies showered over Wade and his comrades as they flung themselves to the ground cheek by jowl with the dead. As a shell approached, Wade could hear 'a sudden enveloping roar and a terrific concussion that rocked the dug-out . . . the pungent smoke nearly stifled us'. If the gunners survived the shell itself, the explo-

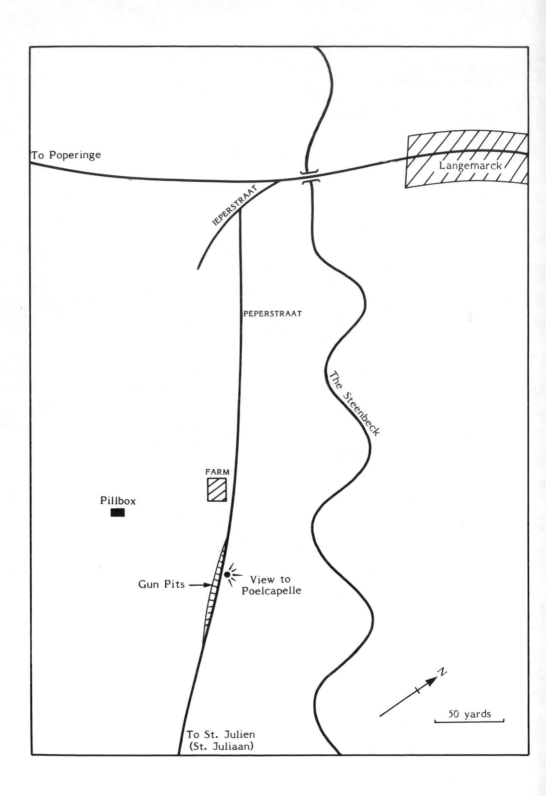

To Poperinge

IEPERSTRAAT

Langemarck

PEPERSTRAAT

The Steenbeck

FARM

Pillbox

Gun Pits → View to Poelcapelle

N

50 yards

To St. Julien
(St. Juliaan)

sion made huge lumps of clay and chunks of red-hot steel fly around, dealing death.

In Wade's battery, even the men who had survived death, injury or shell-shock were getting 'windy' – terrified of every shell, starting at every bang, unable to sleep or, like Wade's friend Ross, sleeping with a set pucker between the brows from strung-up nerves refusing to relax even in sleep. The slaughter never looked likely to stop. Wade never looked likely to get out.

Messages kept coming from HQ which Wade, as a signaller, had to take and pass on to the rest of the battery. Usually the message was to deliver another barrage or to say that ammunition would not be long (the last lot probably having been blown up on its way to them). Other messages contained all sorts of enquiries about materials or the quartering of troops.

At long last, a different message came. 'Strained faces relaxed to smile again with a sense of release and hope that swept over us. We were going out!' They left death behind them but they carried with them the emotional pain and mental scars for ever.

Source
A. Wade, *The War of the Guns*

Third Battle of Ypres, 1917

Sacrifice at Passchendaele: 12 October 1917

The Jaegers, one of Germany's crack machine-gun regiments, held the village of Passchendaele at the beginning of October 1917. They made the defence of Passchendaele long and painful for defenders and attackers alike. By the time the New Zealanders found themselves on the northern approaches to the village on 12 October, all that was left of the quiet farmsteads was rubble pockmarked by shells. Passchendaele had already become a symbol of the decline and death of two great armies.

The New Zealanders struggled up to the front on 11 October to have another go at taking Passchendaele. An attempt by the British a couple of days earlier had ended in disintegration and disaster, with German snipers standing on top of their pillboxes picking off everything that moved. Whole companies were reduced to a dozen men.

Now, Sergeant Jock Stewart found himself advancing up the road from Waterloo Farm towards Passchendaele with the Second New Zealand Machine-Gun Company. The road had been chosen for the attack because the rain had made the mud in the surrounding fields unendurable. Indeed, others in Stewart's company, who were forced to use the fields, spent an icy night up to their waists in water with little shelter from shells. When the time came for the attack, at 5.25 a.m. the next morning, the 12th, the survivors from the fields were exhausted and useless in battle.

The bane of the struggle for Passchendaele, the terrible weather, surpassed itself. As the hour of the attack got nearer, the rain became torrential and the wind whipped up to hurricane force. The whole of the valley between the New Zealanders on the edge of the north spur of Passchendaele ridge and the Australians on the edge of the south spur was flooded, and under the water was the sucking mud which slowly claimed the life of anyone who tried to hide in it or was shell-blasted into it.

The roads were the only places where a man could be sure of being able to stand. They were covered with several inches of mud themselves, but at least they had a firm base. The Jaegers could therefore anticipate the use of the roads and, despite bombardments, their defences along the roads leading up to Passchendaele were still strong. There was some discussion amongst the generals whether to go ahead if the weather were still bad, exactly because of the predictability of using the roads, but they reasoned there might just be a chance of taking the Germans by surprise, by launching a second attack so soon after the first and in such a storm. It did indeed surprise the Germans, but they were still able to defend themselves because they knew the attack would have to be along the road.

Jock Stewart and those who were still fit enough from his company – many of those who were still in one piece had a feverish cold – were quite glad to move up the road when it was time to advance in the morning. They had had a foul night. They had been unable to dig themselves in, since water just poured into any hole they made in the mud. They had not even been able to sit down. They had just stood there in the wind and rain waiting for the cold night to pass and hoping to escape the shelling.

As Stewart and the others came up the road to the top of a small rise of the spur, they recoiled. A dense and massive bank of barbed wire lay straight ahead, completely blocking the road and backed up by the machine-guns of a two-storey pillbox. There was no escape. Stewart was one of the first to go down, shot through the heart.

The pillbox was positively spitting fire. It was remarkable that anyone survived at all. There was certainly not the remotest possi-

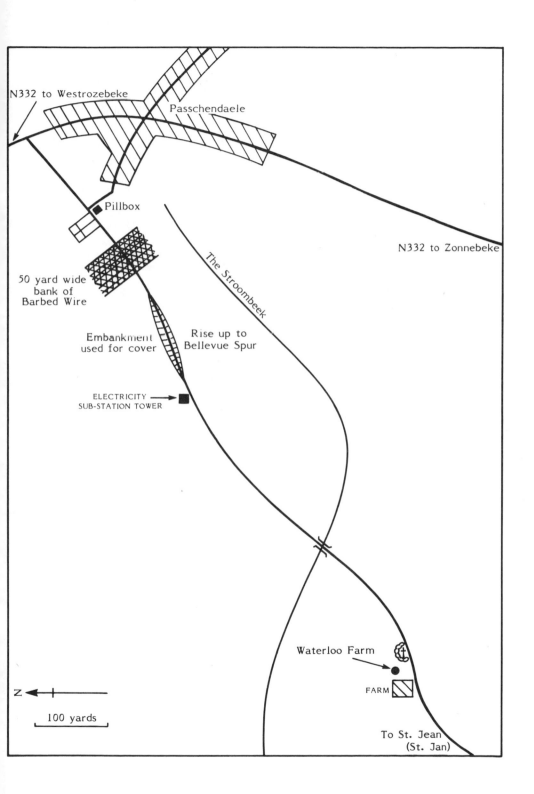

N332 to Westrozebeke

Passchendaele

Pillbox

N332 to Zonnebeke

50 yard wide
bank of
Barbed Wire

The Stroombeek

Embankment
used for cover

Rise up to
Bellevue Spur

ELECTRICITY
SUB-STATION TOWER

Waterloo Farm

FARM

Z

100 yards

To St. Jean
(St. Jan)

bility of pressing a successful attack in these conditions with the men and equipment available. A handful of the attackers managed to fall back to some limited shelter behind a small ridge on a bend of the road. Among them was Sergeant Jock Stewart's young brother, Private Harold Stewart.

Harold Stewart suddenly realized Jock wasn't there. They tried to stop him going but he ran out and was killed next to his brother as he tried to drag his body back behind the ridge. The blood from Harold's pierced jugular vein gushed over his comrades and over his dead brother.

This was the terrible sacrifice by the Stewart family of New Zealand in the struggle for Passchendaele.

Source
L. Macdonald, *They Called It Passchendaele*

Fourth Battle of Ypres, 1918

An Almost Untroubled Advance: 28 and 29 September 1918

Quite suddenly there was a sense that the First World War was nearing its end. A huge British attack was massing. The Germans knew it but did very little about it.

Captain Francis Hitchcock led his company of Leinsters out of Ypres up the Menin Road to Leinster Farm and Birr Cross Road, where they met the pipers who were to lead them up to Hooge to the tune of 'Brian Boru'. They were to be in support of the Worcesters until after Gheluvelt, which the Worcesters were to be given the honour of re-taking after a famous stand they had made in the village in 1914, in the First Battle of Ypres. A measure of German resistance at this Fourth Battle of Ypres was the fact that Hitchcock's company, had no casualties between Ypres and the commanding site of Hooge Château. The Germans had no strength to resist and they were running away.

Hooge Château in September 1918 was a reddish piece of mud where brick was mixed with clay. Hitchcock looked about him. At last he was no longer compelled to keep his head below the parapet of a

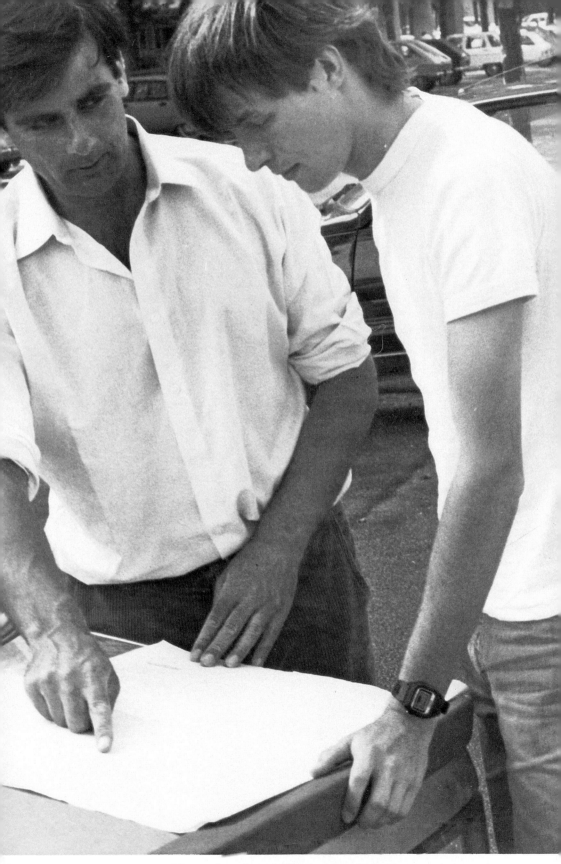

The authors locate Nun's Alley in Lens

Pigs graze around the moat where Bruce Bairnsfather was shelled

Apple trees line the avenue which led to the White Château

The 'Boilerhouse' pillbox where Vaughan set out into the mud

Willow Ditch, which Richards used to approach German lines in
Fromelles (in the background)

The site of Bairnsfather's Christmas Day truce, looking towards Messines. The house on the far side of the field is on the site of the German front line

The Cross of Sacrifice at Neuve Chapelle Farm Cemetery is on the site of the jumping-off trenches for the attack on Neuve Chapelle village over the fields

A crater, now serving as a rubbish tip, on the Hohenzollern Redoubt

View from the Hohenzollern Redoubt south over part of the battlefield of Loos. All the low ground and the edge of the Redoubt were captured by the British on the first day of the battle

The site of the brickworks battleground. The Germans were positioned in front of the site of the modern cooling tower (centre) and the British were on the camera's side of the pipeline which has been installed (foreground)

Gunner's Crater: Hitchcock's men attacked from the camera's position and surprised the Germans on the far side

The town hall at Neuve Eglise where Stoney and his men held out.
This is a view from the back showing where they eventually escaped

Westmann's 'dell', where the German medical student was shelled in the week before the Battle of the Somme

View over Ablain-St.-Nazaire and the Souchez Valley. The remains of the old village church are just visible. The high ground in the distance rises to the left and becomes Vimy Ridge. The photograph was taken from the French war memorial of Notre Dame de Lorette

muddy trench; he could see how vitally important the command of Hooge was to the command of the Ypres Salient. Standing there, drenched by the old Ypres rain, up to his knees in the old Ypres mud, he wondered at the devastation:

'Not one of the old landmarks was left, and the Salient from this ridge looked as featureless as the Sahara. It was impossible to make out the lake, or where Château Wood had been. Earth had been so churned up that the small watercourses had been altered. The only thing that could be seen was the long straight road stretching away behind us towards Ypres and the four solitary tanks spread along the ridge. They had been ditched and knocked out in the third battle of Ypres, July 31st, 1917. The tank near Railway Wood had been bogged in a crater and looked grotesque rearing up its stern.'

They moved east along either side of the Menin road in pursuit of the Germans who had held the whole area the day before. The occasional shell burst harmlessly overhead, but the only other evidence of the enemy was an abandoned gun with smashed sights and an abandoned transport wagon complete with food and horses.

A drying sun came out. Hitchcock decided to give his company a rest by a deserted pillbox. He had never had the chance to have a close look at a pillbox before. It would be a good chance to take off his tunic, wring out his shirt and do some sightseeing at the same time. Hitchcock was fascinated by the pillbox with its steel-framed walls three feet thick and an almost impregnable solidity, dug right into the ground with only its machine-gun slit exposed facing where the British had struggled along the ridge the year before in the Third Battle of Ypres.

They made some tea at the pillbox and made billows of smoke with their fires. At last they attracted enemy shelling, but there were no casualties. Then an enemy plane came after them: 'An enemy Taube, with its fish-like tail, hovered over us as we advanced, its Maltese cross showing out clearly on its silvery body. It fired several bursts from its machine-gun at us, but the bullets went whistling high over our heads like a covey of partridges. It did not carry out its flight unmolested . . .' The pilot was hit and the plane eventually crashed.

They soon got news that Gheluvelt had fallen to the Worcesters. Now the Leinsters were to spearhead the advance. They moved on through the village, still flanking the main road.

After a burst of fierce fighting, but few casualties on either side, the enemy eventually fell back to an easily defended dump of timber, wagons, coal and wire amidst a number of small huts, all of which gave cover; Leinster casualties started to mount.

'It was like disturbing a hornet's nest. I saw a few men falling, and

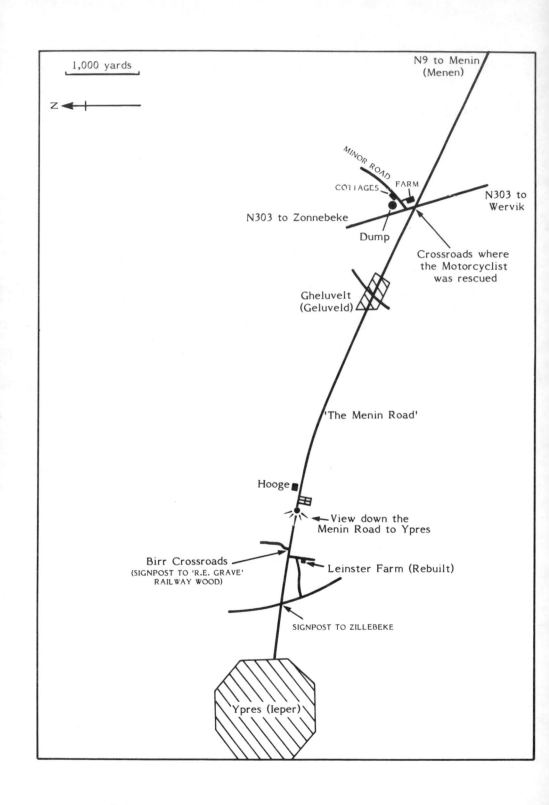

1,000 yards

Z

N9 to Menin
(Menen)

MINOR ROAD

COTTAGES   FARM

N303 to Zonnebeke

N303 to
Wervik

Dump

Crossroads where
the Motorcyclist
was rescued

Gheluvelt
(Geluveld)

'The Menin Road'

Hooge

← View down the
Menin Road to Ypres

Birr Crossroads
(SIGNPOST TO 'R.E. GRAVE'
RAILWAY WOOD)

Leinster Farm (Rebuilt)

SIGNPOST TO ZILLEBEKE

'Ypres (Ieper)

there was a roar for stretcher-bearers. Sergeant Joyce MM was killed, and some men were wounded. I could see them kicking in the long grass. Then some of my men gradually worked their way over to the abandoned coal trucks, and under cover of these engaged the enemy. (One man, Flaherty, actually climbed on top of the coal and commenced sniping.)'

Flaherty silenced several snipers, and survived despite the hail of bullets all about him. Then, suddenly, a roar of engines revealed a detachment of the Motor Machine-Gun Corps coming up the middle of the Menin road – and on past Hitchcock and past Flaherty, although they signalled frantically to them to stop.

'The driver managed to get over the crossroads, when he was bowled over on to the highway by machine-gun fire from a range of less than 100 yards. His companion jumped out of the side-car, turned his gun on the enemy and silenced them. He then picked up his comrade, who was lying wounded on the road, put him in his carrier, turned his bike, and rode off back to our lines. This was one of the bravest acts I have ever seen and we gave the hero a rousing cheer.'

The great advance was stopped, although the Germans were in reality doing little more than covering further retreat, as Hitchcock himself suspected. The Leinsters could only watch sadly when, having learned nothing from the motor cyclists, some French cavalry rode past to be massacred. At the crossroads, the Germans directed withering fire at them from their machine-gun strongpoints. Hitchcock noticed a number of empty saddles and riders propped up on their horses by their comrades riding on either side, when the cavalry returned.

It was a sorrowful end to a great two days. Hitchcock and his men knew perfectly well by the evening of 29 September 1918 that, for all the casualties they might claim as they went down, the Germans were defeated.

Source
F. C. Hitchcock, *Stand To*

LOOS-ARMENTIERES

Introduction

The wide flat valley of the River Lys contains the important market town of Armentières to the north, along with the strategically important Flanders Hills. To the south of the valley lie the hills containing the small mining town of Loos.

Now, as in 1914, this is the industrial heartland of France. The landscape is dominated by slagheaps and factory chimneys. It is not picturesque.

When the lines of the Western Front were being drawn in 1914, the British Expeditionary Force rushed to the Lys to fight the Battle of Armentières. It was still the army of the Boer Wars and the North-West Frontier: hard men of the Victorian era.

The Germans were stopped from breaking through to the Channel ports, but the British were exhausted and counter-attack was out of the question.

The two armies waited and watched each other. Most of the time they waited in primitive trenches, firing shells and reaching for their rifles when any of the enemy moved. Only the remarkable Christmas Day truce of 1914 intervened.

In the following year, the British Expeditionary Force was re-inforced and revitalized by units of the Territorial Army. It was soon strong enough to attack a fortified village a few miles south of Armentières, Neuve Chapelle, and a little later to undertake a major offensive at Loos. These battles showed the shape of things to come. They started off as successes but soon hit the problem of communications. A gap or an enemy weak spot would be noticed at the front, but by the time the generals could order some course of action to exploit the weakness, the enemy had had time to reinforce. No technology at the time could overcome this problem – even telephone wires were blown to pieces. The only way to win, under these circumstances, was to use up enemy reserves so that eventually there would simply be too few men left to act as reinforcements. The war of attrition began. Attempts to break the pattern by using gas and landmines failed. Even when major offensives were going on elsewhere along the front, continuous painful attrition went on everywhere else unabated in the Loos-Armentières sector.

As the war as a whole intensified, the scale of battles elsewhere on the front grew. Major battles in the Loos-Armentières sector – such as the bloody affair fought at Lens in 1917 – were seen as mere sideshows. Eventually, in an attempt to staunch the appalling losses and for political reasons, Prime Minister Lloyd George slowed down the supply of new men and forced the army to reorganize and think again. The structure of the army was changed in the reorganization. The British Expeditionary Force was made up of five armies subdivided into a variable number of corps depending on the importance of a particular sector at a particular time. Each corps was made up of three or four divisions, which each contained three brigades of four battalions of one thousand men. Now the British Expeditionary Force had to reduce its size, and it did so by reducing the size of brigades from four battalions to three, from four thousand to three thousand men.

At the same time, in 1917, as the British Expeditionary Force was cut by a quarter, the German army facing them was increased by a third because of the Russian collapse. The Germans used their temporary advantage and all their reserves to launch a major offensive in spring 1918. An important part of this offensive started with an attack on some weak Portuguese positions near Neuve Chapelle.

Ypres was outflanked and once again the Channel ports were threatened as the Flanders Hills were overrun.

The German Spring Offensive was a success in terms of distance covered and territory taken, but pockets of British resistance cost the Germans dearly. For the most part, however, the British were routed, only to regain all they had lost in September and October 1918 when the exhausted Germans were finally defeated.

Battle of Armentières, 1914

Deadly Riflemen who Stank: 15 October to 18 November 1914

In the first few months of the First World War the ordinary soldier was covered in lice and stank, wore filthy rags, was half-starved and was usually so exhausted that he could fall asleep standing up, with the enemy about to attack. His equipment was faulty and his officers were often ignorant bullies. His was the army of Mafeking and the North-West Frontier. He was a hero in the making, and he was deadly with his rifle.

The enemy had sent the Uhlan Cavalry to see how the land lay in Fromelles. They looked around, looted, forced the locals to give them food and shelter and then reported back – the infantry could advance. The infantry front line was established in a line of trees next to the north-south track through the village.

Private Frank Richards and his fellow Royal Welch Fusiliers dug themselves in 400 yards away to the west. Richards stank. He was covered in lice. Since joining up, he had had only one bath and one pair of clean underpants, which had contained, in their seams, the unhatched eggs of innumerable lice which the heat of the body quickly hatched. He was alive with 'crawlers'. He and his mates used old bully beef tins as latrines and never had the chance to wash.

Richards still had his uniform but it was in a appalling condition. Many of his companions had completely ruined their uniforms and had to scrounge or steal second-hand clothes from local civilians.

Food was scarcely better organized than clothes. Three British firms supplied tins of food to the army, but one invariably half-filled the tins with a little rotten meat and boiled rice: 'The head of that firm should have been put against the wall and shot for the way he sharked us troops,' said Richards. So when they finally arrived at Fromelles, the Fusiliers were nearly starving. They raided a farm with an orchard and one pig. They lived on apples and pork for days. The pork fat was used for greasing their rifles.

Richards and his companions never lay down for weeks on end. Their trench was made for fighting in, not for living in, but they had to live in it for days at a time in filthy conditions. The men had to sleep alternate hours standing up shoulder to shoulder, resting their heads on the edge of the trench. When the Company Commander passed along the trench, the privates had to squeeze their bodies into the mud at the side to let him through.

Foul-smelling, ill-clothed, ill-fed, ill-housed as he was, Richards was still a killer. He relished the enemy's attack.

The enemy emerged from the wood and crossed the road. The Fusiliers kept their heads down. No one gave away their precise position. They lured the Germans closer, ducking the shell fire and rifle enfilade. Then one Fusilier fired. 'You dog!' shouted the Company Commander at the innocent Richards. 'You fired!' and he threw a lump of earth at him and he hit his chest, 'You dirty swine!' Richards shouted back at his Company Commander, nicknamed Buffalo Bill, who had the dangerous habit of waving his loaded revolver at anyone who crossed him. But by this time the attack had begun in earnest.

The enemy advanced out of the wood under cover of the barrage of shells. Meanwhile, the Fusiliers kept their heads down while bullets

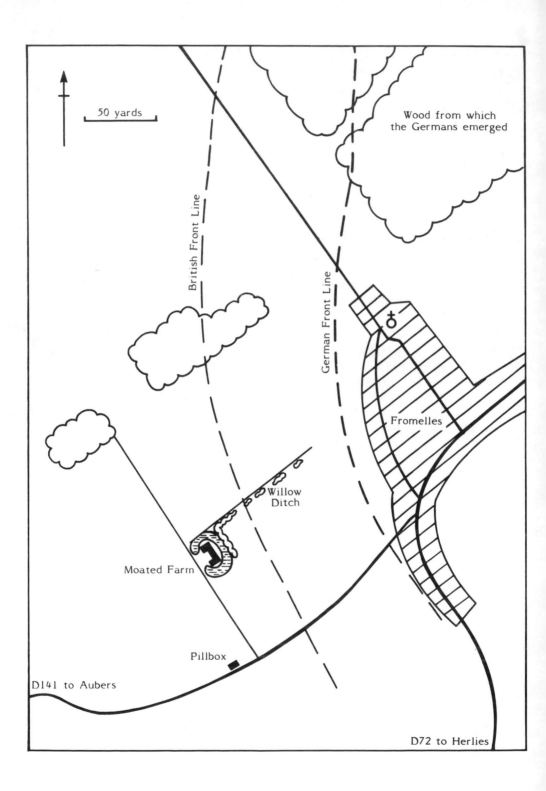

50 yards

British Front Line

German Front Line

Wood from which
the Germans emerged

Fromelles

Willow
Ditch

Moated Farm

Pillbox

D141 to Aubers

D72 to Herlies

thing in the air, this Peace and Goodwill feeling . . .' It was a magic episode but the next day would probably be much the same as others in the trenches, Christmas or not.

Christmas Day dawned. Sunny and crisp. The turnip field looked at its best. The spirit of Christmas Eve, though, had gone. Bairnsfather walked about the trench doing his everyday officer's job. Gradually his mind turned again to Christmas. He wished he was anywhere but at war in a Belgian trench.

He was aware that he could actually see quite a lot of Germans. They weren't hiding in their trench.

'Heads were bobbing about and showing over their parapet in a most reckless way, and, as we looked, this phenomenon became more and more pronounced. A complete Boche figure suddenly appeared on the parapet, and looked about itself. This complaint became infectious. It didn't take Our Bert long to be up on the skyline (it is one long grind to ever keep him off it). This was the signal for more Boche anatomy to be disclosed, and this was replied to by all our Alfs and Bills until, in less than it takes to tell, half a dozen or so each of the belligerents were outside their trenches and were advancing towards each other in no man's land. A strange sight, truly!'

Bairnsfather himself, in his muddy suit of khaki and wearing a green sheepskin coat and Balaclava helmet, followed a minute later.

He was confused. He knew he was supposed to hate the enemy and wrote afterwards, for wartime public consumption: 'The devils wanted to be friendly, these faded, unimaginative products of perverted *kulture* . . .' In fact, the 'Tommies' and the 'Boches' came out of their trenches and mixed cheerfully in the middle of the turnip field. Bairnsfather himself swapped souvenirs with a German officer. 'We both said things to each other which neither understood and agreed to swap; I brought out my wire-clippers and with a few deft snips removed a couple of buttons, and I gave him two of mine.' Meanwhile, the atmosphere was getting even more cheerful and relaxed. A German infantryman was taking snapshots. 'The last I saw of this little affair was a vision of one of my machine-gunners who was a bit of an amateur hairdresser in civil life, cutting the unnaturally long hair of a docile Boche, who was patiently kneeling on the ground whilst the automatic clippers crept up the back of his neck.' It was all trust and good humour.

The party lasted barely an hour but the goodwill lasted for days. The 26th and 27th were peaceful. Bairnsfather and his men never mixed with the Germans again, but they could leave the trenches whenever they wanted. They could stroll into no man's land. They could sing and light fires. It was the same for the Germans.

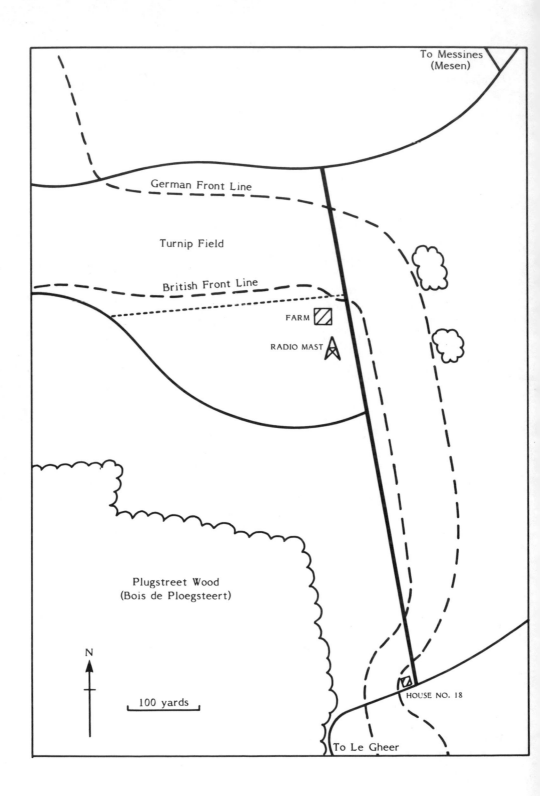

To Messines
(Mesen)

German Front Line

Turnip Field

British Front Line

FARM

RADIO MAST

Plugstreet Wood
(Bois de Ploegsteert)

N

100 yards

HOUSE NO. 18

To Le Gheer

The authorities on both sides were furious. The unwarlike Royal Warwickshires and their German counterparts were ordered out of the line on the 27th. Their replacements had not been softened by the spirit of Christmas.

Source
B. Bairnsfather, *Bullets and Billets*

Battle of Neuve Chapelle, 1915

Britain Claims a Breakthrough: 10 and 11 March 1915

In the early spring of 1915, it was not yet clear that the main British theatre of war would be France. There was still a lot of emphasis on naval operations and on the Middle East. However, Field Marshal Sir John French, in charge of the army in France, had no doubts. He appealed direct to the Prime Minister for more men and materials. He wanted victory and victory for Britain alone not victory for Britain and France together. He met with General Haig, and together they planned a 'battering-ram' attack against the German position at Neuve Chapelle. Strategically, it was nonsense to proceed without France, but an effective tactical blow at Neuve Chapelle did seem a possible way of inflicting serious damage on the Germans – without France. Neuve Chapelle was a strongpoint at the head of a salient jutting about two miles out of the main German lines. It was defended by one brigade, and the British could muster a dozen.

Brigadier David Carter was put in charge of the main support brigade, the 24th. He was to go in to help the 23rd or 25th if either got into difficulties. Although he could see everything that was going on, he could not take decisions about how to deploy his men; that power lay with High Command: the line of command ran back through senior staff officers to General Rawlinson in charge of the whole attack under Haig and French. It took an hour to get a message up or down the chain, a ponderous system that was to cause problems.

The 25th Brigade attacked along a front between Chimney

Crescent and Signpost Lane. Everything went according to plan. The artillery opened up and, since a heavy artillery attack was still a novelty with its stupendous noise and piercing flashes of light and smoke, it smashed and terrified the German front line. There was a quick, simple advance with few casualties, although one notable casualty was the heroic Colonel McAndrew of the Lincolnshires who, with his leg shattered by a shell, lay propped up against a parapet watching the assault with dimming eyes and asking with his last breath, 'Have they taken the trenches?' They had. It took less than two hours. The first substantial British offensive of the war seemed to be a great success; some of the infantry started to believe that it would be the only offensive.

Not everyone in the 25th Brigade was having it all that easy. The Irish Rifles, who had advanced furthest, encountered some resistance and even a minor counter-attack at the château, and there were some heavy casualties resulting from troops dangerously crowded into confined trenches and shell-holes losing touch with other trenches and shell-holes, leaving pockets of German machine-gunners between them.

Overall though, the Germans had, locally at least, been thrown into confusion, and the obvious thing to do was to advance while the going was good, calling in Carter and his 24th Brigade from the support lines. He had plenty of troops to follow up and mop up pockets of resistance and to widen the breach that had clearly and effectively been made in the German lines.

At the same time, it was also obvious that failure to advance would mean that the Germans would get back into their fortified positions and cause grievous casualties in the event of a delay – a fear that turned out to be fully justified in practice.

The problem was that, while everyone was delighted that, two hours after the battle began, the German line had been broken by the 25th Brigade to the south, everyone was in despair about the very different story of the 23rd Brigade at the northern end. The 23rd had attacked north of Signpost Lane, only to find that the artillery barrage in their sector had been light and ineffective, which meant the Germans were in a good position to wipe them out as they advanced. While the 25th jogged to a quick victory, the 23rd ground to a bloody halt.

Carter and the 24th Brigade were now called up to support and, where necessary, replace the 23rd, instead of breaking through behind the 25th. Carter himself wanted to move into an orchard which he could see was undefended but he had first to consult General Rawlinson, who had convinced himself without seeing it that the orchard was a heavily defended strongpoint. Rawlinson

They swarmed up ladders and into no man's land. Bullets and shells were fired at random, for the Germans were unable to see their attackers hidden by a smoke-screen. They knew an attack had started, and they fired blindly.

Although there were quite heavy losses in the first few moments, the London Irish kept good order. They marched forward without hurrying. Every step was taken with regimental precision, and twice on the way across no man's land they halted for a moment to correct their alignment. Macgill also noticed that a group of men on the far right were even confident enough to dribble a football towards the enemy!

Now it was time for Macgill and his fellow stretcher-bearer to go over the top. Suddenly all the fear of anticipation left him and he was standing free. A bullet passed very close to his face like a sharp, sudden breath; a second hit the ground in front and flicked up the dust. The moment had come for Macgill when it was best to stop thinking.

Three young soldiers rushed past him carrying between them a box of rifle ammunition. One of them fell flat to earth. The other two hesitated for a moment before hurrying on alone with the box. The man on the ground raised himself for a moment and looked after his mates, then sank down again to the wet ground.

'Another soldier came crawling towards us on his belly, looking for all the world like a gigantic lobster which had escaped from its basket. His lower lip was cut clean to the chin and hanging apart; blood welled through the muddy khaki trousers where they covered the hips.'

Macgill recognized him.

'Much hurt, matey?'

'I'll manage to get in.'

'Shall I put a dressing on?'

'I'll manage to get into our own trench,' he stammered spitting the blood from his lips. 'There are others out at the wire. Try and get them in, Pat.' He crawled off.

'My cap was blown off my head as if by a violent gust of wind and it dropped on the ground. I put it on again, and at that moment a shell burst near at hand and a dozen splinters sang by my ear. I walked forward with a steady step.

'"What took my cap off?" I asked myself. "It went away just as if it was caught in a breeze. God!" I muttered, in a burst of realisation. "It was that shell passing." I breathed very deeply, my blood rushing down to my toes and an airy sensation filled my body. Then the stretcher dragged.'

Macgill looked round. His fellow stretcher-bearer had gone.

Possibly he had been shelled and possibly he had been swept away in the whirling chaos of an absurd and tragic charge by a Highland regiment which had careered away in the wrong direction. In the confusion of the battle a whole battalion of Highlanders had charged parallel to their own trenches fully exposed to enemy fire.

'Men and pieces of men were lying all over the place. A leg, an arm, then again a leg, cut off at the hip. A finely formed leg, the latter, gracefully putteed. A dummy leg in a tailors window could not be more graceful. It might be X; he was an artist in dress, a Beau Brummel in khaki. Fifty yards farther along I found the rest of X . . .' X and many of his comrades had been Macgill's boyhood playmates in Donegal.

The London Irish fortunately were better organized than the Highlanders. They knew they had to aim for the crucifix in Loos cemetery. They would soon hit the trenches which ran several hundred yards in front of the cemetery.

They advanced. When they reached German positions, they took prisoners. One Cockney who had captured a huge Bavarian told Macgill, '"Kamerad! Kamerad!" 'e shouted when I came up. Blimey! I couldn't stab 'im so I took 'im prisoner. It's not 'arf a barney!' Others were not so sensitive.

'Here's one that I've just done in,' shouted McCrone, whose mother never sent him any money for fear he should take up the evil habit of smoking cigarettes. 'That's five of the bloody swine now!' His bayonet and face were bloodstained. He was a terrifying soldier. His favourite tune which he often whistled as he went about his soldiering was 'There Is A Green Hill Far Away'.

A German gas-bomb exploded nearby, and for a while Macgill hardly knew what was happening. He wandered around vaguely, carrying his stretcher over his shoulder.

'The irritation, only momentary, was succeeded by a strange humour. I felt as if walking on air, my head got light, and it was with difficulty that I kept my feet on earth. It would be so easy to rise into space and float away.

'The sensation was a delightful one; I felt so pleased with myself with everything. A wounded man lay on the ground, clawing the earth with frenzied fingers. In a vague way I remembered some ancient law which ordained me to assist a stricken man. But I could not do so now; the action would clog my buoyancy and that delightful feeling of freedom which permeated my being.'

Friends dying, screaming with pain, eyes bursting from their sockets, passed Macgill airily by. No shock, it seemed, would restore his senses until this sight, at once bizarre, disgusting and sad: 'A man, mother-naked, raced round in a circle, laughing boisterously.

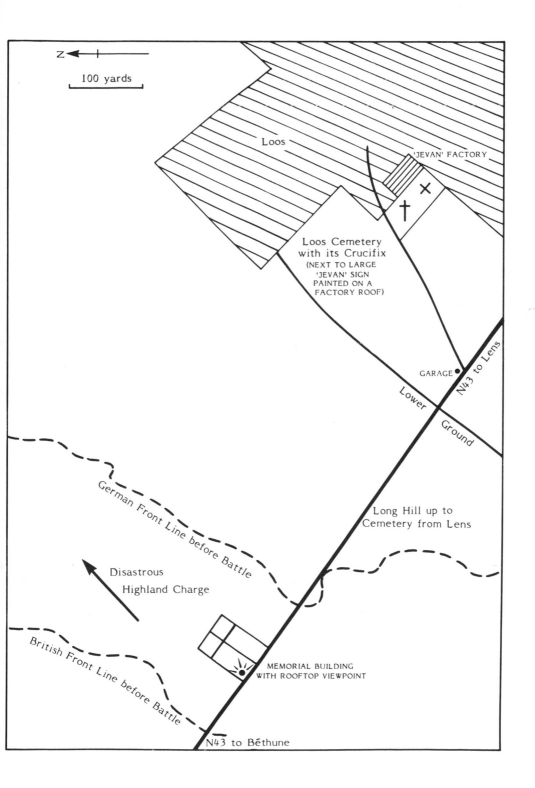

Z ← ⊢──────→

100 yards

Loos

'JEVAN' FACTORY

✝

Loos Cemetery
with its Crucifix
(NEXT TO LARGE
'JEVAN' SIGN
PAINTED ON A
FACTORY ROOF)

N43 to Lens

GARAGE ●

Lower

Ground

German Front Line before Battle

Long Hill up to
Cemetery from Lens

Disastrous
Highland Charge

British Front Line before Battle

MEMORIAL BUILDING
WITH ROOFTOP VIEWPOINT

N43 to Béthune

The rags that would class him as a friend or foe were gone, and I could not tell whether he was an Englishman or a German. As I watched him an impartial bullet went through his forehead.'

This finally brought Macgill back to earth.

The London Irish had now reached the wire in front of the German trenches. They were very near the day's objective. The wire, shells and bullets continued to take their toll, and Macgill busied himself with simple dressings for wounds needing major surgery. A high-explosive shell dropped in a crater fifty yards from him in a little hollow; he saw seven or eight figures in khaki lying prostrate facing the ground; the shell burst and the wounded and dead rose slowly in the air to a height of six or seven yards and then dropped slowly again. It was impossible for Macgill to do anything about soldiers seriously wounded in that way. He felt quite useless and small.

Victorious, the London Irish entered the German trench itself. A final burst of rifle fire, grenades and petrol bombs brought more casualties but the trench was won. Even the football almost made it, but bullet-holes had deflated it, and it was abandoned in land which had been no man's land but which was now safely in British hands.

In the trench Macgill came across an old friend of his called Flannery, lying with his arm around a barbed-wire support. He was a strong, placid, solitary man and an honest friend. He was dying. Macgill knelt down beside him and cut away his tunic where a burnt hole clotted with blood showed under his kidney. A splinter of shell had torn part of the man's side away.

'In much pain, Chummy?'

'Ah Christ! Yes, Pat. Wife and two kiddies too. Are we getting the best of it?'

'Winning all along.'

The survivors of the London Irish were consolidating the capture of the German trench. They were rebuilding it using sandbags and dead Germans indifferently. The day had been fought hard and won.

Source
P. Macgill, *The Great Push*

Battle of Loos, 1915

The Misuse of Gas: 25 September 1915

'The Commander of the gas-company in the front line sent a telephone message through to Divisional Headquarters "DEAD CALM. IMPOSSIBLE DISCHARGE ACCESSORY." ("Accessory" was code for "gas".) The answer came back: "ACCESSORY TO BE DISCHARGED AT ALL COSTS." . . . The spanners for unscrewing the cocks of the gas cylinders were found, with two or three exceptions, to be misfits. The gas-men rushed about shouting and asking each other for the loan of an adjustable spanner. They discharged one or two cylinders with the spanners that they had; the gas went whistling out, formed a thick cloud a few yards away in no man's land, and then gradually spread back into the trenches.

'The Germans had been expecting the attack. They immediately put their gas-helmets on, semi-rigid ones, better than ours. Bundles of oily cotton-waste were strewn along the German parapet and set alight as a barrier to the gas. Then their batteries opened on our lines. The confusion was great; the shelling broke several gas cylinders and the trench was soon full of gas. The gas-company dispersed.'

The colonel was wounded in the hand and out of action. The telephone wires were blown up. All the preparations for the attack were inadequate.

There was a shortage of shells because of an air-raid on the main ammunition dump in the area, so the German wire was still intact. The communication trenches were too narrow – Robert Graves and his companions in the Royal Welch Fusiliers had a terrible time in one of them, Maison Rouge Alley:

'Come on!'
'Get back, you bastards!'
'Gas turning on us.'
'Keep your heads, you men.'
'Back like Hell, boys!'
'Whose orders?'
'What's happening?'
'Gas!'
'Back!'
'Come on!'
'Gas!'

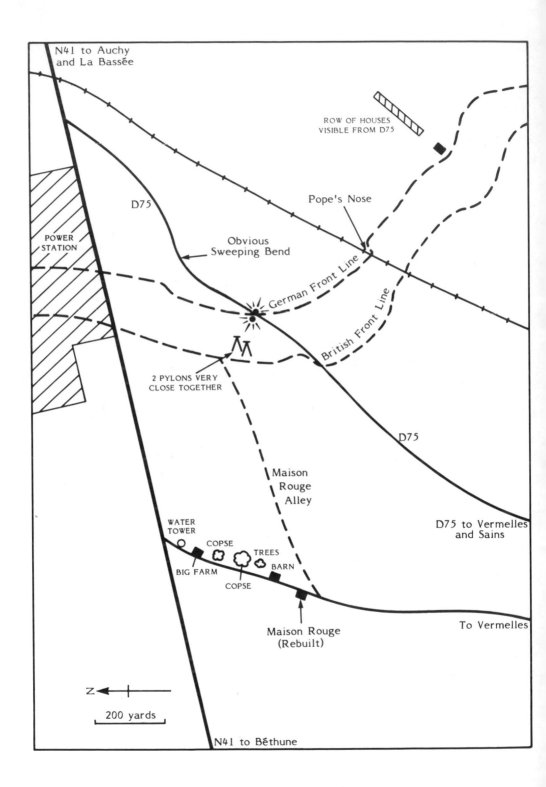

N41 to Auchy
and La Bassée

ROW OF HOUSES
VISIBLE FROM D75

D75

Pope's Nose

POWER
STATION

Obvious
Sweeping Bend

German Front Line

British Front Line

2 PYLONS VERY
CLOSE TOGETHER

D75

Maison
Rouge
Alley

D75 to Vermelles
and Sains

WATER
TOWER

COPSE

TREES

BARN

BIG FARM

COPSE

Maison Rouge
(Rebuilt)

To Vermelles

Z

200 yards

N41 to Béthune

'Back!'

All night long. Even the storeman drank the double rum ration before it could be distributed to the Royal Welch. The death penalty: he was trampled into the mud, face down, and killed.

Still they were eager to go. War had not yet made them cynical. Young officers in the Royal Welch were cross at following the Middlesex. They should go over the top first. They had right of line. They were the older regiment.

They were eager to beat the Scots to glory. 'The Jocks are all the same, the trousered variety and the bare-backed variety. They're dirty in trenches, they skite too much, and they charge like hell – both ways.'

The first Company of Middlesex went over the top three-quarters of an hour earlier than expected. They had been driven out of their own trench by gas. Those who survived being mown down by the enemy machine-gun at Pope's Nose were blown up by their own artillery as they tried to break through the German barbed wire.

The company directly ahead of Graves' went over next. One of the Officers told Graves what happened: 'The din was tremendous. He saw the platoon on the left flopping down too, so he whistled the advance again. Nobody seemed to hear. He jumped up from his shell-hole and waved and signalled "Forward." Nobody stirred. He shouted "You bloody cowards, are you leaving me to go alone?" His platoon sergeant, groaning with a broken shoulder, gasped out: "Not cowards, Sir. Willing enough. But they're all . . . dead." A machine-gun traversing had caught them as they rose to the whistle.'

Graves had had the presence of mind to fill his water-bottle with rum. He drank it. He was ready to take his turn to go over the top. The trench was thick with dead. No one had so far gone over the top and lived.

A runner came with a message. The attack was off for the present.

Source
R. Graves, *Goodbye to All That*

Battle of Loos, 1915

The Hohenzollern Redoubt: October 1915

The mounds and craters at the far end of the battlefront at Loos were the burial ground of thousands of Tommies. The tactical importance of those mounds and craters known as the Hohenzollern Redoubt was dubious. Full control of the redoubt would have allowed some broadening of the feeble Loos Salient but, as Private George Coppard, a machine-gunner from Croydon serving with the Sixth Royal West Surrey Regiment who served on the redoubt, observed, its real importance was probably only the prestige of possessing it. ·

Private Coppard got his first real taste of battle on the Hohenzollern Redoubt.

He was Number Two in a machine-gun team. On 30 September 1915 he and five others carried their Vickers machine-gun up the communication trench running parallel to the Vermelles-Hulluch road and leading up to the ridge running along the old German front line in the Battle of Loos at that time. The Vickers machine-gun consisted of a fifty-pound tripod and a twenty-eight-pound gun and needed continuous supplies of water for cooling as well as ammunition, which it fired at the rate of 600 rounds a minute. All of this, including the supply of water, had to be manhandled uphill to the front line along the communication trench all the way from Vermelles.

Progress under continuous shellfire up the communication trench was slowed by a constant flow of wounded, fatigue parties carrying ammunition and rations, telephone linesmen, runners and parties of relieved troops. Everybody had to pick their way up the narrow trench through wrecked equipment and scores of dead horses. The dead horses were a new and horrible experience for Coppard – as their carcases, hideously blown up by intestinal gases, were punctured, they released the foulest imaginable stench, which poisoned the air in a disgusting way for some distance.

Coppard was certainly not deterred. Supported by the self-confidence of a young man of seventeen – pretending he was nineteen – going up to the front line for the first time, he was quite determined to prove himself. He was also fortunate to be steadied when necessary by the cool experience of the Number One in his team, Lance-Corporal Rankin, who recited heroic poetry and told stories from Arthur Conan Doyle at critical moments.

Still, Coppard had to endure more than the horses on his way to the Hohenzollern Redoubt. On the front-line ridge itself, the blown-up bodies of masses of men from the Highland regiments made a terrible display of colour from their kilts, glengarries, bonnets and blood on their bare limbs. The warm sun had blackened their faces and made them stink.

It was only a few hundred yards from the end of the communication trench to the Hohenzollern Redoubt. The British held the south side of the redoubt and the Germans the north side. The battle raged fiercely.

Coppard and his companions set up their machine-gun near the southern edge of the redoubt, to try to stop any outflanking movement by the Germans on the one side and with a good view of the trenches and craters of the redoubt on the other side. From their position Coppard could see exactly what was happening on the redoubt and how craters were fought over.

The whole of the Hohenzollern Redoubt was scattered with huge mine craters typically a hundred feet in diameter and about thirty feet deep. The object of both sides was to advance by exploding new craters in enemy lines by digging underneath them. The explosions would kill the occupants of that part of the line, and the unoccupied crater would be captured.

Specially selected ex-miners tunnelled furiously to get under each others' positions. Then tons of explosives would be placed and primed ready to blow the enemy sky high. There was a constant underground battle against time, with both sides competing against each other to blast great holes through the earth above. Sometimes they met underground and fought there desperately with picks and shovels, but usually it was a simple, deadly race.

When a mine was ready to go off, the infantry would be prepared to 'go over the top' to capture the resulting crater. 'At the moment of explosion the ground trembled violently in a miniature earthquake. Then, like an enormous pie crust rising up, slowly at first, the bulging mass of earth crackled in thousands of fissures as it erupted. When the vast sticky mass could no longer contain the pressure beneath, the centre burst open, and the energy released carried all before it. Hundreds of tons of earth hurled skywards to a height of three hundred feet or more, many of the lumps of great size.' Panic broke out a hundred yards in all directions. 'There was nowhere to run for shelter in the crater area. Troops just pinned themselves to the side of a trench, muttered a prayer of some sort, and cringed like animals about to be slaughtered.'

The infantry would then rush into the hot, smoking crater. Coppard and the machine-gunners would rake the German trenches

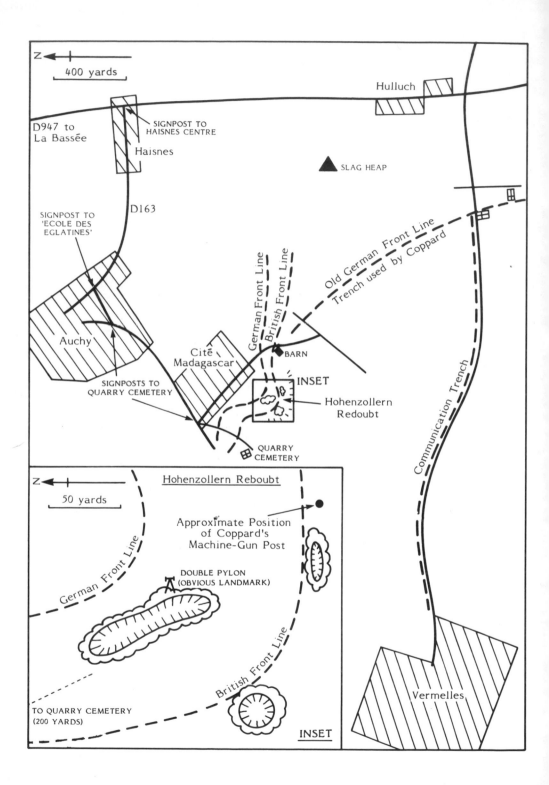

Z ←—————
400 yards

Hulluch

D947 to
La Bassée

SIGNPOST TO
HAISNES CENTRE

Haisnes

SLAG HEAP

D163

SIGNPOST TO
'ECOLE DES
EGLATINES'

German Front Line

British Front Line

Old German Front Line

Trench used by Coppard

Auchy

Cité
Madagascar

BARN

SIGNPOSTS TO
QUARRY CEMETERY

INSET

Hohenzollern
Redoubt

QUARRY
CEMETERY

Communication Trench

Z ←—————
50 yards

Hohenzollern Reboubt

German Front Line

Approximate Position
of Coppard's
Machine-Gun Post

DOUBLE PYLON
(OBVIOUS LANDMARK)

British Front Line

TO QUARRY CEMETERY
(200 YARDS)

Vermelles

INSET

with fire to fend off German machine-gunners and snipers as the infantry moved forward. Then the new crater had to be defended although enemy-held craters were often only twenty feet away. Grenades were lobbed from all sides into the pit of the crater behind the men clinging to its crumbling sides trying to defend it. These grenades caused shocking injuries.

The machine-gunners knew that their post was likely to be a target for a mining attack. They had no means of knowing where the digging was going on, and so there was a permanent cold fear. Coppard and his companions never knew if they were about to be blown up. They knew it was likely. Rather feeble attempts were made to disguise the exact location of the gun by covering it with sacking by day by fitting on a funnel by night so the sparks could be seen only from straight ahead (which was an unsafe place to observe from); the machine-gun also had a Heath Robinson arrangement to avoid visible steam emissions from boiled water which had been used for cooling.

Coppard was not blown up on this occasion. After eighteen days he and the five out of six who survived from the machine-gun team went back to Vermelles. This was a much higher than average survival rate for the Battle of Loos and especially for the Hohenzollern Redoubt.

Sir John French paid with his command for the sixty thousand dead and negligible gains of this battle. He was replaced by Sir Douglas Haig. Coppard remarked: '. . . not that it made any difference to us Tommies . . .'

Source
G. Coppard, *With a Machine-gun to Cambrai*

Cuinchy, 1916

Confusion Among the Brickstacks: April 1916

The British Army and a German spy both occupied Cuinchy. The chemist shop was the British command post where orders were issued on everything from rations to raiding parties. The shop was also the base for a German spy who tapped electric cable which crossed the front line. It was only the utter confusion of orders emanating from Cuinchy that rendered the spy more or less harmless. Order and counter-orders from behind the lines were often irrelevant to the reality up front. Edmund Blunden, the poet, serving as a lieutenant in the Royal Sussex Regiment, put it this way: 'One's mind was more filled with one's relations to superior beings behind us than to those who were not losing the war in front of us.' This was a sure road to disaster.

Edmund Blunden had scrambled around the confusing web of trenches and saps among the brickstacks east of Cuinchy to find his dug-out. As he lay down in it, the roars and flashes of an exploding mine ripped through the wet night outside. The dug-out shook but held. Blunden was sent up with stretcher-bearers to see what could be done to help. They ran along the narrow communications trenches, support trenches and front-line trenches with shells burst-ing all around lighting up the night sky eerily. They were also bombarded with 'Minnies' or 'Airy Devils', huge mortar-shells which looked like oil-drums packed with high explosive and shrap-nel; these were fired high into the air, where they wobbled menacing-ly for a few seconds, while the people underneath scattered, and fell to earth with murderous effect. And they were bombarded with hand grenades. When they at last got to the scene of the mine disaster, they found sixty men had been blown up but that more stretcher-bearers were not needed and should therefore return the way they had just come. As they got back to the dug-out, incredibly without loss, they found an unexploded 'Minny' in their path. Walking by a primed and detonated bomb which might go off any second was a heart-stopping exercise. They managed though, and they got back safely.

The response from headquarters in Cuinchy to these acts of bravery and the mine disaster was a request for a statement of the number of picks and shovels in the sector; this request was accompa-nied by a note, 'Please expedite.'

After a couple of hours rest, Blunden was out again, dragging himself through the thick wet clay of the trenches to the furthest forward point of the front line, a fire-step supported by gas cylinders, overlooking Jerusalem Crater. The crater was an enormous hole in brown exploded soil with a pool in the bottom of it. Blunden splashed through the pool and up on to the sniper's fire-step nearest the German front line which he thought was some fifty yards away. He peered through the sentry's periscope to see to his horror that the enemy was in fact near enough to hurl bombs right into and beyond Jerusalem Crater itself.

Grenades landed around and flew behind him, where they pro-duced terrible screams of agony from a group of young soldiers in the trenches.

Blunden made his plans for a night attack on the German advanced position and started back. He came across two young men from the hand-grenade attack: 'Brothers should not join the same battalion. When we were at the place where some of the wounded had been collected under the best shelter to be found, I was struck deep by the misery of a boy, whom I knew and liked well; he was half-crying, half-exhorting over a stretcher whence came the clear but weakened voice of his brother, wounded almost to death, waiting his turn to be carried down. Not much could be said at such times; but a known voice perhaps conveyed some comfort. In this battalion, brothers had frequently enlisted together; the effect was too surely a culmination of suffering.'

That night Blunden took a patrol, perilously, to the German advanced post near Jerusalem Crater. Nobody was there. What apparently happened each day was that a small group of German soldiers led by a grenade-hurling Goliath of a man, made their way to within ten or fifteen yards of the edge of the crater to harry the British front line. At night they would creep to the safety of a dug-out away from the battle. Once again, Blunden had been made to risk his life and the lives of his men without cause.

The following day, grenades were again flung at the men in the crater. The order came through from Cuinchy to ensure that every man had porridge for breakfast that morning. It was precisely this kind of nonsense from headquarters, thought Blunden, that made officers at the front insecure and unwilling to take initiatives. The young officer in charge of the crater became so deeply concerned about contravening regulations that he sent back the following message to Cuinchy: 'The Germans have thrown 6 bombs into Jerusalem Crater. Shall we throw any back?'

By the time this exchange of messages was going on, Blunden was asleep. He had crawled along winding trenches to a new and relatively safe dug-out hidden on the lee side of one of the brick-stacks, and climbed through a gap in the sandbags and gas cylinders which blocked his entrance, down the smoky black stairway and into the corner to sleep.

He woke to a hive of activity. British tunnellers, at the front, trying to dig under German lines, had got half way into no man's land when they heard German tunnellers going the other way. They realized the Germans had probably detected them too, and the decision had been taken to explode a defensive mine which would stop either side getting any further. Engineers rushed backwards and forwards with wire and detonators. The tunnellers retreated as quickly as possible past Blunden's dug-out. At length, a loud thud came from deep underground; then the earth of thousands of square feet of no man's

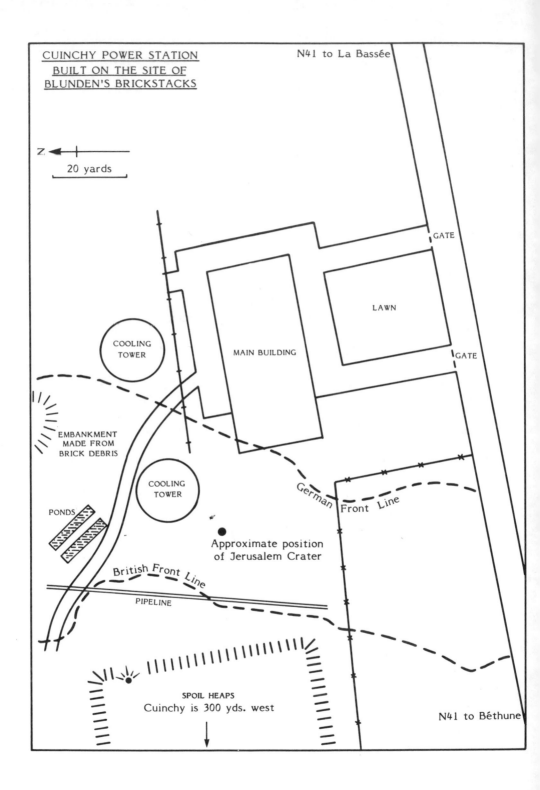

CUINCHY POWER STATION
BUILT ON THE SITE OF
BLUNDEN'S BRICKSTACKS

N41 to La Bassée

Z

20 yards

GATE

LAWN

COOLING
TOWER

MAIN BUILDING

GATE

EMBANKMENT
MADE FROM
BRICK DEBRIS

COOLING
TOWER

PONDS

German Front Line

Approximate position
of Jerusalem Crater

British Front Line

PIPELINE

SPOIL HEAPS
Cuinchy is 300 yds. west

N41 to Béthune

land heaved up to a great height in solid crags and clods amidst huge clouds of dust. There was a flame and a roar, and a whole great column of material hung in the air before collapsing with hisses and thuds indiscriminately over the British, the Germans and no man's land.

Cuinchy headquarters at least found a relevant response to this disaster in which hundreds died. They sent out large quantities of lime.

A little way back from the front, near where he had been sleeping, Blunden noticed a profusion of poppies, blue and white cornflowers, yellow cabbage-flowers and giant teazles. It was a warm day, and butterflies were plentiful. As he got nearer where the mine had gone off, nature gave way to man-inflicted death, and lime mercifully rotted the horrifying remains of men of the Royal Sussex Regiment.

Source
E. Blunden, *Undertones of War*

Lens, 1917

Trenches in the Streets: 14–19 August 1917

They practised trench warfare in Lens with tape and coloured flags. Then, in the evening of 14 August, there was a church service with a stirring rendering of 'Onward Christian Soldiers' and 'Nearer My God to Thee'. Everyone took communion. The colonel gave a brisk pep talk on the parade ground at seven o'clock and then shook hands with each officer. The officers, including Captain James Becton, then led their men of the 24th Canadian Battalion to the front.

Zero hour was to be 4.20 a.m. Becton and his company would go over the top then. First, they had to get to the front line:

'As we followed the ingoing communicating trench, part of which ran through the middle of the street, there were houses on both sides. These the German artillery was constantly playing on, so bricks and mortar flew in all directions. The few houses that had been left standing were demolished as if they had been made of cardboard. You can well imagine that when a shell hit anywhere near a house it made things very unpleasant for those of us passing through these trenches.'

When a shell came over, all they could do was to huddle in the trenches and hope for luck. One of Becton's lieutenants unwittingly committed suicide by climbing out of the communication trench to see how his men were coming up from the rear. When Becton passed him, he gave a cheery wave. Shortly afterwards he was dead. A sergeant took over his platoon.

By midnight they had reached the front line directly in front of the suburb of Lens called Cité St. Edouard. To prepare for the attack and to avoid the danger of being shelled in a trench whose exact location the Germans knew, Becton ordered his men into forward shell-holes on the edge of no man's land.

At 3.45 a.m. he crawled from shell-hole to shell-hole serving rum. This was extremely dangerous since the Germans were sending up Very lights which every few seconds lit up the whole of no man's land like day. Becton had no wish to die serving rum. 'I never wanted to appear so small in my life . . . if I had to "go west" I wanted to go fighting at the head of my men.' Becton survived.

'At 4.19 a.m., a heavy barrage was laid on our front line and rear trenches. We knew then that the Huns had anticipated our attack and had by some means found out our Zero Hour. We were still not able to move forward until the Zero Hour.'

When Zero Hour came, the British artillery barrage and the explosion of the mines laid under German positions all along the line had a cheering effect on Becton. Despite some early casualties, he and his men advanced quickly to within fifty yards of German lines, ready to attack the Germans hand to hand when the barrage lifted.

When that time came, however, there was no one left alive in the German front line. Even the German second line was manned only by terrified Saxon boys who surrendered at once.

The going got tougher as they entered the suburb of Cité St. Laurent. Shells and machine-guns from what had now become the German front line were assisted by ferocious machine-gunning and bombing from German aeroplanes. Eventually British planes intervened and two bombers were brought down but not before they had caused a good number of casualties among Becton's men. Not only this, but in the confusion of smoke and shells, Becton lost his way and headed in the wrong direction, exposing himself even more as he found he had left the ruins and rubble of Cité St. Laurent and somehow ended up in Commotion Trench.

He nevertheless eventually reached his special objective, a trench called 'Nun's Alley', and his men suffered further as the Germans decided to make a strong stand to defend it: 'We had to fight our way up this trench dodging German stick bombs and rifle

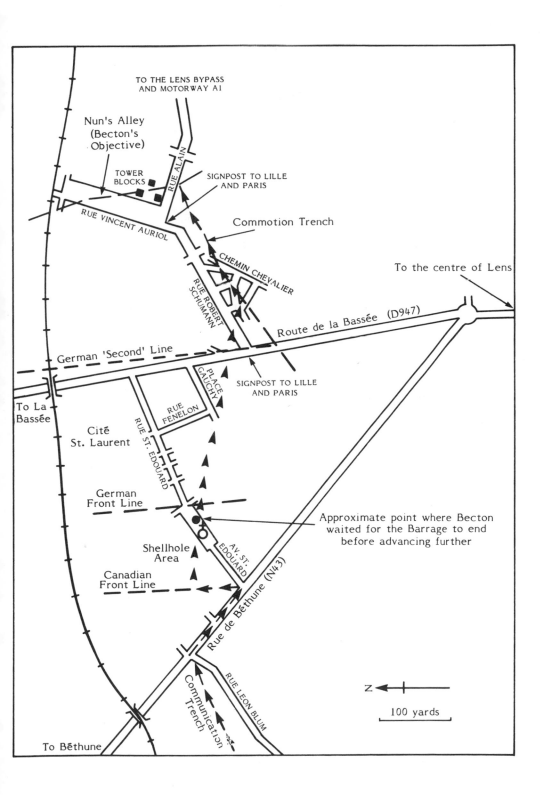

TO THE LENS BYPASS
AND MOTORWAY A1

Nun's Alley
(Becton's
Objective)

TOWER
BLOCKS

RUE ALAIN

SIGNPOST TO LILLE
AND PARIS

RUE VINCENT AURIOL

Commotion Trench

CHEMIN CHEVALIER

RUE ROBERT SCHUMANN

To the centre of Lens

Route de la Bassée (D947)

German 'Second' Line

PLACE GAUCHY

SIGNPOST TO LILLE
AND PARIS

To La
Bassée

RUE FENELON

RUE ST. EDOUARD

Cité
St. Laurent

German
Front Line

Shellhole
Area

AV. ST. EDOUARD

Approximate point where Becton
waited for the Barrage to end
before advancing further

Canadian
Front Line

Rue de Béthune (N43)

Communication Trench

RUE LEON BLUM

Z

100 yards

To Béthune

grenades, walking over dead German bodies, until we reached
our objective . . .'

Becton took the view that the Germans were a good, disciplined
fighting force but weak in this kind of hand-to-hand battle. The
fighting was personal and vicious, the bayonet was used, and each
man tried to tear the gas helmet from his opponent. A gas helmet
pulled off a man meant his death when the fumes were thick.

Nun's Alley was secured, although with heavy casualties. Becton
and his men were then required to hold it against up to four
counter-attacks a day for four days until 1.30 a.m. on 19 April. It
took the whole of the remainder of the battalion to hold 300 yards of
this front line: there was no sleep and little food, and the men used up
their iron rations.

As they made their way out of the lines they had won, the nervous
strain began to wear off. Men dropped exhausted by the wayside.
Those who made it back to billets discovered a reputation had gone
before them. The bagpipes struck up 'The Campbells are Coming'.
Everyone turned out to cheer them.

Source
J. Becton and E. L. Odell, *Hunting the Hun*

Battle of the River Lys, *1918*

A Brilliant Colonel Goes Too Far:
11–15 April, 1918

All that stood between the advancing Germans and the sea was
Hoegenmacker Ridge with its mill. From this ridge, Colonel Seton
Hutchison's machine-gunners delayed the advance for nearly a
week, until the French arrived in force. The cost was appalling.

Hutchison left his peaceful camp at Meteren to lead a bicycle team to
the battlefield just to reconnoitre. The British were in full retreat.
The Germans were advancing fast. Under these circumstances, it
was not in Hutchison's character just to carry on reconnoitring.

He soon abandoned his bicycle for some emergency action. In no
time, he rallied enough infantry to establish a temporary defensive

line to allow a casualty clearing-station to evacuate before it fell into German hands.

Hutchison now had the bit between his teeth.

He commandeered one of the casualty clearing-station's Ford ambulances for his own use and rushed off to organize his machine-gunners to make the temporary defensive line permanent. The command post and mid point of the defensive line would be Hoegen-macker Mill.

It was urgent to get his machine-gunners to the line quickly if they were to have any effect. There was no transport except his comman-deered ambulance and some Army Service Corps trucks. The officer in charge of the trucks explained to Hutchison that they were needed elsewhere. Hutchison answered by hitting the officer on the head with the butt of his revolver and taking charge of the trucks himself.

By the time the trucks had been filled with machine-gunners, guns and ammunition and had been driven back to the defensive line, the mill had almost been lost. Hutchison himself, from the front seat of a truck, shot dead some German machine-gunners, and their gun was captured. Everywhere else the Germans were advancing and the British were in retreat – or rout.

Hutchison had become obsessed with his defensive line. Hoegen-macker Mill must be held!

One North Country infantry battalion was fleeing past the mill. Hutchison punched their major and threatened to shoot him dead there and then if he failed to turn his men round. He did turn them round, but the survivors slipped away in the next hour or so.

By now, the mill had been recaptured but was perilous.

Hutchison was ready to murder. He discovered some drunk British stragglers. He routed them out and, with a machine-gun trained on them, sent them forward towards the enemy. They perished to a man. 'He was a filthy sight, the whole body churned with machine-gun bullets, the clotted pools of blood stinking with wine – so this pack at least was successful in drowning, once and for all, their sorrows in drink.'

The mill again fell and was again recaptured by hand-to-hand fighting in which Hutchison revelled, but its final fall to the Germans was now inevitable. They were achieving such complete victory elsewhere else on the line that soon six divisions would be able to concentrate on Hoegenmacker Ridge.

In the meantime, the mill and most of the defensive line held out through acts of individual bravery by Hutchison's men.

Hutchison exploited the bravery of his signallers: 'The equipment for my signallers was with the transport, but I put two men into the top of the windmill with handkerchiefs tied to sticks, so that from its

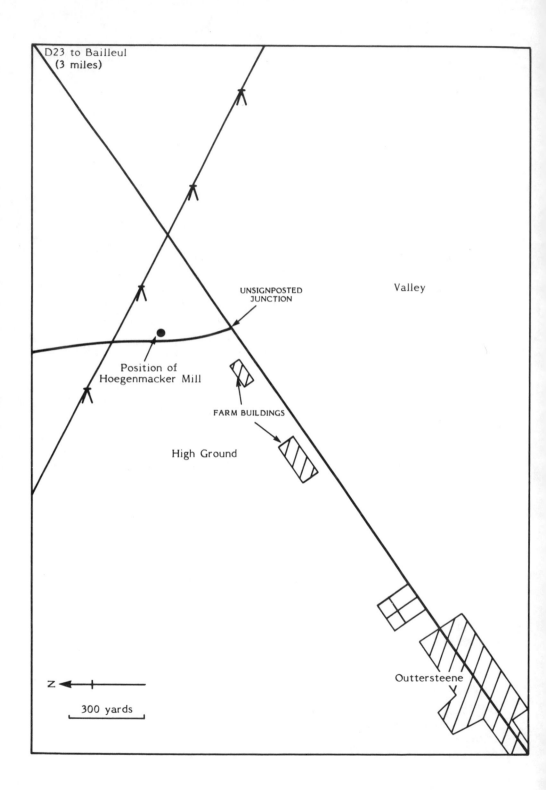

D23 to Bailleul
(3 miles)

UNSIGNPOSTED
JUNCTION

Valley

Position of
Hoegenmacker Mill

FARM BUILDINGS

High Ground

Outtersteene

Z

300 yards

eminence they could watch the moves of the enemy. One of these men was Corporal Noblett, who looked like his name, a great hulking fellow from the wide Yorkshire moors. He remained in the Mill-top for three days until long after it had fallen again into German hands, and finally escaped back to our lines after the Mill had been blown down by our artillery fire, attired in the uniform of a German soldier . . .'

He exploited the bravery of his transport officer: 'Transport Officer McQueen . . . arrived in a style reminiscent of the Royal Horse Artillery at an Aldershot field day. The fighting limbers with belt boxes and small-arms ammunition were galloped through a hail of shell and machine-gun fire to our gun positions.'

He exploited the bravery of his driver: 'Driver McKay, riding my big black horse, "Old Bill" fleet of foot and a magnificent jumper, rode the whole length of the line under a hail of fire for three miles along the front of our posts, while I, observing him, noted his trail upon my map, and thus was able to make clear the whole of our front. As he rode past the front of the First Queen's, the men rose from the little trenches which they had dug and cheered him to the echo.'

He backed up his exploitations with a terrible threat: 'I issued orders to my sergeants in charge of gun teams that any time that they saw British troops retiring they were to fire on them; and from the Mill I saw one of my gunners destroy a platoon of one regiment in full flight.'

Inevitably, the situation became quite desperate. Hutchison's defensive line became completely indefensible. He jumped on a horse and charged back to his headquarters at Bailleul for orders. He was lucky to get a few New Zealand pioneers to help cover his retreat.

The survivors retreated to a new and possible defensible line.

The maddened colonel once again took up his bicycle and went out to reconnoitre. He was struck down by gas before he had time to make any new plans. Over and over again he had issued gas-mask instructions, but he himself had never bothered to learn how to put a gas mask on. It was minutes before he could get his mask over his face, and by then his lungs were filled with gas. A little white dog coughed itself to death at his feet. Hutchison staggered to a nearby building and collapsed on the floor.

Source
G. S. Hutchison, *Warrior*

Battle of the River Lys, 1918

The Town Hall Siege: 13 and 14 April 1918

The German offensive was well advanced by 13 April 1918. Field Marshal Haig had sent out a 'backs to the wall' appeal but it fell mainly on deaf ears. The army was in rout. Acts of individual heroism hardly delayed the advance, pointless self-sacrifice. 'If the section cannot remain here alive it will remain here dead, but in any case it will remain here . . .' was a common enough sentiment. A much more effective sort of bravery was shown by Lieutenant-Colonel Stoney and his men at Neuve Eglise. They gave the Germans hell and got away to give them hell again.

Lieutenant-Colonel Stoney and the Padre, the Reverend E. V. Tanner, had sat down and started their breakfast in the brewery in Neuve Eglise. They were interrupted by the Germans coming into the village from the north, south and east.

Stoney rushed out past the church and across the square and organized small groups of signallers and runners to keep the Germans at bay while he got a company of his 2nd Worcestershires together to counter-attack to get the Germans out. This time the British were successful but they clung on only by their fingernails. Next time would not be so easy. Neuve Eglise stuck out further than ever in front of the retreating British front line.

Some German snipers had remained behind – one almost killed the Padre when he stooped to give a dying German a drink of water. The village was only slightly damaged but the streets were strewn with debris and dead bodies. The residents had long since fled. The Germans were expected back soon. Hope of reinforcements was fading.

Stoney moved his men into the town hall. It was tall and commanded a good view of the whole village; they would be able to see where and how the Germans were entering the village. And they were entering it. Stealthily.

By nightfall, only the town hall remained firmly in British hands. By 4.30 a.m. the Germans had even occupied a barn at the back of the town hall and were in a position to drop grenades into the cellars.

The town hall held. Stoney, the Padre and sixty men defended it.

A frontal attack on the town hall from across the square failed. It was repulsed by a machine-gun in one of the top windows and

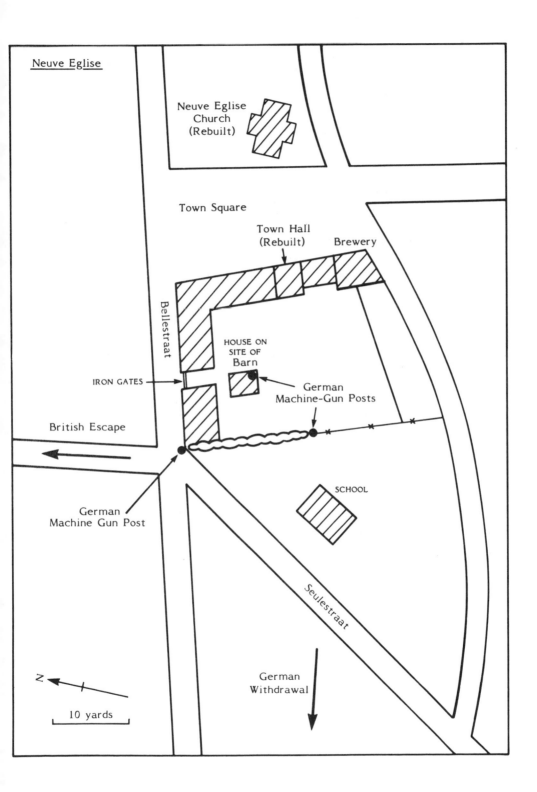

snipers in every other window. German dead and the wounded littered the square.

The Germans now planned a large-scale dawn attack from the front and the rear. Stoney realized the situation was now hopeless unless some way could be found to escape. The square was completely open, and no British soldier could cross it and live. The town hall was hemmed in on either side by buildings in German hands. The British lines were to the rear but there was a German machine-gun post in the barn and another twenty yards further on, covering the main road and any possible break-out beyond the barn.

In an extraordinarily brave surprise attack on the two machine-gun posts, Stoney's lieutenants, Crowe and Poynton with just five men forced their quick but temporary withdrawal.

At least there was for the moment no machine-gun trained on the town hall's back door.

The sixty men left the town hall in single file; they hurried across the courtyard and through the now-deserted barn. The bullets flew round them but they kept low and there were no casualties from the machine-guns which had been forced back by the lieutenant's raid. Out of the village. Back to the British lines. Eager and alive.

Source
J. Toland, *No Man's Land*

Battle of the River Lys, *1918*

The Defence of the Outpost of Merris: 14 April 1918

Twenty-year-old Lieutenant W. Allbeury of the 31st Division headed a platoon of exhausted and depressed troops. After 3½ years of war the Germans were advancing again.

Allbeury found his way to brigade headquarters in the convent at Merris and was told at first, amidst the confusion, when he asked for orders, to 'Go to Hell.' It was finally agreed that his platoon would march on to Strazeele, a village a few miles away. Nobody seemed to know why.

They marched across countryside unspoilt by battles and came

under fire near Strazeele. Allbeury's platoon of seventy or so bands-
men, cooks and storemen did not react well. Allbeury shouted at one
man whose greatcoat was burning to 'Lie down and roll in the road',
and within seconds the whole panicky company were lying down and
lining the road, expecting an instant attack by massed German
infantry. After their meandering dangerously around the countryside around Strazeele, a further order was received: 'Go back to
Merris and defend the approach from the Outtersteene road.' When
the colonel gave that order, Allbeury asked about rations for the
men: 'Rations! You won't want any rations! There won't be any need
for them! I believe they feed you all right in Ruhleben or wherever
some of you may be lucky enough to go!'

The defence of Merris was to be a holding operation at best, a
sacrificial operation at worst. The Germans were moving in that
direction in force. Exactly where they had got to no one was quite
sure, but at the same time no one doubted that they would be moving
through the village of Merris which stood out on a slight hill on the
way to the west. So uncertain was Allbeury of the precise where-
abouts of the Germans that in the fields north of Merris, on his way
back to defend the village, he thought for a while that his company
had somehow got behind German lines.

Finally, in the small hours of 14 April 1918, they reached the
hedgerow to be defended on the eastern outskirts of the village,
placed a listening post in a small depression further out in a hop field,
overlooking all the ground between Merris and Outtersteene, and
placed a platoon with two Lewis guns in a paddock south of the road
looking down to the railway and beyond. They were now the only
troops in Merris; brigade headquarters had long since evacuated the
convent.

Two young Geordies were at the listening-post and soon ran back
with news of fearsome moaning and groaning from the field beyond –
it turned out to be the wind blowing through the wire and poles
supporting the hops. The next news was more concrete. Two
German scouts were out from Outtersteene. Two shots disposed of
them as they reached the hop field. By now, however, an entire
German battalion was emerging from Outtersteene and was a bare
thousand yards away.

A morning mist descended.

All that Allbeury and his platoon could do was to wait and hope
that their inevitable extermination would be as painless as possible.

Time passed and no Germans emerged from the thick mist.
Allbeury and the two Geordies hardly dared to breath as they peered
out into the hop field. Not a movement. Not a sound.

The silence was suddenly broken by the machine-gun in the

paddock south of the wood. The sergeant in charge was calmly directing an enfilade of fire over the advancing mass of Germans who had bypassed Merris and were unexpectedly exposed, as the fog cleared, moving south of the railway line, easily within range, up to Celery Copse.

'We poured a steady fire into as fine an enfilade as ever offered in the whole course of the war. Gleefully we congratulated ourselves that we had not yet been spotted. Even so, things could not last. We must sooner or later be observed, and the inevitable would take place – we were bound to be overwhelmed in no time. But we felt that it would almost be worth it now, because we had taken a toll, which he would be bound to feel. Those lads, trained as they were only upon ranges at home, had acquitted themselves valiantly against their first live targets, judging from the host of still figures which lay about in curious twisted positions on the low ground before us.'

After forty minutes or so, the ammunition ran out. Allbeury's orders had been to stand and fight to the last, but he was not prepared to sacrifice seventy men for nothing and he had spotted a safe path back through the village. He gathered the company together and they made their way along a narrow track hidden by hedgerows back past the convent.

To Allbeury's astonishment, a nun appeared at the door:

'Is there any danger, M'sieur?'

Allbeury exclaimed that there was imminent danger, that he was the last British soldier and that she should leave instantly!

'But, M'sieur, I have many refugees in the cellars, sick women – women in child-bed who can go no further.'

'Listen, Mother, the enemy are about to occupy Merris. You must go to your people and get them ready. When the enemy come you must go to them quite openly, and ask them to protect you. They will send you safely to the rear through their lines. Do you understand? You must not delay, for Merris may well be bombarded in an hour.'

'I understand, M'sieur. We shall trust in our religion. God bless you!'

By now, Allbeury had got well behind his retreating men, and the first German bullets were starting to fly through the village. Still he found time at one point to nip into a hen hutch to help himself to a breakfast egg which ended soon after as a squashed mess up his sleeve when a machine-gun started up and he flung himself into a ditch.

The platoon retreated down the Strazeele road and were ordered to defend the line west of the orchard, a few hundred yards outside the village. There they had a rough time in half-dug trenches without

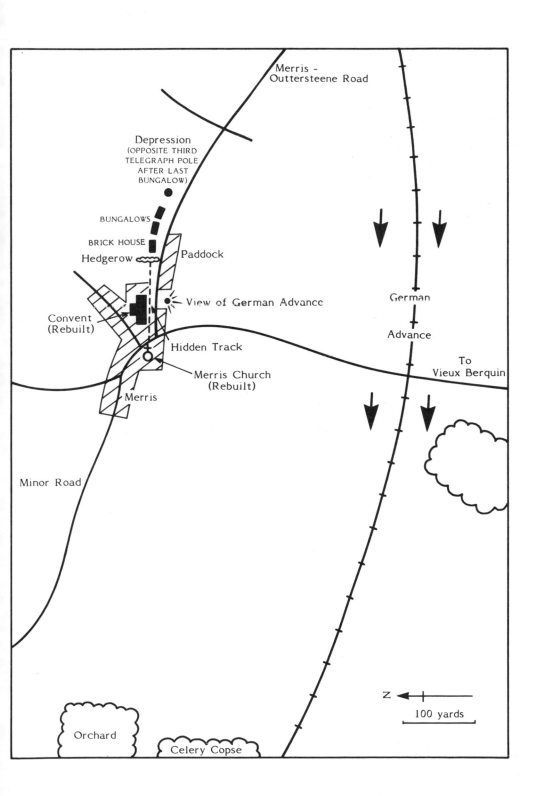

Merris -
Outtersteene Road

Depression
(OPPOSITE THIRD
TELEGRAPH POLE
AFTER LAST
BUNGALOW)

BUNGALOWS

BRICK HOUSE

Hedgerow

Paddock

Convent
(Rebuilt)

View of German Advance

German

Advance

To
Vieux Berquin

Hidden Track

Merris Church
(Rebuilt)

Merris

Minor Road

Z

100 yards

Orchard

Celery Copse

sleep or rations and under constant fire from a machine-gun set up in Merris church clock.

At last, in the evening, the decimated platoon were allowed to withdraw to Australian lines on higher ground behind. Merris had been given up.

Source
Great War Adventures

ARRAS

Introduction

By the seventeenth century, Arras was already a vital fortress. Marshal Turenne had considered it the key to the northern defence of France. With his back to the wall in 1918, Field Marshal Haig took a similar view.

Arras stayed French throughout the war, although the hills to the south changed hands in fierce battles. The ridges of Vimy and Notre Dame de Lorette are now preserved as memorials to the Canadians and French who fell there. They commanded a dominating view over the industrial region to the north and were fought over at enormous cost by the French, who succeeded in wresting back from the Germans the ridge of Notre Dame de Lorette and forcing them half way up Vimy Ridge.

The French attitude to trench warfare was rather different from the British. When not actually pursuing a major offensive, the French preferred to live and let live. When the growing British Army was able to take over the front line in the Arras sector in 1916, relieving pressure on the embattled French at Verdun, they found it quite tranquil in comparison with the more vicious fighting to the north. The British generals thought the troops (on both sides) would get complacent if they just waited around like the French. They felt especially that command of no man's land by laying mines and making trench raids during the hours of darkness was essential to demoralize the enemy.

In spring 1917 the British agreed to assist the French attack a hundred miles to the south, on the Aisne, by a diversionary offensive to capture Vimy Ridge. The success of such an operation depended on the destruction of enemy defences by artillery fire, which depended in turn on observations from aircraft and balloons. It also depended on the skill and courage of the Canadian infantry, who were operating in their own corps for the first time. The Canadians stormed the ridge on 9 April 1917.

The success of the Canadian Corps (the physique and determination of the Canadian troops were generally of a higher standard than the British) led directly to the formation the following year of the Australian Army Corps. Colonial troops fought well and were held in high esteem. Their pay was five shillings a day compared with one shilling a day for the British. They were rewarded with the toughest tasks, such as taking Passchendaele and storming Vimy Ridge.

Vimy Ridge was just the first objective of the Arras diversionary offensive. Other advances in the area were much less successful and soon ground to a halt as the Germans got over the first shock and as it became clear that the French offensive on the Aisne had lost momentum completely, the attacks at Arras – which had cost 159,000 casualties – were wound up.

After the offensive, the routine of trench warfare resumed around Arras. Reinforcements arrived to replace the losses, fresh, enthusiastic and often fearful young men who had to learn quickly the truth about the trenches.

In 1918 the German Spring Offensive broke through both north and south of the Arras sector. If Arras itself had fallen, the entire line would have collapsed; the responsibility on the troops there was heavy. In the event, the Arras sector as a whole held out well, and the war moved away finally in the wake of the last allied offensive, which started on 27 September 1918.

City of Arras, 1916

Peace of Arras: August 1916

It was hot August weather when Captain Victor Kelly MC of the Leicestershire Regiment took up his post in Arras. Battalion headquarters in the city was in a brewery where officers held convivial dinner parties and slept in four-poster beds. One officer had a gramophone which kept grinding out 'Let the Great Big World Keep Turning' and the general used to enjoy a duck-shoot in a swamp about a hundred yards from the German trenches.

Life was probably just as easy on the German side.

The trenches were rarely shelled, 'and the general holiday atmosphere was only disturbed by occasional bursts of trench-mortar fire on the front line and, at four in the afternoon, with comic regularity, by a few shells on Arras Cathedral. We were usually having tea at that time on the second floor of our brewery, and the shells flew straight overhead to the Cathedral a few hundred yards away, but we had complete confidence that the efficiency of the German artillery would prevent any shells falling short and hitting our headquarters by mistake'.

Inspecting the trenches in the suburbs east of Arras was Captain Kelly's job. Every day he strode out along the silent cobbled streets to the Pont St. Nicolas over the Scarpe and from there to the candle factory. Iron trays from the factory had been used to line the communication trenches which led out to the support line and front line. The banks of the trenches were overgrown with weeds but just occasionally a pathetic French skeleton from the offensive of 1915 could be seen, a reminder of more warlike days.

Kelly would always make his way to the furthest forward post by the river, which was connected back to headquarters by a long wire with bells on the end of it. But there were no occasions to sound this alarm. The officer in charge spent most of his time with a net intercepting floating messages on their way to German lines. He never found any evidence of espionage, just frivolous messages from British soldiers addressed to 'Dear Jerry . . .'

Then tragedy struck. The enemy were suspected of trying to mine the front lines, and some precautionary digging by civilian miners from New Zealand drafted in for this special work was going on around the three mine craters called 'Cuthbert', 'Clarence' and 'Claude'. At five o'clock one morning, Kelly and his brigadier were called out to the craters – there had been an underground explosion. The Germans had blown a small mine right in the centre of the tunnelling operations and some twenty men were buried. The brigadier asked a survivor if there was any chance of finding the others alive; the miner, hands in pockets, a cigarette in his mouth, mumbled, 'Naw, flat as winkles!'

The idyllic near-truce was coming quickly to an end. A raid was ordered on the German front line. It was unsuccessful. Far from being a surprise, a bombardment warned the enemy of the size, location and timing of the attack. (No messages down the river were necessary.) The Germans withdrew to the flanks of the threatened trench and, when the attack came, gave a signal to their artillery and machine-gunners who bombarded and enfiladed until the raiders were blown to pieces, cut down by bullets or forced to retreat.

Soon afterwards the Germans counter-attacked without a warning bombardment, and it was a lot more effective than the British raid. They never left their lines but instead concentrated their deadly trench-mortars on very short stretches of the British lines. One post with twenty men was annihilated and the British reply was so much less accurate that it had almost no effect on the Germans at all. In fact, one British mortar bomb landed short in a British gun-pit, and it was only a brave corporal who reloaded it and re-fired it – though he must have known it was only a matter of seconds before it burst – that saved the whole crew.

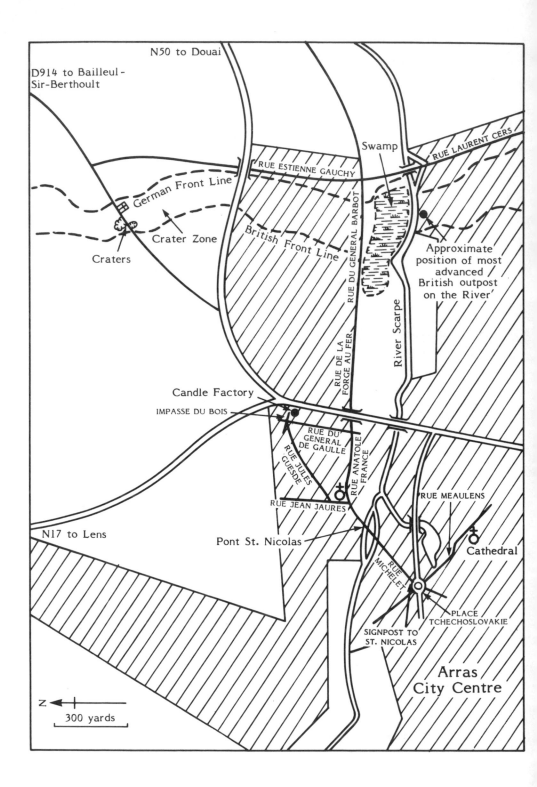

By the time Kelly moved on, the peace of Arras was at an end. The hate had started again.

D. V. Kelly, *Thirty-nine Months with the 'Tigers'*

The Battle for Vimy Ridge, 1916

Showing the Offensive Spirit: 21 September to 26 October 1916

A 'Cook's Tour' to inspect the lines to be taken over by the Leinster Regiment was enjoyed by all. The weather was fine and the scenery was good; the trenches were dry and for once were on the ridges rather than at the mercy of them. 'Good visibility,' said the brigadier, and Captain Francis Hitchcock from Tipperary agreed with him: 'The trenches were well-built . . . my Company Headquarters was bomb-proof. . . A regiment of the Saxon Corps were opposite us. They seemed tame.'

The next day Hitchcock and the Leinsters marched to this peaceful section of the front where they were to stay for over a month. The order of the day was: 'We are going to worry the Boche and have the offensive spirit all during the tour.'

There was no battle taking place when the Leinsters arrived. Hitchcock intended to change all that. He sent over salvoes of grenades at unpredictable intervals to lower the enemy's morale, and he kept a careful look-out for sniping opportunities.

At Sap 8 sentry-post, a Saxon came across to the British sentry for a chat and a swap of mementoes; the lance-corporal in charge of the post encouraged him until he was close enough to see the number of the regiment on the shoulder-straps; then he shot him.

This was just the sort of thing that was needed to get the front active again, and General Capper was delighted to hear about it when he came to inspect. He certainly felt no love for the enemy: 'The General seemed very upset, and I learnt that he had received news that very morning that his son had been killed with the Gunners on the Somme.'

Still more aggression was demanded. A letter came from regimental headquarters accompanied by a helpful list of burial grounds,

known to the troops as 'rest camps', ordering more raids to be carried
out by specially selected parties of seven men. Also, more mines were
to be laid in no man's land to make craters into which these élite
groups could advance.

Hitchcock's mining operations went badly. He had a number of
men buried alive as a result of enemy shelling, and he had to depend
on erratic punishment parties being sent up by night from the rear to
remove the tell-tale blue subsoil which could be spotted by enemy
aircraft during the day.

His raiding operations were much more successful. For several
days, mortar-shells had been used for cutting enemy wire along a
short stretch of the German front line from Kennedy Crater to
Gunner's Crater; in addition, daring patrols had crept out from the
craters by night to cut the German front-line barbed wire. On 5
October, the night of the raid, Hitchcock waited behind with
stretcher-bearers, telephone operators and orderlies at the head of
Sap A1 while four of the élite groups under Lieutenant Gately (who
had recently gone on a special course on trench raids) slipped out
into Gunner's Crater, into no man's land and through the remnants
of the German defences into the enemy front-line trench. They killed
at least six Germans, wounded many more, caused great destruction
and returned with a talkative prisoner – who had a wife and ten
children and was taking no risks. They suffered six wounded,
including Gately, who needed attention to some grenade splinters in
his eye. Congratulations all round were followed by a scurrying to
cover as German artillery attempted its revenge.

Successful raids like this one livened up a front which had
deteriorated to fraternization and a quiet life. It helped to take the
minds of the soldiers off the grisly and pervasive reminders of the
fierce trench battles of the year before. The skulls, the skeletons and,
above all, the rats. Complete battalions of the French Army had been
wiped out on this ridge, and most were not buried but decomposed in
the sun. They provided a feast for the rats, which grew to a colossal
size, almost as big as dogs.

When the Canadians took over on 26 October, they certainly had
no time to worry about the rats. The front they inherited from
Hitchcock was very different from the one that he had taken over in
September. Gone were the summery days of September and non-
aggression. The weather broke and it was cold and foggy. The
Germans were out for revenge on a front which Hitchcock and the
Leinsters had fairly warmed up.

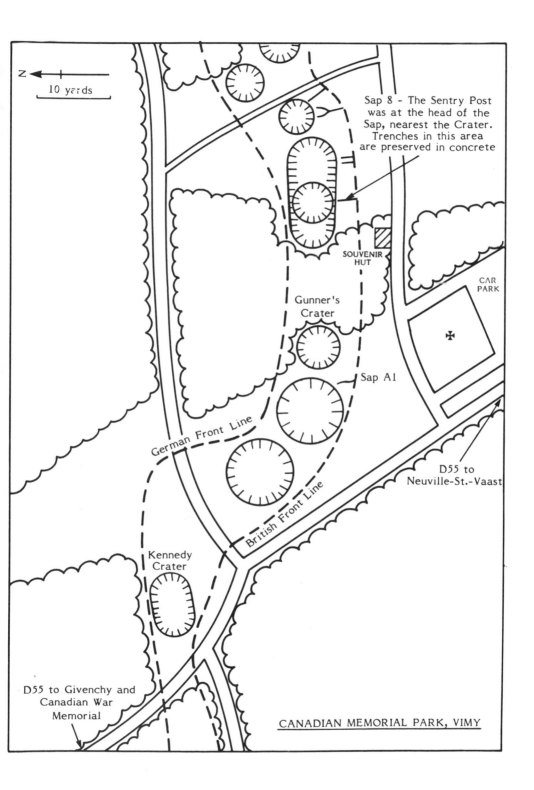

Z ← | 10 yards

Sap 8 - The Sentry Post was at the head of the Sap, nearest the Crater. Trenches in this area are preserved in concrete

SOUVENIR HUT

CAR PARK

Gunner's Crater

Sap A1

German Front Line

British Front Line

D55 to Neuville-St.-Vaast

Kennedy Crater

D55 to Givenchy and Canadian War Memorial

CANADIAN MEMORIAL PARK, VIMY

The Battle for Vimy Ridge, 1917

Simple Patriotism Wins the Day: 8 and 9 April 1917

The Canadians crossed the Atlantic to fight for King and Country. They did so with enthusiasm and gusto, as volunteers. Their feelings of patriotism were uncomplicated. Like most soldiers, they relished the excitement of war and loathed its horrors, but their simple belief in the rightness of the Empire's cause made them brave – more effective than the reluctant British drafts of 1917 and more fervent than the 'blood and steel' Germans.

At St. Eloi on Vimy Ridge, the Canadians looked forward eagerly to their formidable task: 'The boys were in high spirits and glad of the opportunity to demonstrate again the quality of the New World troops . . . We would uphold all the traditions of the Canadian Army and our battalion would prove to be one of the best in France!'

Most of the Canadians had only recently arrived in Europe; they were shocked by destroyed villages and churches and by the pitiable state of refugees. They marched to the front determined to get back at the monstrous enemy who had caused all that they had seen. The Canadians were fresh to the battle; they had not been sharing terrible winters in trenches with the enemy; they had not been around to hear '*Heilige Nacht*' at Christmas. They knew they would beat the Germans and that the Germans deserved to be beaten.

Lieutenant Ernest Odell and his platoon entered the Aux Rietz Communication Trench from the Arras-Béthune road, which was being shelled intermittently. It was pitch dark, late on 8 April 1917.

As they started to move down the trench, they got a message to speed up because the shelling had become serious and queues of men waiting to enter the trench from the road were in great danger. Hurrying down Aux Rietz Trench was perilous. Telephone wire, barbed wire and rivulets of muddy water criss-crossed the trench, and when barbed wire caught a running man under his chin, his injuries could be fatal.

Aux Rietz Trench led to the front line. From there, the platoon crept across a stretch of no man's land, dangerously illuminated by German flares, to their jumping-off trench whence they would attack at 5.31 a.m. the next morning.

The time started to drag. Odell and his men simply wanted to get it over with. It started to drizzle, and there were still over two hours to go. Waiting and wondering.

'Suddenly, I was aroused from my reverie by a voice that sounded between us and our own front line. I listened, and heard the same voice shout out these startling words, "Where in Hell is the end of this damned ditch?" The voice was clear and distinct and betrayed no sign of nervousness or fear. The Huns were strafing our front lines, we all knew he was not a soldier, therefore he must be a civilian . . .' He seemed to be carrying a heavy machine-gun and Odell trained his revolver on him and told him to drop his weapons or he would fire. 'Don't shoot, friend, don't shoot. I'm a moving picture man . . .' It turned out to be an American Press photographer who had come to see the Canadians go over the top in daylight for the first time, for the newsreels! He was determined to be in the thick of it and to advance with Odell and the first assault troops after the artillery barrage.

The photographer and the rum distribution made the men of Odell's platoon almost unrestrainable. At 5.30 exactly, the shells of the bombardment whistled overhead to the German lines, one shell every fifteen seconds on every twenty yards of line.

There were desperate Germans SOS signals, and then, at 5.31, 'I blew my whistle. I knew they could not hear it, but I pointed in the direction of the enemy and everyone was "over the top" like a shot. I cannot describe how I felt. My blood ran quickly, my head seemed to throb, and my heart felt as if it was going to come through my chest.'

Few Germans were left alive by the bombardment. Those that fought on were shot or bayoneted by Odell's platoon. Those that yelled 'Kamerad' were taken prisoner. The French Canadian 'moppers-up' took no prisoners – they were following behind Odell's platoon and could see how many of their fellows were dead or bleeding to death; their special response to 'Kamerad' was a bullet.

Odell's platoon reached their ultimate objective, the Stellung in the fourth line of German trenches. They had lost quite a few men but, compared with others down the line who had met with stiffer resistance, they got off lightly. The Stellung was a well-built trench with a luxurious dug-out full of German coffee, eggs, bacon, sausages and fresh water, well appointed with comfortable furnishings and specially decorated notepaper for holders of the Iron Cross.

The photographer recorded the victorious Canadian platoon, and its lieutenant, tucking into a hearty celebration breakfast!

Source
J. Becton and E. L. Odell, *Hunting the Hun*

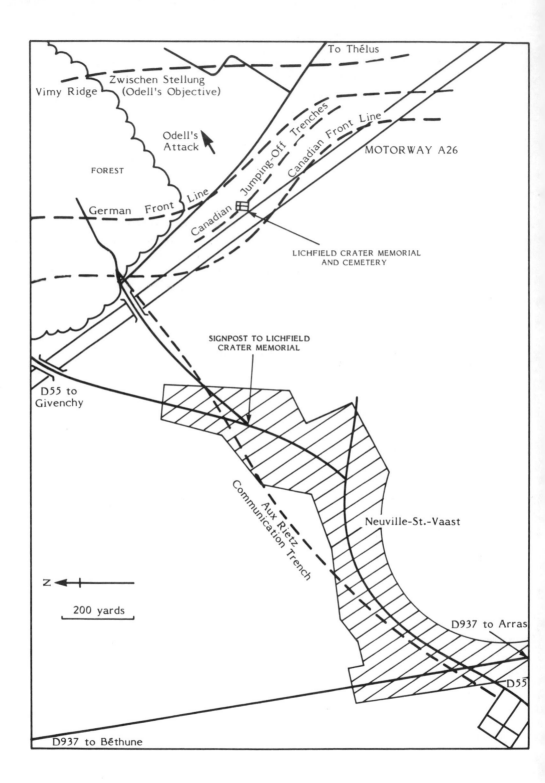

To Thélus

Vimy Ridge
Zwischen Stellung
(Odell's Objective)

Odell's Attack

FOREST

Canadian Jumping-Off Trenches

Canadian Front Line

MOTORWAY A26

German Front Line

Canadian

LICHFIELD CRATER MEMORIAL
AND CEMETERY

SIGNPOST TO LICHFIELD
CRATER MEMORIAL

D55 to
Givenchy

Aux Rietz
Communication Trench

Neuville-St.-Vaast

Z

200 yards

D937 to Arras

D55

D937 to Béthune

Battle of Arras, 1917

Balloon Lost: 9 April 1917

Great sausage-shaped kite-balloons, sixty-five feet long and twenty-seven feet wide, were a feature of all the major battlefields by 1917. Like monstrous bugs, they were winched slowly from the ground to guide gun batteries and infantry attacks from vantage points 1,000–1,500 feet above the ground. They were vulnerable to shrapnel shells, sitting targets for planes equipped with incendiaries and at the mercy of bad weather. It was the last of the three enemies that Captain C. N. Down of the Royal Flying Corps and his boss, Major Roxby, encountered 1,200 feet above the church of Ablain-St.-Nazaire shortly after breakfast on Easter Monday 1917.

Down and Roxby made their way to their balloon hidden in a copse just west of the village; it was close-hauled and swaying uneasily in the breeze. Its basket, a few feet above their heads, was also swaying. The balloon was attached to a winch by a slender cable of steel wire, and the winch was bolted to the floor of a lorry which looked substantial enough to allay passing fears that it might rise from the earth and follow the balloon into the air. Two men in Royal Flying Corps uniforms were standing by to operate the winch.

The winch-corporal was told to take the balloon to 1,200 feet, and Down and Roxby clambered into the basket, which was made of wicker with sides about chest-high. Inside, there was just room for two to stand upright. The equipment consisted of a telephone, an aneroid barometer, a compass and parachutes.

Their rate of ascent was slow but steady, and soon they were out of earshot of the winch gear. They moved up and, as the wind caught them, eastwards over the village. The balloon was reassuringly large but the cable seemed woefully thin. The previous day, in a blizzard, a cable had snapped and the occupants of the balloon been killed as they jerked and soared to 12,000 feet over German lines.

All of a sudden, the steady motion of the balloon being winched up ceased and both balloon and basket swayed and swung in the wind. They had reached 1,200 feet. The balloon was now anchored, and quite severe air sickness was likely in the gale.

They could see down into the Souchez Valley where the Canadian Corps faced Bavarian regiments, and they had a clear view of Vimy Ridge with its wooded eastern slopes harbouring German artillery

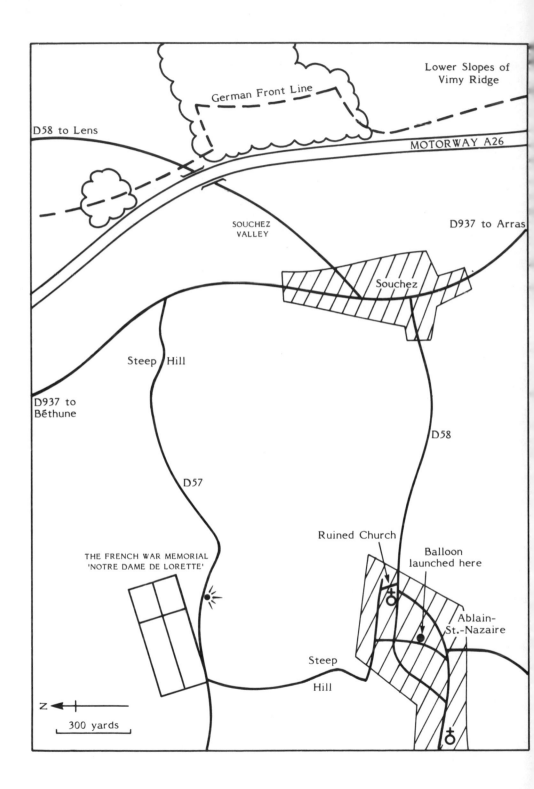

and its battle-scarred western slopes dropping steeply to the Douai Plain.

As the wind got stronger, they laced themselves in and out of the rigging to avoid being tipped from the shaking swaying basket. Active artillery below seemed silent puffs of smoke. All they could hear was a buffeting wind.

Without warning, the starboard fin of the balloon cracked and they were in peril of their lives.

The balloon hurtled down to 200 feet and then zoomed back up to 1,200 feet, pulling the winch-lorry several yards. It repeated this terrifying course time and again until at length the cable snapped and they shot skywards. The basket was hurled over the top of the balloon, and Down thought it was miraculous that they stayed tied into it: 'I remember vividly looking over the side of the basket into the rigging through which I had wound my arms and seeing the greeny-grey belly of the balloon below me, with the tops of the trees just below that, and beyond the winch a crowd of men with upturned faces. The wire cable in great coils seemed to be lying all over the place.'

Down and Roxby grabbed their parachutes, unravelled themselves as fast as they possibly could as the balloon soared inexorably past 10,000 feet. They jumped. Down recalled that by the time his parachute opened – a heart-stopping few moments late – the balloon was at 15,000 feet.

Down and Roxby landed in icy mud and were 'bounced like corks'; they were lacerated as they smashed through British support lines. Down finished up in a ditch and Roxby stopped only when he slammed into the brick wall of a roofless house. Neither was badly injured.

For their lowly section of the Royal Flying Corps that day they had done enough.

Source
A. Morris, *The Balloonatics*

Battle of Arras, 1917

Beyond the Front Line and Back through a Drainpipe: 23 April 1917

The quiet fields around the village of Gavrelle were the scene for violent action in April 1917. Able Seaman W. A. Downe of the Royal Marines had participated in the recapture of Gavrelle from the Germans, and now the British were pressing home their advantage with an attack across the fields to the east of the village. Soon the flanks of the attack were repulsed. A depleted company, including Downe, which had spearheaded the attack, found themselves dangerously isolated.

Downe was pleased to be leaving the front line. True, he was going further forwards, but it would be a while before the Germans realized that there were any British further forward than the front line. In the meantime, he would be out from under the heavy German bombardment which had been going on ever since the fall of Gavrelle. Also, Downe was a gritty soldier. He was experienced and pleased to be back in the attack.

Downe's company was spearheading the attack. They set off before dawn, using a small drainage ditch leading from the village as cover. About 150 yards into no man's land they came to a light railway line which they had to cross:

'The first four men jumped into the open and dashed across, but three were immediately hit, a machine-gun appearing to open at them from the Mayor's garden right in advance of the German line . . . with my heart beating at a tremendous pace I held my breath and made a frantic dash. Wonderful luck – the machine-gun fired short, the bullets tearing up the dust round my feet while a revolver spat by my ear. I covered the distance in about three leaps but fell on top of Wilmer, who had been hit, and was lying on the other side.'

Ten men got across, about a quarter of those who tried. The rest stayed behind.

Downe and his comrades went thirty yards further and dived out of the ditch and into a shell-hole. Every move was punished. One man stood up, 'And as I watched he seemed to hang in the air as he stretched himself to his full height, and crumpled, falling on top of the men following, shot through the heart.' From then on that man's body was useful for hiding behind; the impact of the bullets in his body sounded 'like the action of a grocer's assistant patting a slab of butter'.

The morning was all too much for eighteen-year-old Private Charlie Jennings. He had a comical round face with a little turned-up nose, and his steel helmet was always cocked over one eye, but even his appealing features could not make him seem cheerful today. The morning had started with the death of a wounded friend crying deliriously for his mother. Several more friends had been mown down crossing the railway line. Two more friends' heads were blown off their shoulders in the shell-hole he shared with them. When Downe stood straight, Jennings clung to his feet and ankles. When he lay flat, Jennings heaved himself up so he could put his arm round his shoulders, seeking comfort. It made Downe himself feel easier, as if sheltering a small child.

Meanwhile, it was plain that the attack had ground to a halt and the pathetic little spearhead with Downe and Jennings in it had best withdraw before very long. Khaki figures could be seen in the enemy lines with their hands up. Germans were everywhere. Trying to get back to the railway line, the little group got separated. At one time, Downe, belly-crawling through the mud with bullets actually slamming into his haversack, was fired on by the panicking Charlie Jennings. Luckily it was a very bad shot.

They scrambled back into the ditch only to find that the Germans were firing straight down it. There seemed to be no escape.

The railway line loomed.

A young infantryman called Staley, who had a day or two before heard the news that he had become the father of a boy, had found a drainpipe twenty-five feet long leading under the railway. Downe described it as 'a large-bore stoneware drain'. A man could just possibly get through it. Staley's dead body would have to be moved first.

Munching some of Staley's biscuits, Downe investigated the drain. Any chance was better than trying to cross the railway line.

'My shoulders were not over-wide, and I just got in; my arms, bent at the elbows, were squeezed tightly, so that it was impossible to push them over my head. I could only make progress with the movements of my legs, and progress was slow. Andrews was still in the pipe and I could not see daylight at the end, while Carter had followed me quickly, for I could feel his head against my feet. Exertion left me breathless, and with the air almost blocked at both ends and sweat pouring into my eyes, which I could not wipe, my head began to whirl.'

Downe was suddenly gripped by cold fear. He couldn't move.

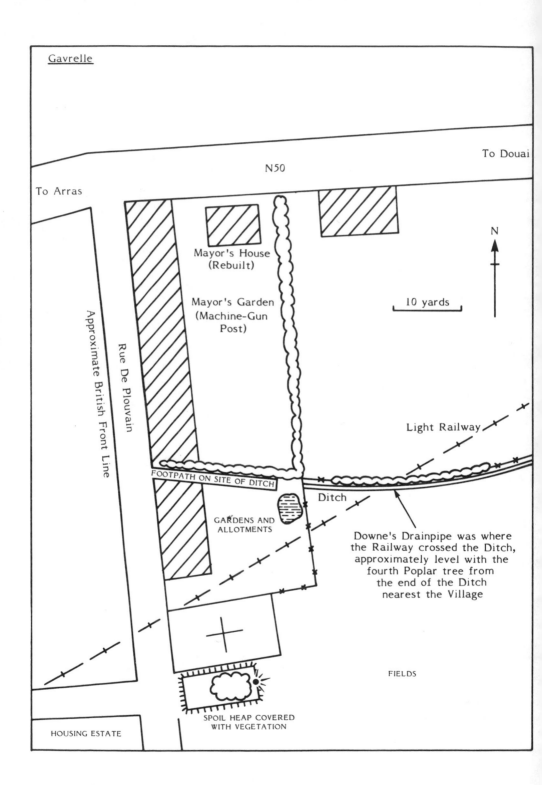

Gavrelle

To Douai

N50

To Arras

N

10 yards

Mayor's House
(Rebuilt)

Mayor's Garden
(Machine-Gun
Post)

Light Railway

Approximate British Front Line

Rue De Plouvain

FOOTPATH ON SITE OF DITCH

Ditch

GARDENS AND
ALLOTMENTS

Downe's Drainpipe was where
the Railway crossed the Ditch,
approximately level with the
fourth Poplar tree from
the end of the Ditch
nearest the Village

FIELDS

SPOIL HEAP COVERED
WITH VEGETATION

HOUSING ESTATE

His bayonet was tied to his leg and stuck in a broken joint in the pipe.

'Daylight appeared at the far end. Andrews was out. I shouted, but what was the use? My leg was held in a vice. I jerked and pulled, and pain shot through my wrenched hip. I went limp and lay helplessly looking at the circular opening showing daylight. Terror-stricken, I pulled the equipment till it twisted like a knot round my ankle, while against my feet Carter's head nosed.'

'Thoughts raced through my mind – horrible imaginings. I felt too weak to pull. And what was the use? Carter was tight against my feet; I could not ease myself backward to loosen the grip. Carter must have been in a worse plight. A huge fellow, how he got into the pipe I never knew, and he had no air. His head, down at my feet, in a frenzy urged me on.'

Every few minutes, Downe was fired with bursts of energy, but each time they were weaker than the last. Carter, behind him, frantically struggled against exhaustion and suffocation.

'His head beat against the obstacle which barred his progress, loosened the bayonet, pushing my legs against the sides of the pipe. I was free, and with seeming ease, which the relief brought, worked my way forward and out again into the ditch, where I lay gasping amongst several wounded.'

Back to the front line and back to base. The attack had failed completely. Downe, Jennings and half a dozen others were neither casualties nor prisoners. They would fight another day. Most of their comrades would not.

Source
J. Hammerton, ed., *I was There!*

Avion, 1917

Fumbling in the Trenches: December 1917

Lieutenant J. H. Pedley had heard about the horrors of Passchendaele and about the battle for Vimy Ridge but had not yet been in the trenches. He had only recently arrived from Canada and, since his arrival in France, the more he heard, the gloomier he felt about the trenches. His gloom was enhanced by the inevitability that it was to the trenches, indeed to the front-line trenches, that he would be going very soon.

Pedley hated the colonel of the Fourth Canadian Infantry Battalion who sent him to the trenches:

'My first impression of Harry Lafayette Nelles was not altogether favourable. He was too well dressed, too smooth, and in the few moments we spent at Headquarters even a newcomer could see that the accord which should exist between a commander and his officers was lacking. He had pushed himself, so the word went, into prominence through his concentration on the display side of soldiering and had become a sort of "Brasso King".'

And he hated his immediate superior, Captain Eric Davis: 'He had not grown with the job, and did not get the co-operation of his officers, because it was always too apparent that he distrusted, envied and feared them. If there is such a thing as an inferiority complex, Davis had one.' When Pedley was late on parade one day, Davis publicly rebuked him. The humiliated Pedley never forgave him.

Davis gave Pedley command of a section to take up to the front. Pedley was immediately made a fool of by his sergeant, who told him that the men all had dirty, unusable rifles because they had been forced to use them for rifle grenades. 'I was glad after hearing the Sergeant's explanation that I had not gone after the men with dirty rifles.' The next day he discovered by chance that they had not in fact fired a rifle grenade in years. 'I had a talk with Sergeant Bradley which I don't think he altogether enjoyed.' But it was too late – Pedley had been made to look foolish in his own platoon.

Although he got tough with his NCOs as he grew more confident, Pedley tended to idolize his private soldiers in a patronizing salt-of-the-earth way: 'Their bodies still warm with the tingle of rum, their hearts beating high and breath coming full, they would stretch out in their great-coats and fall into the deep sleep that children and soldiers know.'

The order came through to proceed to Red Line Trench, and Pedley enjoyed the trip by light railway followed by a few hours' march. The journey to the front seemed like an adventure, and he started to get a taste for war, helped by the fact that the fighting for the ground he was covering had been some months before and now there was hardly a shell or a gun to be heard.

Pedley nevertheless soon found plenty to complain about. First there were the lice breeding in the leather knots in a thong round his neck which held his mother's locket. Then there was the menu, which never varied – although it was more and better than the food endured by the rest of his section; every day Pedley got fried bread, cheese and bully beef with a spoonful of jam for pudding.

After a few days in the Red Line Trench, Davis ordered Pedley's section to the front. Now the adventure would end and the fear would begin. They proceeded up Cyril Trench and into Beaver Trench.

'I felt the general oppression most keenly perhaps as I ducked across the low place in Beaver Trench where the railway crosses, and realised that the peewits sweetly singing in the air a few feet above my head were not peewits at all but bullets from Fritz's machine-guns. And now, in Sullivan Trench, I could hear the relentless hammer-hammer of the Emma-Gees (machine-guns) themselves, and the sharp reply of our Vickers firing from higher ground behind; while the star-shells that had looked beautiful from Notre Dame de Lorette now were more sinister.'

Pedley was determined to be a man. When shells burst around them in Beaver Trench, he ignored the danger-signals and continued at 'trench slouch':

'Should I increase the pace, and show myself timorous? A second shell screamed its way to earth, a little closer. I felt that this was the testing point for me. They would see, those fellows behind, that I was no poltroon. I continued at the former deliberate pace, and did not change even when a third shell exploded not more than twenty-five yards off, sending some fragments of earth among us. But I was beginning to feel shaky. "What the hell does this damned fool think this is – a funeral? If he doesn't stir himself he'll have us all killed." I needed no second hint and gladly broke into a half-trot. By the time the next shell came we had got ourselves out of danger.'

Pedley soon developed a particular fear of trenches at night. He always seemed to be catching himself on wire or slipping down holes. Once his imagination completely ran away with his sense. He thought he had missed his turning and had somehow reached no man's land. He grew more and more scared at every step. He heard some footsteps coming towards him and pointed his revolver into the darkness ready to fire. A stranger was upon him – 'Who goes there?', Pedley yelled, ready to fire if the stranger moved another muscle. 'Just another fella from T'ronto.' It turned out to be a Canadian corporal who, badly frightened, ordered Pedley, his superior officer, to put away his gun as he might kill someone!

Although Pedley claimed to be in favour of 'tickling Fritz', there were only two aggressive actions during the whole of his week at the front and both of them failed. His machine-gunners missed an officer jumping from shell-hole to shell-hole not a hundred yards away, and then they missed a working party on a hillside in the distance.

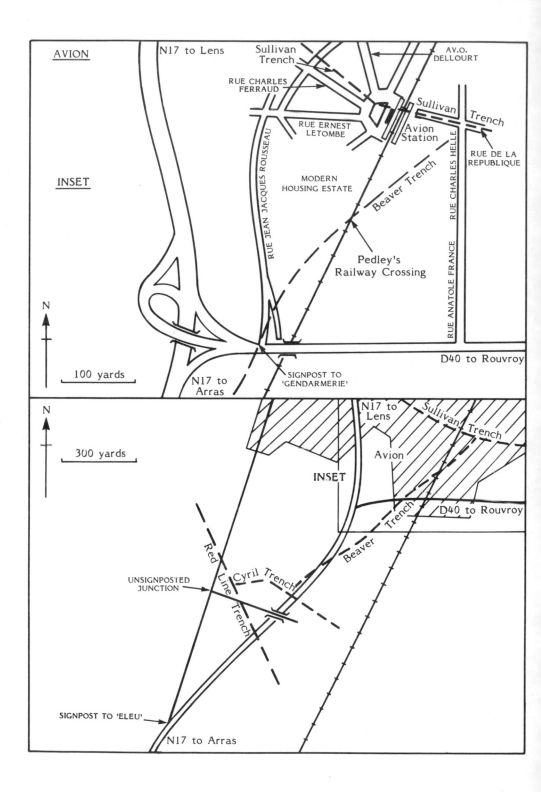

AVION

INSET

N17 to Lens

Sullivan Trench

RUE CHARLES FERRAUD

RUE ERNEST LETOMBE

RUE JEAN JACQUES ROUSSEAU

MODERN HOUSING ESTATE

Beaver Trench

Pedley's Railway Crossing

AV.O. DELLOURT

Sullivan Trench

Avion Station

RUE DE LA REPUBLIQUE

RUE CHARLES HELLE

RUE ANATOLE FRANCE

D40 to Rouvroy

N

100 yards

N17 to Arras

SIGNPOST TO 'GENDARMERIE'

N

300 yards

N17 to Lens

Sullivan Trench

Avion

INSET

D40 to Rouvroy

Beaver Trench

Red Line Trench

Cyril Trench

UNSIGNPOSTED JUNCTION

SIGNPOST TO 'ELEU'

N17 to Arras

A day or two afterwards, Pedley was taken out of the front line and sent away to training school.

Source
J. H. Pedley, *Only This*

German Spring Offensive, *1918*

Holding Telegraph Hill: Early April 1918

Lieutenant J. H. Pedley of the Fourth Canadian Infantry Battalion had found his headquarters and got the orders for his battalion in spite of the appalling muddle and confusion of the retreat from the great German Spring Offensive of 1918. The orders were to shift from the present backward position in the village of Dainville, through Arras, to relieve and to hold the front line on Telegraph Hill.

Arras had been evacuated the day before as the German guns came into easy range. It was sorrowful to go through a city which only the day before had throbbed with life but which now echoed emptily. All the shops and houses were locked and bolted, except for a handful which had had their fronts exploded away by shells, exposing the rooms. Here and there a dead horse gently rotted but the dead people had all been buried.

On the first part of the road out of Arras towards Telegraph Hill, Pedley's battalion marched behind a brass band, but the going soon got difficult and the band returned to Arras. A shell landing near Pedley's mare made her bolt and throw him into the mud. He walked from then on; an infantryman, he was never happy on horseback. Now he was a caricature of a foot-soldier, head to toe in black slime.

More shells fell on his men as they advanced up the Neuville Vitasse road to a point well forward where a shallow switch line, or oblique communication trench, led round Telegraph Hill. As they advanced, they left some of their comrades' shell-exploded bodies by the wayside to be buried later and they also encountered some older, unburied bodies. When they reached Telegraph Hill, they found the decaying remains of men from the battalion they had relieved, including two dead officers left behind in the officer's dug-out – which was considered inexcusable – but the battle was now becoming less intense. The full-scale battle was subsiding. In the trenches of Telegraph Hill the full horror of war continued but the intensity of panic of the British retreat and German advance had died down.

The losses of the last week sank in: 'Any day might mean an attack, our defences and communications were none too good, and we stood in front of Arras. Arras taken, Vimy Ridge might be turned, and the work of the preceding summer entirely undone.'

As the panic of constant retreat ended, the administration took over. The air was heavy with messages asking for information to be dug up; for one thing, High Command needed to know exactly where the front line was now drawn; there followed a furious row about whether or not the right outpost on the side of Telegraph Hill was in line or stuck out dangerously into no man's land. Pedley was given the job of finding out – not of doing anything about it, just of risking his life finding out.

From the start, Pedley's rather pointless little expedition to the outpost did not go well. As soon as he left the officers' dug-out, there was a thud and a crash. He, his batman Paddy Nugent and a third man were blown back together into the dug-out, and the third man screamed that he was blinded: 'I got my arms around him and soothed him as much as I could (his elbows were jabbing into my face, for he had buried his head in his arms) and Paddy re-lit the candle. Our hero was not badly blinded for he recognised the first gleam of candle-light; it was just a bad scare. He had been standing in the trench a few feet from the burst. His rifle lay outside, twisted and ripped to the semblance of a corkscrew.'

Pedley decided he could do with a smoke: '. . . baked rope, he called it. I had been doubtful myself if some foreign substance had got into the pipe for there was a roughish smell in the place. So I dumped out the bowl and refilled it. But the stench grew worse, and Paddy protested again. As I was about to make some smart retort the Colonel woke with a start, yelled "Gas" and grabbed for his mask. Hurriedly putting on my own I made my way outside and shouted a warning, which was repeated up and down the little trench. Through the eye-pieces I could see the whole basin milky-white, the vapour moving fog-like. Shouts multiplied, someone beat on a shell-case, and the boys came tumbling out of their rabbit-holes, clutching their masks.'

A little later on, the gas cloud lifted. The alarm had been given just in time, there were no casualties.

At last Pedley and Nugent got out again into the maze of trenches around Telegraph Hill. They found their way down the switch trench which they knew led to the front and then tried a short-cut. At this very moment the shelling started again in earnest:

'It soon became apparent that we were in for a bad time. Chilled, scared and filthy wet, we squirmed like so many rats along the trench floor. The shelling and the machine-gun fire multiplied. Big ones crashed in before us and behind, seemingly ranged on our trench. My morale began to slip. Once or twice we crawled by a corpse and more than once I brushed against a soldier crouched over a wounded comrade, fumbling for the first field dressing and the iodine.'

Pedley and Nugent were ignored by the trench garrison, who simply wondered why officer and batman had emerged from their dug-outs.

'Neither of us had been hit as yet, though some big crumps had landed much too close. It got to the point where we listened for those likely to come in our vicinity, and on hearing the whistle of one, lay flat. After a while we came to a dead stop. Flat on our bellies in the mud we waited the end of the strafe. Hearts palpitating, expecting dissolution any moment, we squeezed close to the earth, listening to the crash of TNT, the whine of shrapnel and the whistle of the bullets, while the rain beat on us and we wished we were home. But no strafe strafes forever.'

When the allotted time was up, the shelling died away and they found themselves shaken but unharmed.

They got up, shook themselves down and carried on following in the darkness what seemed to be the short-cut. A machine-gun started up and they sheltered in a shell-hole or an old gun position, they were not quite sure. Pedley realized he had lost his compass. They had lost the short-cut. They were completely lost.

For three hours they dived from shell-hole to shell-hole, probably a few yards out in no man's land, only realizing they were near German lines at first light. They scrambled back to the front line.

Then they saw that they had (at last) had a stroke of luck: they were in the trench which might (or might not) have been sticking out from the front line. Pedley established with a borrowed compass that in fact it was sticking out.

The battle quietened a little, and Pedley was able to have a scratch breakfast with an old friend from his schooldays in Canada, Lieutenant John Gordon, who was in charge of the sticking-out trench. He even agreed to accompany Gordon on 'his morning jaunt down the sap', but they had only just set out when Gordon's batman noticed that they had no bombs. 'All right – get me a couple,' Gordon said, and stood holding up a strand of wire for Pedley to stoop under. They were his last words, for two shots rang out and he dropped.

'I knelt down and lifted John's head into my arms. The eyes were open, but glazed, and there was no response in them when I called him over and over by name. As I watched, still speaking to him, the

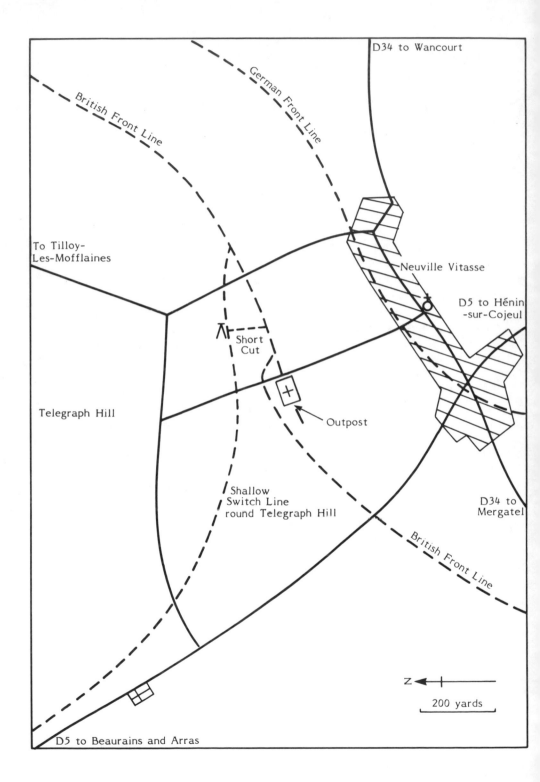

D34 to Wancourt

German Front Line

British Front Line

To Tilloy-
Les-Mofflaines

Neuville Vitasse

D5 to Hénin
-sur-Cojeul

Short
Cut

Telegraph Hill

Outpost

Shallow
Switch Line
round Telegraph Hill

D34 to
Mergatel

British Front Line

N

200 yards

D5 to Beaurains and Arras

colour that was in his cheeks faded out more and more. He was indeed gone, gone past power of mine to recall him.

'A rough hand on my arm, Sergeant Mackay's rough burr in my ear: "Get him back out of there for God's sake and get yourself into shelter, or there'll be two of you to be carried out."'

Pedley took the hands, which he disentangled from the barbed wire. The sergeant grabbed the corpse's feet. They laid John Gordon in the trench.

'As I composed the hands across the breast, I noticed that he had been shot through the stomach as well as the neck. I took a watch and a silver identification disk off his wrists and gave them to his batman.'

Deeply depressed, Pedley returned from his worthless excursion. A few days later, his battalion was relieved and he left Telegraph Hill. There is no record of whether or not the front line was ever straightened.

Source
J. H. Pedley, *Only This*

SOMME

Introduction

In spring 1916, Britain's brand-new volunteer army arrived in France. Its destination was a quiet sector of the French-held front line north of the River Somme, an area of rolling chalk hills cut across by slow-moving swampy rivers. It is still much the same – farmland and sleepy villages.

The reason why the new army was sent to the Somme sector was to take part in the major allied offensive of 1916. The British would have to take the leading role because the French were just four months into the ten-month struggle of Verdun.

The quiet conditions on the Somme front had enabled the Germans to choose defensive positions, making the best use of the landscape to put any attackers at a disadvantage. Furthermore the soft chalk enabled them to dig deep dug-outs, some equipped with electricity and water.

The date set for the offensive was 1 July. During the week before, over a million shells were fired into German lines. Yet, when the British actually left the trenches, the Germans were still sufficiently well organized to co-ordinate artillery, machine-guns and rifle fire to repulse the assault along most of the line.

There were 60,000 British casualties on the first day, probably the most ever sustained by an army in a single day. Still, the battle was immediately continued and what advantages had been gained were pressed home. For the next five months, the army attacked. Bloody battles revolved around fortified woods and fortified villages.

Non-stop attacks and counter-attacks accompanied by heavy artillery fire wore the chalk hills into an unrecognizable desert.

Wave after wave of attack and counter-attack cost the British 415,000 casualties and the Germans (who had a far more experienced army) 350,000 casualties. At one point in September, British hopes were raised by a new invention, the tank, but they were too few and proved too unreliable, and the costly grind carried on as before. The offensive was finally called off on 18 November. About six miles had been gained along a six-mile front.

By the winter of 1916–17 the mud had become unbearable. The new front had to be patrolled in conditions where a few yards' walk was an endurance test. The glutinous mud sucked off boots and puttees, and a man stuck fast was an easy target.

With such bad conditions, and in view of the casualties, the

Germans decided to withdraw. The Somme and Verdun, the Italian and Russian fronts, were causing the Germans to lose the war of attrition. Of all the battlefronts, though, General Ludendorff selected the Somme as 'the muddy grave of the German field army'.

The Germans withdrew to the Hindenburg Line in March 1917, a shorter line, comparatively easy to defend, leaving the Somme battlefields in the rear of the new British positions.

Exactly one year later, in spring 1918, British and colonial troops were back on the Somme trying desperately to contain the German Spring Offensive. The Germans were making for Amiens and were finally stopped five miles short of their objective, on the high ground around Villers-Bretonneux. During the battle of Villers-Bretonneux, the first tank-to-tank battle occurred and the British prevailed.

By now, both sides were using all their resources and inventions to gain any advantage. As well as tanks, a chemical weapon, mustard gas, was used in increasing amounts to saturate areas before attacks, and aerial bombardment was also becoming more important. Yet, despite these innovations and ever-increasing artillery and machine-gun firepower, trench warfare resumed while the German offensive was halted and the Allies prepared a counter-attack.

On 8 August 1918 the last great Allied counter-offensive started with the most successful day of battle in the War. The Battle of Amiens started with a huge barrage, and then Canadian, Anzac and British troops followed mass tank formations right through the German lines. The fighting was hard at first, but later on German forces began to surrender in large numbers. Germany's eventual defeat was put beyond doubt. The Allied pursuit forced the Germans out of the Somme sector and back, once and for all, beyond the Hindenburg Line.

Battle of the Somme, 1916

A German Doctor on the First Day of the Somme: 1 July 1916

The Germans were desperate for doctors. Kurt Westmann was a student of medicine with only limited skills and no experience but he was drafted to the front and sent to a first-aid post in a dell south of Beaumont-Hamel in the German support line. On 1 July the British attacked.

For a week up to 1 July, British artillery had bombarded German lines continuously with heavy shells, light shells and gas. Westmann recalled:

'Again and again we had to dig ourselves and our comrades out of masses of blackened earth and splintered wooden beams. Often we found bodies crushed to death, or bunks full of suffocated soldiers. The "drum-fire" never ceased. No food or water reached us. Down below, men became hysterical and their comrades had to knock them out, so as to prevent them from running away and exposing themselves to the deadly shell splinters. Even the rats panicked and sought refuge in our flimsy shelters; they ran up the walls, and we had to kill them with our spades.'

Westmann's first-aid post was damaged, partly buried, but survived.

The worst slaughter was to come. And it was not to be the slaughter of the Germans but of the British. On the morning of 1 July the British artillery directed their fire to German rear positions and the British Army went over the top in solid formation. They even tossed footballs over their parapets and started to run after them because they expected nobody to be still alive on the other side. 'But German machine-gunners and infantrymen crawled out of their holes, with inflamed and sunken eyes, their faces blackened by fire and their uniforms splashed with the blood of their wounded comrades. It was a kind of relief to be able to come out, even in the air still filled with smoke and the smell of cordite. They started firing furiously, and the British had frightful losses. It has been estimated that their dead amounted, within the first ten minutes, to at least fourteen thousand men.'

The British advance, on Westmann's part of the front, was nowhere more than a mile or so, and in some places the attackers hardly left their trenches. The whole mighty offensive ground to a halt. The British and French generals had not yet learned that it was useless to let human beings run against machine-gun and intense infantry fire, even after softening up.

The German wounded started to pile up too, and Westmann was kept very busy. Shells landed all around him, often interrupting his work and making it impossible to reach the dying.

Two stretcher-bearers set out to rescue a wounded man screaming for help a few yards away, when the whine of a shell was heard. Westmann and his medical orderlies flung themselves to the mud and missed the worst, but it hit the stretcher-bearers.

'Over the spot where the two men had been, hung a cloud of black smoke. We could not see the men, and we ran out to try to discover what had happened. At first, all we found were several pieces of the

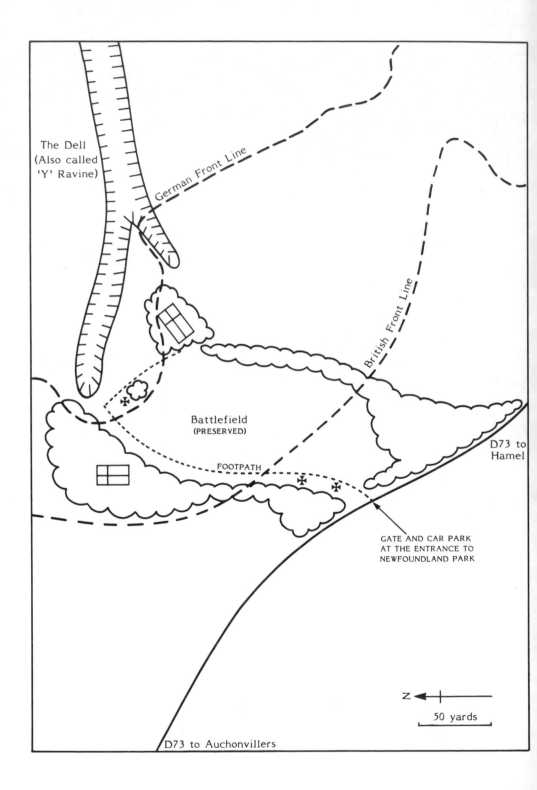

The Dell
(Also called
'Y' Ravine)

German Front Line

British Front Line

Battlefield
(PRESERVED)

FOOTPATH

D73 to Hamel

GATE AND CAR PARK
AT THE ENTRANCE TO
NEWFOUNDLAND PARK

N

50 yards

D73 to Auchonvillers

stretcher, then one man, with one foot dangling out of his trousers without its boot, and blood spouting out. We laid him on a stretcher with a piece of string as a tourniquet over his trouser and above his knee in order temporarily to stop the bleeding. On the spot where I knew the main artery was I put an unopened field dressing so as to exert special pressure.'

At last they found some pieces of the second man. An orderly spotted a half naked torso impaled on the spike of an exploded tree stump. 'Apparently the blast of the explosion had cut him in two and had hurled one half so high up that it was impossible to take it down. More shells were landing in our vicinity, and so we had to leave the torso to rot away, the torso of a man who had gone out to help his fellow creatures.'

The man with the blown-up leg was dragged into the first aid post and, once again, Westmann's studies in anatomy came in useful. He knew just where to apply pressure on the arteries and just how to get the balance right between preventing a man bleeding to death and avoiding gangrene from lack of circulation. He placed forceps on the artery and left the stretcher-bearer, now unconscious, eventually to be taken down the line.

He discovered later that he had saved the stretcher-bearer's leg but that he had still had to have his foot amputated.

Two hours at the front on the first day of the Battle of Somme taught Westmann more about anatomy – the hard way – than he had learned in his years of medical school. In the course of a few hours he saved many lives through a combination of courage, skill and common sense, and he also lost lives through simple inexperience. He had no time to worry; it was instinctive surgery.

Source
S. K. Westmann, *Surgeon in the Kaiser's Army*

Battle of the Somme, 1916

The First Minutes of Battle: 1 July 1916

The model in plasticine which Captain Duncan Martin had made while on home leave was soon the subject of anxious discussion among the officers of the 9th Devonshires. The model was based on the orders Martin had received for his company for the first minutes

of the Battle of the Somme. They would have to climb a small rise by
some trees called Mansel Copse and then advance across open
country to the German lines. Martin was certain that German
machine-gunners at their post, which was built into the base of a
crucifix in Mametz, would be able to mow down his whole company.
General Rawlinson and other senior officers in charge of the preparations did not like to have their orders put into question – even Haig
himself preferred not to interfere with 'Rawly' – so Martin stayed
silent. Anyway, the Fourth Army waiting to go into action had been
assured that the preceding artillery attack would be so intense that
there would be no German machine-gun posts, German barbed
wire, German trenches or living German soldiers left on the Somme
by the time Zero Hour, 7.30 a.m. on 1 July 1916, arrived.

Although they were somewhat disturbed by reports that living
Germans could still be seen and that German barbed-wire defences
were still apparently intact, Martin and his men felt more cheerful
about the impending attack as the artillery pounded night after
night, blasting the Germans' positions some 500 yards away across
no man's land. The return fire caused some inconvenience, including
the destruction of the trench which was supposed to be Martin's
jumping-off point. But on the whole German fire was light. A
support trench was quickly allocated to Martin and his men as a new
jumping-off point.

The infantry were fully equipped. They had their normal packs,
plus a rifle, a bayonet, two gas helmets, 220 rounds of ammunition,
two grenades, two empty sandbags, a spade, a pair of wire-cutters, a
flare and other smaller items. Most men's loads weighed about six
stone.

With loads like this, the men were not very mobile, and there was a
lot of cursing and delays in the communications trenches on the way
to the front the night before the battle. Progress to the front was
interrupted constantly by all kinds of confusion and by constant
shellfire. At least one soldier put his foot through a broken duckboard and broke his leg, causing Martin and his men a long delay.
Soldiers who had lost their platoon or even their regiment pushed up
and down the trenches all night, tripping over soldiers trying to
sleep.

Yet, as Zero Hour approached, the comradeship was immense.
Martin's men did not know of his doubts, and they tended to believe
that the vast majority, at least, of the Germans would be dead. They
had been told to expect very few casualties and they had believed
what they had been told.

Rum was issued. The artillery on both sides stopped firing for an

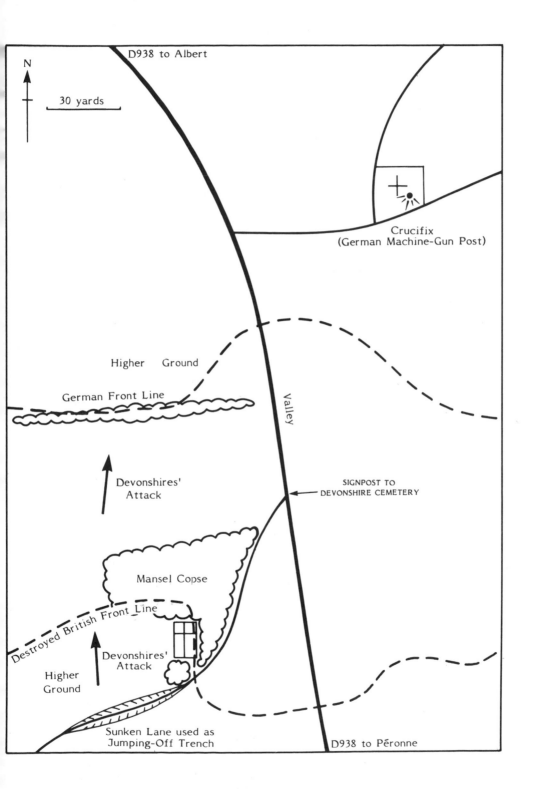

eerie few seconds at 7.30 a.m. precisely. Captain Martin blew his whistle and climbed onto the parapet of his trench. He shouted encouragement and helped some of his men with their heavy loads scale the ladders out of the trench and into no man's land.

It was the first time for two years that anyone had climbed the rise by Mansel Copse in broad daylight. The sun shone and the birds sang, and the Germans seemed to be dead after all.

Martin was shot about where he had predicted on his plasticine model. Directly the Devonshires appeared over the top of the hill, a German bugle sounded. Martin and his company were mown down by machine-gun fire coming from that shrine in Mametz. They had, as instructed, formed into a line, rifles held across their chests, bayonets at the ready; they advanced slowly in a disciplined way – they could do little else carrying six-stone packs. They walked and watched. They presented a facile target. The German gunners laughed and beckoned them on. As men fell, their comrades still carried on in the same way, slowly, walking in a line. There was almost no panic. They felt terror and anger but they were numbed. The survivors of the first wave, the first of six tragic waves, carried on walking in a line.

Martin's men did in fact reach and hold the German trenches, but in pitifully depleted numbers. All along the front, as far as the eye could see, wave after disciplined walking wave of men were being slaughtered. The second wave of men and all those who followed them had not only machine-guns to cope with but also German artillery, which was now directed to the centre of no man's land as well. As for the hill by Mansel Copse, the Germans realized that new waves would follow and they took advantage of the gentle curve of the hill and fired over it, killing a good many soldiers before they could even see the German lines. 20,000 men were killed that day and 40,000 wounded or captured by Germans who were supposed to be dead. The dud shells of the British artillery littered the few German lines that were captured.

Source
M. Middlebrook, *First Day on the Somme*

Battle of the Somme, 1916

A Soldier and his Camera: 1 July 1916

A great and glorious offensive was about to be launched on the Somme. Posterity was intended to see the bravery of heroes in the field (and the genius of heroes in the War Office). Generations of British men and women yet unborn would witness with their very eyes the expected victory of the Somme, the battle to end the war to end all wars, for it was to be the first great battle recorded on film from the moment the first soldier climbed out of the relative safety of his trench to the moment of victory over a great mass of the German Army.

The man chosen to film the battle was Lieutenant Geoffrey Malins. He had filmed for the War Office before, but only soldiers training in Britain. He was now to film the Battle of the Somme in the sector of Beaumont-Hamel, where the toughest fighting of all was expected.

The last time Geoffrey Malins had filmed the Lancashire Fusiliers they were just pretending. This was now reality. He was in the advanced front line specially prepared for the attack. Some men were placing bets on who would be first across no man's land and some were making arrangements how to pay if they didn't make it. Most of the men were quietly, perhaps contemplatively, smoking Woodbine cigarettes. The picture Malins took showed good spirits on the whole – banter, Woodbines, joking – and fear too – there was perspiration, there was talk of 'Going West'.

It was 6.30, and Zero Hour was 7.30. Malins had to get back to his camera position at Jacob's Ladder for filming the start of the attack. One last shot of the front-line soldiers fixing their bayonets and he was off.

He had to wait for ammunition-carriers to pass down the sunken road behind the front line and then crawl across the road feeling horribly exposed to German machine-guns on the hill opposite, Hawthorn Redoubt. Then, with an assistant helping with the heavy tripod and camera, he dived into the tunnel, crawling and clawing his way past murky lines of troops moving forward in the gloom from the support trenches up to the front.

Finally, he made a dash back fifty yards to Jacob's Ladder, only to find that his carefully prepared filming position had been blown away by the Germans. Five minutes before, it had been a hide-out in a small sandy cliff; now it was flat.

Malins quickly found another location on the side of a small bank where he could film the start of the great attack to his left and the blowing of the mine under the German machine-gun and artillery position on Hawthorn Redoubt. The mine would be fired ten minutes before Zero Hour.

The enemy's machine-guns and shells caused little alarm. Behind the front line, everyone was cheerful about the drubbing the Boche was about to receive. Mental and nervous excitement as the moment of attack grew near was very great. Everyone was in a state of suppressed excitement.

'Are you going over?'

'Rather. The whole lot of us. Some stunt, eh!'

'Don't forget, the camera will be on you; good luck!'

Tension mounted as the time for exploding the mine under Hawthorn Redoubt approached. The minutes dragged on. The men got their final instructions crouching down in the trenches, ladders ready for the assault. The officers who were to lead the assault waited, looked at their watches, shuffled their feet and perspired.

7.19 and 30 seconds. Malins started his camera and fixed his eyes on Hawthorn Redoubt. His hands started to shake. It was an unbearable half minute. A drum beat deep in the earth. The ground shook, then swayed. Hawthorn Redoubt lifted from the hill, broke into a thousand pieces and crashed down again. The terrible strongpoint which had cost so many young British soldiers their lives was no more. Only a mountain of smoke remained. Soon the attack started. The engineers rushed over (too late) to stabilize and secure the crater, the soldiers with their heavy packs responded to blowing whistles and yelled commands and clambered up and over, the guns redoubled their fire. Swarms of men were over the parapet and marching slowly and relentlessly across the grassy expanse of no man's land towards the German lines.

The camera showed the British Army advancing to a great victory. Cheerful but watchful soldiers, bayonets at the ready, even stopped to light their cigarettes in the middle of no man's land. It was a stroll to victory.

By the time his film ran out and Malins had replaced it with another, his viewfinder showed a very different scene.

Enemy machine-guns opened up and the Lancashire Fusiliers were being strewn all over the ground. Most of them were dead. Never in two years of war had there been so many dead in such a small area. At first, all the casualties were from machine-gun fire, and so the bodies were whole, although where enfilade fire had

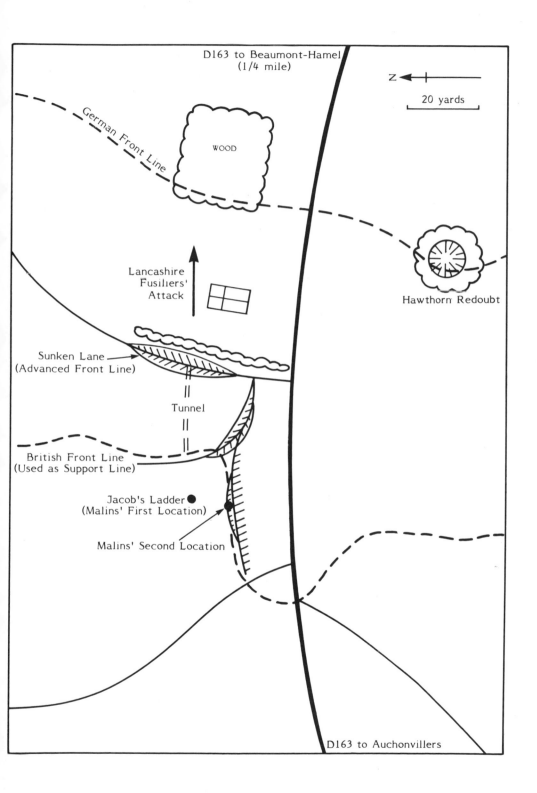

D163 to Beaumont-Hamel
(1/4 mile)

Z

20 yards

German Front Line

WOOD

Lancashire
Fusiliers'
Attack

Hawthorn Redoubt

Sunken Lane
(Advanced Front Line)

Tunnel

British Front Line
(Used as Support Line)

Jacob's Ladder ●
(Malins' First Location)

Malins' Second Location

D163 to Auchonvillers

caught them from both sides they lay three or four deep. Later, shells fell among them, killing their comrades who were trying to clamber over them, and dismembering the dead bodies.

Malins turned his cameras to the photogenic shellbursts going on around him. He even wished that one or two would burst nearer the camera for a better view. He was granted his wish: 'The next moment, with a shriek and a flash, a shell fell and exploded before I had time to take shelter. It was only a few feet away. What happened after I hardly knew. There was the grinding crash of bursting shell; something struck my tripod, the whole thing, camera and all, was flung against me.'

He got the equipment going again, but the War Office would have little use for the rest of his film. The slaughter by shellfire of the young fusiliers going on in the captured German front line fortunately was out of range, but the wounded, picture-stories of disaster, were not what the War Office needed to stiffen morale back home. Torn limbs, ripped and hanging flesh were not required.

Source
G. Malins, *How I Filmed the War*

Battle of the Somme, *1916*

Ten Days to Live or Die in No Man's Land: 1–14 July 1916

Private Matthews had that kind of experience which is rarely found in the history of a battle. He was presumed dead. No one searched for him. He was injured and couldn't move. Even if he could have dragged himself along, he probably would still have been unable to find his way out of no man's land back through the maze of zigzagging trenches, new British lines, old German lines, new German lines, and through the inevitable rain of bullets and shells.

He was left for dead in a trench in no man's land, and there he would probably die not a soldier's death but a death of hunger and thirst.

The assault on Gommecourt was a key part of the first day of the Somme offensive. Private Matthews and the 4th City of London Rifles had rehearsed it a lot and knew exactly what to do.

When the assault took place, everything went smoothly. The German first and second lines were taken with hardly a casualty. The battle was to get a good deal hotter later but by then Matthews would be well and truly out of it as far as the fighting went.

He was given the job of escorting a few prisoners back from the German second line. After just a few yards, he was struck by a bullet in the thigh; it caused a painful multiple fracture, preventing him from moving at all. He would certainly be blown up by a shell where he lay – in the middle of the battlefield – but he was lucky. A few men in a nearby disused trench, now a good hiding-place on the battle-field, dragged Matthews down to them, and they roughly bound his wound. He would clearly need proper medical attention soon.

Matthews had lost a lot of blood and was in a state of shock. The bullet had pierced the lymph ducts in his thigh, and his body fluids oozed away: he was desperately thirsty. The bullet had also passed through his water-bottle.

He was lucky again in his next visitor, a company messenger who sheltered in the same trench and left his own water-bottle behind for Matthews. It was a noble act, for that messenger could not have known when he was likely to get any further store.

The messenger departed and Matthews was left quite alone. For three days and three nights he was alone with one water-bottle, five hard biscuits, a twelve-ounce tin of corned beef and, mercifully, a packet of Woodbine cigarettes. Deep in his trench he was quite unable to move an inch. His wound chained him to a small patch of ground. No one could see him to fire at him, and no one could see him to rescue him.

On the fourth night, there were footsteps nearby. Matthews yelled. Four British soldiers approached unsteadily. They could only help him by gathering up some dead soldiers' rations and water-bottles and by promises to give his position when they got back to the British lines; however, they themselves had also been lying out in the battlefield wounded since the start of the battle three days before and they were trying to find their way back.

These lost soldiers went off and returned more lost than ever a couple of hours later. They had no idea which way to go now. The fighting was still fierce and shells were bursting all round. They were all in a bad way, and one of them was actually crawling on all fours. They went away and were never seen again.

Matthews went into a dazed sleep.

When he woke, a shell had burst above him and blown in the side of his trench. His food was destroyed and shrapnel had broken the water-bottles the lost soldiers had left him. He had no more food at all, and for two days he had no water either. When it rained, he

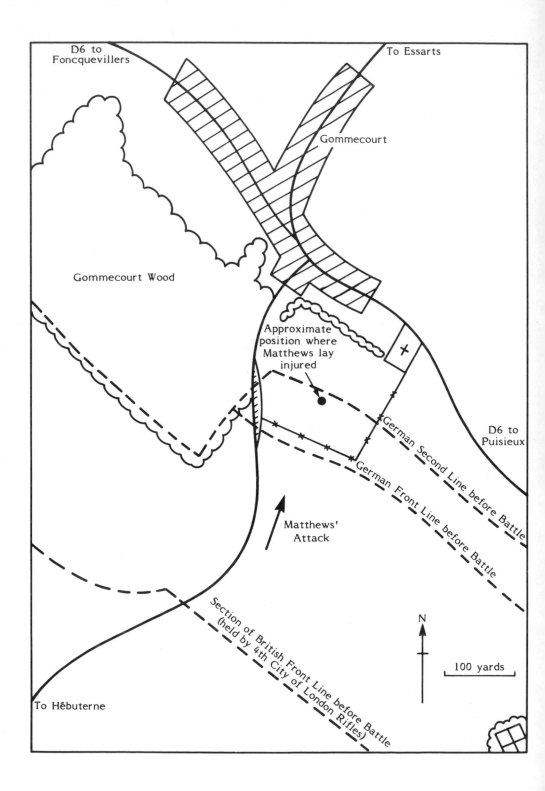

D6 to Foncquevillers

To Essarts

Gommecourt

Gommecourt Wood

Approximate position where Matthews lay injured

German Second Line before Battle

D6 to Puisieux

German Front Line before Battle

Matthews' Attack

Section of British Front Line before Battle (held by 4th City of London Rifles)

To Hébuterne

N

100 yards

caught some of the water in his helmet and, when that was soon gone, he drank from the filthy puddles around him.

He became weaker.

He hallucinated. He dreamt that he had been rescued and was safe and warm; then he woke up and found he was still lying in the trench. He felt himself dying.

Gradually he became too weak even to shout for help. Death would soon end all the anguish and all the pain.

Matthews was rescued by a patrol of the London Scottish after ten days in the open. He was stuck so fast to the ground that he literally had to be dug out and, even in his weak state, he cried with pain. After a perilous journey across no man's land, Matthews had his wound examined. It was serious but, amazingly, not septic. Soon he was able to have a good drink and a nourishing meal.

He was delirious with joy.

Source
J. Hammerton, ed., *I Was There!*

Battle of the Somme, 1916

Lieutenant Siegfried Sassoon Captures a Trench Single-handed: 6 July 1916

Lieutenant Siegfried Sassoon was an extraordinary soldier. He was awarded the Military Cross and even recommended for a Victoria Cross for his extreme bravery. He was brought back to Britain three times, wounded or sick. Once, while he convalesced, he felt impelled to write a violent attack on the conduct of the war and expected to be court-martialled (but was declared to be suffering from shell shock). He was a famous poet and writer of prose, and he was inspired by his war adventures.

Sassoon had just seen his first dead German. He was with the Royal Welch Fusiliers marching beside a battalion of the Royal Irish south of Mametz Wood which was thought to be empty of Germans. It wasn't. They were fired on as they went along the road and forced to take cover in a quarry. Since all the men were carrying picks and shovels for digging trenches and were short of sleep and soaked with

rain, they were not well-prepared for an unexpected fight. The Royal
Irish were ordered forward to deal with the Germans in the wood,
and the Royal Welch, including Sassoon, were kept in support.
Sassoon felt nervous and incompetent while he wondered what on
earth he should do if called on to lead a party out 'into the blue'.

The little attack quickly failed and the Brigade withdrew in the
direction it had come. Sixty casualties in the Royal Irish had enabled
the generals to discover that Mametz Wood was absolutely full of
Germans. 'This sort of warfare was a new experience for all of us,'
remarked Sassoon.

A different approach to Mametz Wood was needed. The two
battalions were marched round the west of the hill to the edge of
Bottom Wood, there to await the signal to attack again, this time in
force.

Quarter to one in the morning of 6 July was Zero Hour. It was
pitch dark and the ground was mud. As the softening-up bombardment started and the Germans responded, Sassoon wondered
whether shells ever collided in the air. The first wave went over the
top; Sassoon's platoon waited in reserve.

The confusion and the darkness made an effective attack impossible but there was heavy shelling, and it was terrifying. Sassoon was
supported by a young friend he had made, a nineteen-year-old
Lance-Corporal in his platoon, called Kendall. 'Young Kendall was
remarkable for his cheerfulness and courage, and cheeky jokes.
Many a company had its Kendall, until the war broke his spirit.'

Now, in the darkness, it became obvious that the attack needed
support, but no one knew exactly what Sassoon's platoon should do.
So Sassoon set off on his own to try to get clear orders for his platoon.
A figure loomed up beside him, to offer companionship. 'It's me,
Kendall, sir.'

'We groped our way into the wood, and very soon I muttered that
unless we were careful we'd get lost, which was true enough, for my
sense of direction had already become uncertain. While we hesitated, some shells exploded all round us in the undergrowth with an
effect of crashing stupidity. But we laughed, encouraging each other
with mutual bravado, until we found a path.' Together, fortified
by each other's company, Sassoon and Kendall got back to headquarters and got their orders. 'Take the bombers up at once' – for a
grenade attack starting in Quadrangle Trench newly captured from
the Germans.

Sassoon, Kendall and their platoon advanced through Bottom
Wood out into the open and into the northernmost edge of Quadrangle Trench. Just as they got there, a runner overtook them to say
they weren't needed. Sassoon sent his platoon back. 'I sent them

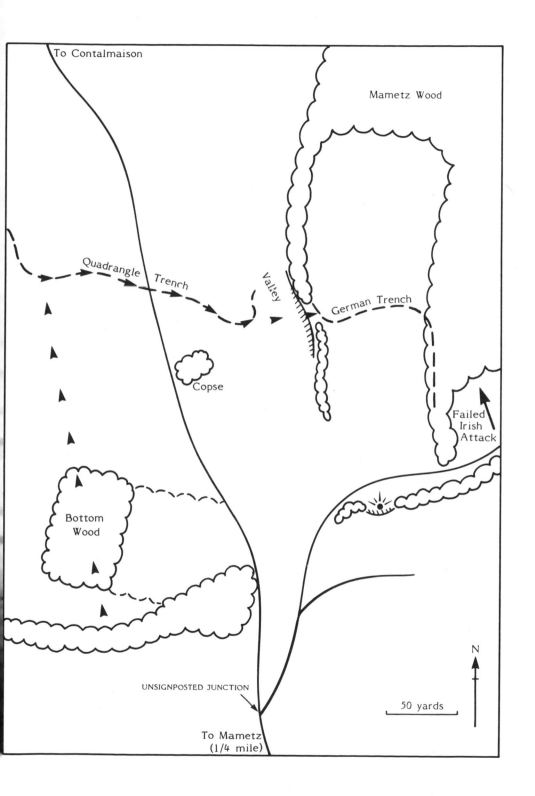

To Contalmaison

Mametz Wood

Quadrangle Trench

Valley

German Trench

Copse

Failed
Irish
Attack

Bottom
Wood

UNSIGNPOSTED JUNCTION

To Mametz
(1/4 mile)

N

50 yards

back. I cannot say why I went on myself, but I did, and Kendall stayed with me.'

It was now nearly six in the morning. Sassoon and Kendall crawled up Quadrangle Trench towards the small valley which separated the end of the trench from German-held trenches in and around Mametz Wood. The nearer they got to the Germans the more inadequate the trench became until it was only twelve inches deep in places. As they crawled, they exchanged rifle shots in a desultory way with a group of Germans occupying a short trench leading straight out of the wood. The Germans found their mark. One shot gave Kendall 'a blotchy mark where the bullet had hit him just above the eyes'. He slumped into the mud.

'All feelings tightened and contracted to a single attention, to settle that sniper.' Maddened by the killing of his friend beside him, Sassoon discarded his helmet and equipment and rushed across the valley and up the opposite bank: a hundred yards of total exposure.

I found myself looking down into a well-conducted trench with a great many Germans in it. Fortunately for me, they were already retreating. It had not occurred to them that they were being attacked by a single fool . . . Idiotically elated, I stood there with my finger in my right ear and emitted a series of "view-halloas" (a gesture which ought to win the approval of people who still regard war as a form of outdoor sport). Having thus failed to commit suicide, I proceeded to occupy the trench – that is to say I sat down on the fire-step, very much out of breath, and hoped to God the Germans wouldn't come back again.'

Sassoon explored the trench he had taken and found no dead Germans. His bombing was not so accurate and he was a bit disappointed. He noticed there were between forty and fifty packs abandoned in a hurry, 'a fact which I often mentioned (quite casually) when describing my exploit afterwards'.

He returned to the sniping post at the end of the trench and sat down for a few minutes to decide what to do, 'somewhat like a boy who has caught a fish too big to carry home . . . Finally I took a deep breath and ran headlong back by the way I'd come'.

Back in the safety of the deeper part of the Quadrangle Trench, Sassoon saw a dead German. 'His blond face was undisfigured . . . gentle. He didn't look more than eighteen. He and Kendall had cancelled each other out in the process called "attrition of manpower".'

Source
S. Sassoon, *Memoirs of an Infantry Officer*

Battle of the Somme, 1916

From Enthusiasm to Terror: 7 July, 1916

Harold Mellersh was just nineteen. The Somme was to be his first battle. He was the greenest second lieutenant in his regiment, the 2nd East Lancashires.

It would be exhilarating to lead his platoon into battle for the first time. He wouldn't be scared. The only reason why he was shivering the night before was because he didn't have his trench coat to cover him.

The first attack from Fricourt to Contalmaison was already going on while Mellersh was leading his men up the Fricourt road from the west. They were not shelled on their advance to the front but it was a long unpleasant march. Soldiers' bodies lay unburied and were turning green in congealed pools of blood. Ambulances passed continuously with groaning passengers.

By late afternoon on 6 July, Mellersh and his men reached the dug-out where they were to spend their last night before the battle. It was a captured German dug-out and was altogether better built and more permanent than the British ones. The entrance at trench level (protected by an impregnated anti-gas blanket) led to half a dozen stairs going down to a small room made to look cavernous by small pools of light from candles stuck to a trestle table. Mellersh and his companions 'got a good fug up' to get rid of the dank atmosphere, and got what satisfaction they could from some mildly alcoholic French syrups they had bought, citron and grenadine.

Mellersh tried to think of England. He failed, trembled and fell asleep.

At 7.53 a.m. he and his men arrived at the trench where the attack was to start. Artillery fire was slight. Mellersh was exhilarated, walking up and down 'supervising'.

He looked at his watch. Eight o'clock: 'In thoroughly approved style I was blowing my whistle, giving the overarm signal, and commanding "advance!"'

Nothing happened at first. They ran slowly and kept alert. Mellersh noticed it had begun to rain.

They arrived at a low muddy gully, rested a few moments and advanced again over the grass in a line. Now the enemy machine-gunning started, first one gun, then many, raking Mellersh and his men systematically from right to left, left to right, right to left . . .

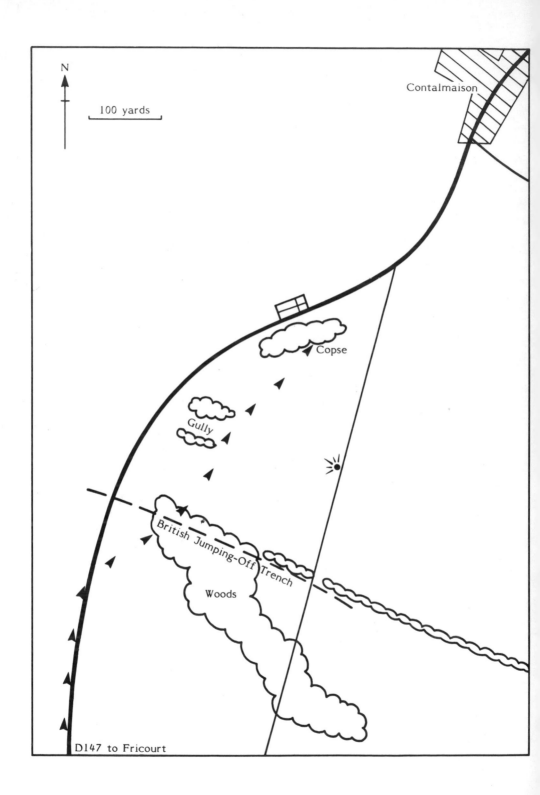

N

100 yards

Contalmaison

Copse

Gully

British Jumping-Off Trench

Woods

D147 to Fricourt

Lying flat on their faces, they had a good chance of survival but standing up almost none. They lay still and a few were picked off. What could they do? Paralysis.

A textbook answer to this situation was a 'sectional rush'. One half or 'section' of the platoon would stay still, covering the other advancing half with rapid rifle fire. They tried 'sectional rushes'. The textbook said nothing about what happens if, as in this case, the enemy machine-gunners are hidden from the riflemen and probably out of range too. More men fell.

There was obviously no point in allowing the slaughter to continue but there was no order to retire. Mellersh used his initiative. Sheltering in a nearby copse looked possible. They sprinted to it with back and knees bent. The copse sheltered them from machine-guns but made a perfect target for 'whizz-bang' shells. They were still in a death-trap; the shelter offered by the copse was an illusion.

After an agonizing few minutes in which Mellersh himself was saved only by a 'whizz-bang' shell failing to explode at his feet, an assistant adjutant from brigade headquarters arrived and ordered the retreat. Stooping, they ran back to the gully, now lower and muddier from the shelling and the rain: 'We struggled on through the mud and the rain and the shelling. Then came a terrific crack above my head, a jolt in my left shoulder, and at the same time I was watching in an amazed, detached sort of way my right forearm twist upward of its own volition and then hang limp.'

Razor-sharp steel shrapnel had smashed into his shoulder. 'You're for Blighty alright!' said the doctor. Mellersh had achieved in his first battle what many soldiers prayed for throughout the war, a Blighty wound to get him back home.

'That I had just taken part in a failure, that I had really done nothing to help with the war, these things were forgotten – if ever indeed they had entered my consciousness. I had been through the Somme battle and I was alive. That was enough.'

Source
H. E. L. Mellersh, *Schoolboy into War*

Battle of the Somme, 1916

Too Far Advanced: 13 and 14 July 1916

Captain Charles Carrington was frightened of being frightened. He was a teenager, and he was leading his company of Warwickshires into attack just a fortnight after the Somme offensive had opened. It so happened that he encountered almost no resistance, got lost and over-excited and never stopped until he was over a thousand yards too far ahead, on the German side of the village of Ovillers. In this way, the Germans in Ovillers found they were surrounded, but troops attempting to relieve Ovillers in turn soon surrounded Carrington and isolated him in his advanced trench.

Carrington's introduction to the Ovillers region had been a pair of two smartly booted and gaitered legs protruding into the old German front-line trench at La Boisselle. No other part of the German body remained. Carrington was shocked but the older tougher soldiers took an easy-going view of dead bodies, rummaging around the swelling flesh, which usually contained maggots and often rats as well, and taking souvenirs. Sometimes they made a necklace out of a set of teeth and used protruding limbs as clothes-horses. Carrington was getting hardened very quickly.

In the officers' dug-out, he washed quickly in grey, slimy water already well used, and went for orders from the colonel. He wrote down his instructions very carefully, but out in the dark with his company he was soon lost. The night of 13 July was black, and once past a broken ambulance there were no landmarks at all.

Shells were falling and the prospect of attacking a German trench and fighting hand to hand with bayonets was extremely unpleasant.

'I don't want to go over the plonk,' wept Private Elliot, who presented himself to Carrington just as he was getting lost. 'I'm only seventeen, I want to go home.' 'Can't help that now, my lad . . . You'll be alright when you get started. This is the worst part of it . . . Jump to it!' Carrington was nineteen.

The time had come, Carrington calculated, for his company to leave their trench and head in the rough direction of Ovillers. A torrent of men climbed over the parapet of their trench and charged down the hill, and no one spotted them and not a shot was fired. Across the valley and up to a battered unoccupied trench. Across the road, over a high bank – which took a lot of nerve – and finally down into a well-built German trench. The trench turned out to have some

Germans in it, but they were not in the portion entered that night. So Carrington had led, more or less accidentally, a thousand-yard advance on the Somme without losing a single man. One man even cheered, but they quietened him and waited.

It was the next day before the Germans realized what had happened and tried to work their way along the trench to get the British company out. Some grenades were thrown and new-fangled egg-bombs which exploded with a great deal of noise but little effect. A sniper started to cause a lot of damage: three dead and a young corporal with his brains blown out but refusing to die. Carrington's men started filling in the trench between themselves and the Germans, to make a 'bomb-stop', and they wondered bitterly where the rations, the water, the rum and the rest of the battalion had all got to.

It dawned on them slowly that their advance had been over a thousand yards of exposed rough grass further than their comrades who were still stuck back on the La Boisselle-Posières road. Nobody could cross that grass by day. They were very lucky that the Germans decided to concentrate on the main road first and to mop up Carrington and his company afterwards.

That night, Carrington's boss, the colonel, arrived. He told Carrington calmly how the rest of the battle had gone. The fighting along the road had been fierce but, at the cost of half the battalion, the British had at last won through and would eventually be able to relieve this trench and take Ovillers.

The men were hungry, exhausted and terribly thirsty. The colonel provided a drop of whisky and soda from a flask for Carrington, but the rest had to wait several more hours for cans full of petrol-flavoured water.

More important, the colonel provided a calming and confident air. The men would be safe. They could even attack up the trench. They would shortly be relieved. They were soon all singing (in low whispers) in keen anticipation:

> 'A-love the la-dies
> A-love t'be among the girls . . .'

The Germans lost Ovillers two days later. By that time, Carrington's company were resting in the rear. The trench they had gained, more by luck than judgement, was never lost again.

Source
C. Edmonds (C. E. Carrington), *A Subaltern at War . . .*

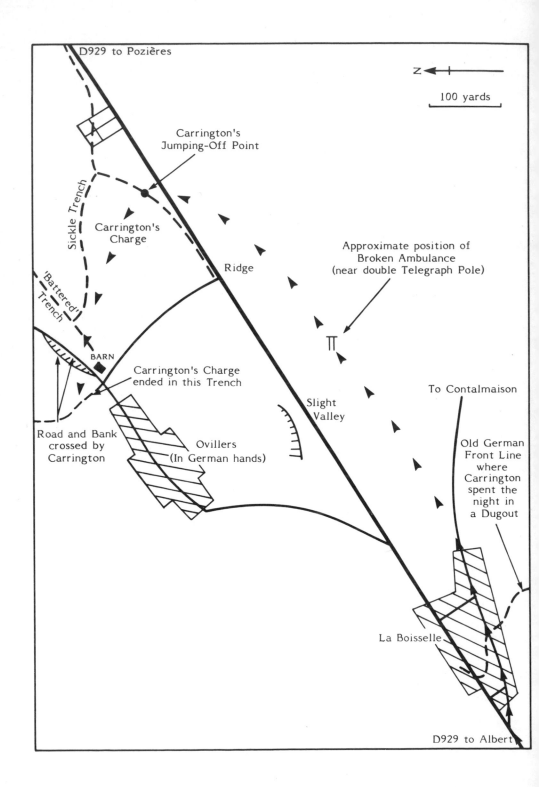

D929 to Pozières

Z

100 yards

Carrington's
Jumping-Off Point

Sickle Trench

Carrington's
Charge

'Battered'
Trench

Ridge

Approximate position of
Broken Ambulance
(near double Telegraph Pole)

BARN

Carrington's Charge
ended in this Trench

Slight
Valley

To Contalmaison

Road and Bank
crossed by
Carrington

Ovillers
(In German hands)

Old German
Front Line
where
Carrington
spent the
night in
a Dugout

La Boisselle

D929 to Albert

Battle of the Somme, 1916

Danger Signals: 20 July 1916

To stand in the middle of a battlefield waving flags and shining mirrors to attract attention took a lot of nerve. It was, however, the only effective way of getting messages from headquarters to the battle-front and back again to the rest of the world. Telephones were no use. The wires were smashed by artillery almost as soon as they were laid. So Private Frank Richards was sent out on the fourteenth day of the Battle of the Somme expecting to relay back to his brigade headquarters (and thence to the world) a victory at High Wood.

As soon as the Royal Welch Fusiliers, including Frank Richards, reached the relative safety of Mametz Wood from a bloody battle in the village of Bazentin-le-Petit on 19 July 1916, they were told about the plan to launch an attack on High Wood the next day. This had all been worked out at brigade headquarters, which was in Mametz Wood.

Richards and seven others were sent at 2 a.m. with their primitive equipment to a most exposed position, a large mill about 600 yards on the Mametz side of High Wood: 'We had a good view of everything from here, but we also found that when we were exchanging messages with the wood, the enemy would have an equally good view of us, especially when we were flag-wagging.' Richards predicted heavy shelling.

The battle raged from 10 a.m. the next morning, and the prediction Richards had made came true. Shells of all types and from both sides burst around them and on top of them. One shell splinter flew between Richards's legs and slammed into the thigh of the man behind him. Five of the signallers were so struck with terror that they refused to move from the shelter of a shell-hole. Richards was braver and carried on.

Messages were received from the battle-front and sent on to brigade headquarters despite the shelling. Through the fog of battle, Richards soon picked up the victory sign – THE WHOLE OF HIGH WOOD IS TAKEN.

The victory at High Wood was short-lived.

Within a few minutes, a massive German counter-attack began. It wiped out not only the victory but three-quarters of the Fusiliers, the Manchesters, the Argyll and Sutherland Highlanders and the Public

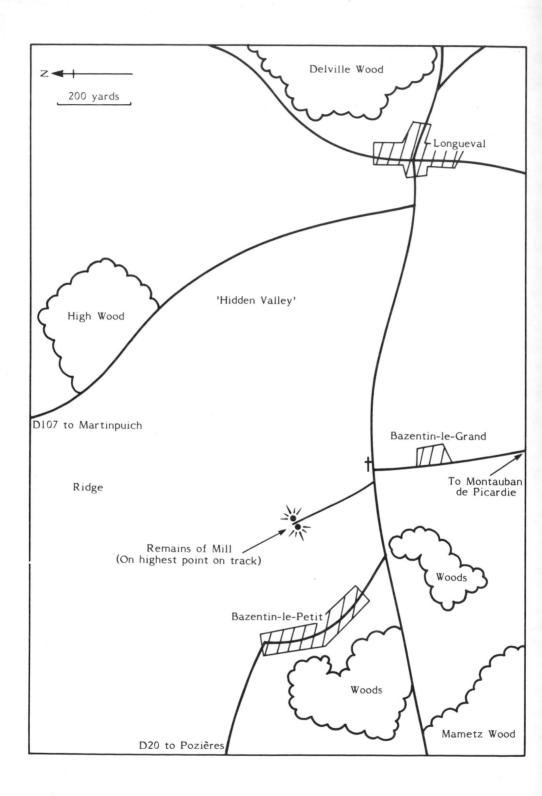

Z ← ⊢

200 yards

Delville Wood

Longueval

'Hidden Valley'

High Wood

D107 to Martinpuich

Ridge

Bazentin-le-Grand

To Montauban
de Picardie

Remains of Mill
(On highest point on track)

Bazentin-le-Petit

Woods

Woods

D20 to Pozières

Mametz Wood

Schools Battalion. No more messages reached the signallers – the flag-wavers and the runners from the front had been killed.

Chaos turned to defeat and defeat to calamity.

No more signals were needed. Richards was ordered back from the mill.

He returned past the remains of the Argyll and Sutherland Highlanders: 'I could only see heads, arms, legs and mangled bodies.'

And past the Public Schools Battalion: 'One shell burst just outside the trench not far from me, and a man had one side of his face cut clean away by a piece of shell. He was also hit low down but was still conscious. His two pals were deliberating whether they would put him out of his misery or not; fortunately they were spared that, as he died before they had made up their minds.'

Finally he regained his own regiment: 'One of our old stretcher-bearers went mad and started to undress himself. He was uttering horrible screams, and we had to fight with him and overpower him before he could be got to the Aid Post. He had been going queer for the last month or two.'

The 'blood-tub' was living up to its name.

Source
F. Richards, *Old Soldiers Never Die*

Guillemont, 1916

High Hopes Machine-Gunned to Death: 18 August 1916

Three earlier attacks had failed. They had all ground to a halt half a mile before Guillemont ridge. The valley the Leinsters had to cross to get to the new British front line had been appropriately named 'the Valley of Death'.

This time though, Francis Hitchcock of the Leinsters thought there was a chance of attacking from the new front line across to the Guillemont Ridge without that much bloodshed. He had special confidence in his regiment and in the immense artillery barrage taking place – surely no German would survive it. The only disadvantage was the very hot weather, which caused overloaded men to groan and sweat and made it virtually impossible for them to do anything other than move slowly and steadily in attack.

The plan was very simple. Two battalions to be in the first line. First objectives to be the German front line in front of Guillemont village to be taken by leading units. Second objective the village of Guillemont to be taken by support units, including Hitchcock's. There was to be a 'creeping barrage', which meant that the artillery would keep about thirty yards ahead of the attack as it made its way uphill to Guillemont:

'They had got to within thirty yards of their objective. Our barrage had then to lift off the Hun lines and, when it did, up rushed the Boche from his deep dug-outs with machine-guns and directed a withering fire on the attackers. Machine-guns which had been lying out concealed in a sunken road which ran between the advancing battalions also enfiladed the flanks of the two units.'

The machine-guns in the sunken road were devastating.

Streams of wounded, walking and on stretchers, were now drifting back past Hitchcock and the support battalions; men with smashed arms, limping and with the worst of all to see – facial wounds. They all muttered about the machine-guns in the sunken road.

Suddenly it was no longer just the 'walking wounded' coming out of the smoke – wounded don't come back in lines. A failure! It had been a fine sight seeing the leading battalions advancing into action, but it was a most depressing one seeing them retiring.

Hitchcock's new role was to take over the front-line trenches from the remnants of the attacking battalions who had fallen back into them, and to defend them against counter-attack.

The artillery preparation by the Germans for their counter-attack was fierce:

'Shell-fire was hellish all afternoon . . . the heat was intense . . . crouching in the trench, hugging the forward side, one could feel every minute small stones and lumps of earth ricochet off one's helmet. Now and then one would be almost smothered by the parapet being blown in. The dirt flying about and the fumes from the lyddite added to our discomfiture. During a bombardment one developed a craze for two things: water and cigarettes. Few could ever eat under an intense bombardment, especially on the Somme, when every now and then a shell would blow pieces of mortality, or complete bodies, which had been putrefying in no man's land, slap into one's trench. Shell-fire, too, always stirred up swarms of black flies, of which there was an absolute plague on the Somme battlefields . . .'

No significant counter-attack materialized to follow up this barrage. The Germans were exhausted too. By ten o'clock at night,

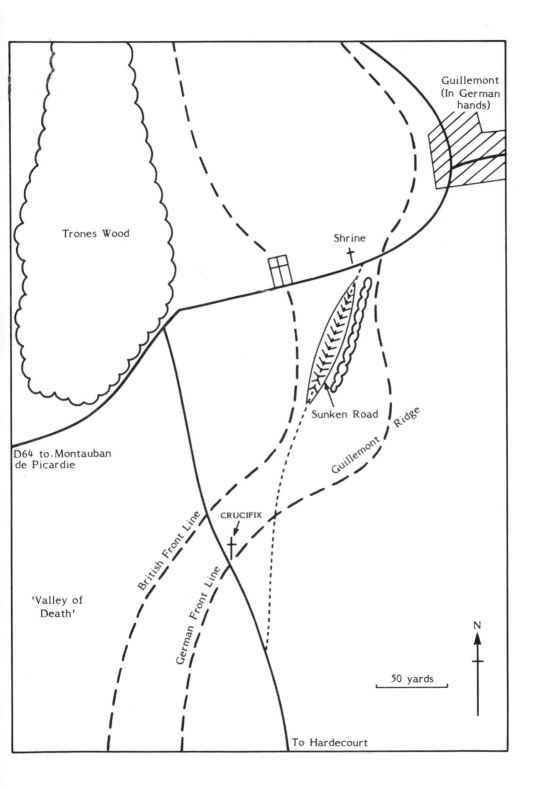

Guillemont
(In German
hands)

Trones Wood

Shrine

Sunken Road

Guillemont Ridge

D64 to Montauban
de Picardie

British Front Line

CRUCIFIX

German Front Line

'Valley of
Death'

N

50 yards

To Hardecourt

Hitchcock felt it safe to post sentries and get some sleep. It was much quieter.

He crawled into a protected undercutting in the trench, known as a funkhole, only to wake up the next morning next to two dead bodies he had not even noticed were dead the night before – indeed, he had spoken to them.

Hitchcock's men now found themselves in a rather quiet front line but with no rations, so they searched for breakfast through the kits of the dead. Hitchcock found tinned lobster and crab and enjoyed a superior breakfast.

He and his colonel thought they could carry on the fight. They wanted to stay in line and perhaps have another go at Guillemont, but they were ordered to a reserve line a mile or so back, to hold themselves in readiness and to be prepared to move to the Guillemont front within an hour.

In the event, they were not needed and had a few days' well-earned rest.

Source
F. C. Hitchcock, *Stand To*

Martinpuich, 1916

The First Tank of the War:
15 September 1916

'Can you get away in the morning Malins? The boat train leaves early.'

'If there is something doing I wouldn't miss it for worlds.'

'There is: they want you urgently.'

'I've only got to get my supply of film stock. I'll manage it during the night somehow and meet you at Charing Cross in the morning.'

The next day, Lieutenant Geoffrey Malins was in France and heading for the front line at Martinpuich.

'So you're Movies, eh?' the general asked Malins, 'What are you after?'

Malins replied that he would like to be right at the front at 6.20 a.m. for the attack with the new secret weapon.

'There's a machine-gun position in a sap head. I am sure that would suit you, but you'll get strafed. Boche can't fail to see you.'

A rumour had reached Malins of a British secret weapon. No one had seen it. No one knew what it was like. They simply called it the 'Hush! Hush!'

'I haven't seen them,' said the general. 'All I know is that we have two of them going over with our boys. This is their line; they will make straight for the left-hand corner of the village, and cross the trenches on your left about two hundred yards from your sap. They are a sort of armoured car arrangement and shells literally glance off them. They will cross trenches, no matter how wide, crawl in and out of shell-holes, and through barbed wire, push down trees and . . .'

'He'll tell me next they can fly as well,' Malins murmured. 'The war must be getting on his nerves.'

At three o'clock in the morning of 15 September, Malins set out from a former German dug-out. It was icy there, deep underground. An occasional shell whistled over as he made his way to his sap but caused little damage. The Germans seemed to know something was up for they flooded no man's land with Very lights, making the scene, for a moment, like daytime. Whenever this happened, Malins and his companions, who were carrying his equipment, froze.

The trenches gradually warmed into life. The men were quite cheerful and ready for the attack (particularly since they knew they were to be supported by the new secret weapon). Malins stopped for a cup of tea round a cheerful little trench fire on his way to the front.

Day was breaking as he got to his filming post in the machine-gun sap at the front.

'What's that, sir?'

Gingerly Malins raised himself above the parapet and peered in the direction in which his companion's finger pointed.

For a moment he could discern nothing. Then, gradually, out of the early morning mist a huge, dark, shapeless object appeared, about three hundred yards away. It moved and, judging by the subdued hum and a slight smoke emitted – like the breath of an animal – it lived!

He had never seen anything like it before. What was it?

For the moment, Malins forgot about his camera. He and his companions (and also the Germans two hundred yards away on the other side of no man's land) just gaped.

Malins could not take his eyes off it. The thing – he really could find no words to describe it – ambled forward, with slow, jerky, uncertain movements. The sight of it was weird enough in all conscience. At one moment its nose disappeared, then, with a slide

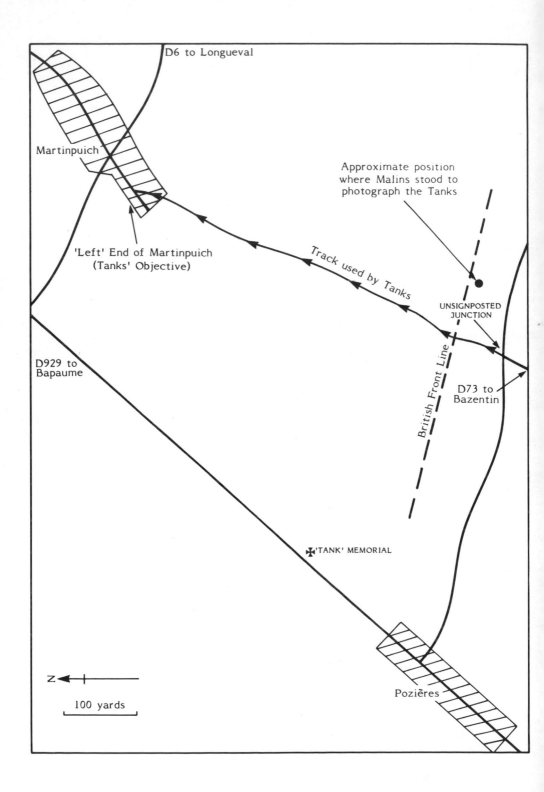

D6 to Longueval

Martinpuich

Approximate position
where Malins stood to
photograph the Tanks

'Left' End of Martinpuich
(Tanks' Objective)

Track used by Tanks

UNSIGNPOSTED
JUNCTION

D929 to
Bapaume

British Front Line

D73 to
Bazentin

✠'TANK' MEMORIAL

Z

100 yards

Pozières

and an upward glide, it climbed the other side of a deep shell crater which lay in its path. Malins stood amazed.

He forced himself to concentrate on getting his film and camera out and trained on the advancing tanks and the Argyll and Sutherlands and the Scottish Rifles following in their wake.

Malins recalled, 'All this time I had scarce taken my eyes off the ugly-looking monster. It wobbled, it ambled, it jolted, it rolled – well it did everything in turn and nothing long – or wrong. And most remarkable of all, this weird-looking creature with a metal hide performed tricks which almost made one doubt the evidence of one's senses. Big, and ugly, and awkward as it was, clumsy as its movements appeared to be, the thing seemed imbued with life, and possessed of the most uncanny sort of intelligence and understanding. It came to a crater. Down went its nose; a slight dip, and a clinging, crawling motion, and it came up merrily on the other side. And all the time as it slowly advanced, it breathed and belched forth tongues of flame; its nostrils seemed to breathe death and destruction, and the Huns, terrified by its appearance, were mown down like corn falling to the reaper's sickle.'

The frantic Germans hailed rifle and machine-guns' fire on the tank but to no effect. Some courageously edged close to it and even clambered onto it. They were knocked aside or crushed. Others cowered in the trenches and shell-holes and surrendered to the British infantry following behind.

Some Germans were killed by the infantry but most were machine-gunned or crushed by the tank, or buried alive as the tracks trundled over their dug-outs. Three hundred Germans died in the assault on Martinpuich.

Source
G. Malins, *How I Filmed the War*

Near Lesbœufs, 1916

Taking Over No One's Land: December 1916

Scrambled eggs, bacon and coffee made a luxurious breakfast indeed. Captain Sidney Rogerson and his second in command, Lieutenant Skett, deserved it. They were going straight off afterwards to supervise the take-over by their company of the 2nd West Yorkshires of an extremely vague front-line trench, a long, primitive ditch stuck out in no man's land at present held by the Devon Regiment. Skett ate practically nothing. He was young, and this was to be his first tour of the front line. 'Leave him alone and he'll be all right.' Skett missed his last meal.

To get to the front, Rogerson and Skett had to cross a heavily shelled valley north of Lesbœufs where the headquarters of the Devon Regiment was situated in a sunken road. They were then led by guides from the Devon Regiment up to the stretch of front lying between the villages of Lesbœufs and Le Transloy. They crossed another low valley, with Dewdrop Trench, the scene of earlier heavy fighting and once a substantial German reserve line, running through its midst. 'The shell-ploughed ground was carpeted with dead, the khaki outnumbering the field-grey by three to one.' Halfway up the ridge on the far side of the valley they slid into a shallow ditch, Autumn Trench. The front itself lay beyond Autumn Trench over the top of the ridge and could only be reached by a scooped-out muddy ditch, nowhere more than three feet deep, which led to a series of shell-holes on the far side of the ridge which joined up to make a sketchy front line.

In fact, this so-called front line was little more than no man's land with primitive ditches leading backwards and forwards, some of them nominally British and some nominally German, around the same area. They were largely uncontested; any sort of real combat in this immediate area was made almost impossible by the thick, glutinous mud through which the ditches and trenches had to be dug.

'No one could struggle through that mud for more than a few yards without rest. Terrible in its clinging consistency, it was the arbiter of destiny, the supreme enemy, paralysing and mocking English and German alike. Distances were measured not in yards but in mud.'

In these conditions, Rogerson's tour of his sector, the few hundred yards of front for which he was responsible, took over two hours. He had to rely on officers like Skett to mind part of the line, taking their own initiatives and not waiting for detailed orders. Skett took over the northern part of the sector.

'The impression left on my mind was that we were as much at the mercy of the elements as of the enemy.' There were no ordinary trench amenities. Two stretchers slung across the top of the trench signified Rogerson's 'company headquarters', and they were the only shelter. There were no holes where men could hide. 'They slept

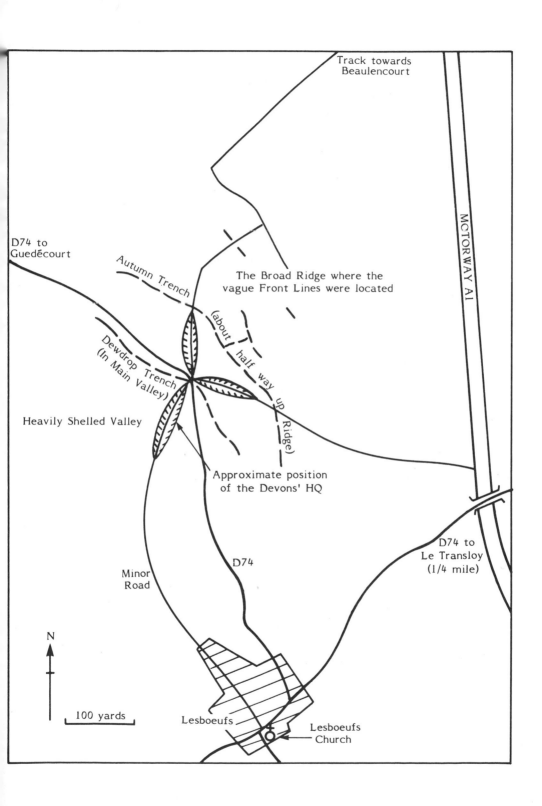

Track towards
Beaulencourt

MOTORWAY A1

D74 to
Guedécourt

Autumn Trench

The Broad Ridge where the
vague Front Lines were located

(about half way up Ridge)

Dewdrop Trench
(In Main Valley)

Heavily Shelled Valley

Approximate position
of the Devons' HQ

D74 to
Le Transloy
(1/4 mile)

Minor
Road

D74

N

100 yards

Lesboeufs

Lesboeufs
Church

as they sat, huddled into themselves, in positions reminiscent of prehistoric burials. As cooking was out of the question, there was no apology for a cook-house. The one latrine was a hole dug into the side of a support trench. In short, there was as much to be done to make the place habitable as defendable.'

On their first night at the front, Rogerson and Skett supervised improvements to the trench system throughout the sector. As normal, they sent out patrols to ensure the diggers were not surprised by an attack. Everything was very quiet, although they knew there was a sniper about because one new recruit had been shot (not seriously) in the mouth. Skett sent out a subaltern called Pym on patrol and he disappeared. Nobody ever knew if he was captured by a German patrol or slipped into the mud and suffocated. He just disappeared. Skett went after him, but as he climbed over the improved parapet of the trench he became the sniper's first victim to die.

Rogerson had been devoted to Skett. Now, the only officer within several hours' walk, he was to bury him in this mud desert – 'Mile upon mile of emptiness, never a hedge or a tree or a spot of green to mark the absolute monotony of tint and feature.' A mud hole in the side of Autumn Trench was Skett's tomb.

Rogerson soldiered on. Keeping low. Making the best of the shelter he could get. Counting the minutes of his twelve days' tour of the front line. Risking life and limb as little as possible. Resenting his superior officers who never came near the front. What could they know of this place, of the mud, from their maps?

Source
S. Rogerson, *Twelve Days*

Battle of Villers-Bretonneux, 1918

A Franco-Australian Alliance Saves the Day: April 1918

The enemy broke the British Fifth Army in March 1918. To the Australian reinforcements who rushed south to try to plug the gap, the Fifth Army presented a spectacle of a force broken and scattered. Its breaking had flung the whole British war machine out of gear. To weld it together again into a solid hard-hitting force was going to be a

View from Avion Station: 'Sullivan' front line trench ran down the road which now lies opposite. The Germans were about a hundred yards to the left

A copse on the site of the exploded Hawthorn Redoubt

The valley crossed by Sassoon: the trench he captured single-handed
led into Mametz Wood on the far right

Mellersh tried to advance towards Contalmaison (behind camera) and was
forced to shelter in Peake Wood (far right)

The mound is the remains of
Richards's windmill. The view is
south-west in the general direction of
Mametz Wood, to which Richards
was signalling

Looking towards the bend in the
sunken lane where German
machine-gunners were hidden. They
surprised the Leinsters whose attack
on Guillemont village failed with
heavy casualties

A crucifix overlooks the 'Valley of Death'

The tractor is following the track in the foreground used by the first tank in the attack on Martinpuich in the trees in the distance. The camera position is similar to that of Malins

Looking down the valley containing Dewdrop Trench, which Rogerson crossed from the heavily-shelled valley beyond. Rogerson was heading for the vague front line (behind the camera)

The first tank-to-tank battle took place in this field. Cachy, where the Whippet tanks emerged to rout the Germans, is behind the trees in the background

This view is from the most advanced Indian positions over the Hindenburg Line — a group of trees half a mile away (centre right) marks the line of main fortifications. The copse, used by Junger and his men is at the bottom of the foreground slope on the left. Junger's outpost was halfway up the foreground slope, some fifty yards left of the camera

View from the Hindenburg Line to Yorkshire Bank (hill left of motorway). Bacon's tank advanced along the line where the motorway now lies, towards the camera

Coppard's machine-guns were on the slope on the right; the Germans were on the left of the canal

very difficult task. In the meantime, the Australians and French set out to fill the gap. They were to meet in Hangard Wood.

No one knew the true extent of the German breakthrough in March 1918. What struck Captain Maxwell VC and his fellow officers and men of the 18th Australian Battalion after they had detrained at Amiens was confusion. The confusion of rumours about the breakthrough, the confusion of the thriving city of Amiens abandoned in a day, and the confusion of groups of refugees with pathetic bundles of a few belongings. Leaving Amiens in the direction of the front, the nature and effects of the German breakthrough itself were soon apparent. Companies and platoons were scattered and men wandered about aimlessly, and in the background the grey-black smoke-cloud that overhung the advancing force.

Maxwell's orders were to round up any individual British 'strays' and include them in his own company. After the defeat they had just suffered, it did them a power of good to be among the Australians, the 'Diggers', with their reputation for high morale even in the face of dangerous odds.

On their way to the front, they passed many of the inhabitants of the village of Villers-Bretonneux, which was about to become a battlefield. One old couple, about seventy years of age, stumbled along. 'The woman was weeping. The old man crouched at her side with a few treasures tied in the folds of a shawl. He paused for a moment near our concentration, raised a battered felt hat in solemn farewell to the little village, for so long the centre of all his joys and hopes, and then ambled on.'

Reaching the battlefield itself, on the wet night of 31 March, the most surprising thing to Maxwell was that there was no front line. There were no clear trenches, just occasionally a few shell-holes joined together – highly vulnerable, with German snipers very close. And not only snipers, for the German artillery attack on these makeshift defences was also fierce. The British artillery support was distant and slight, as far back behind the battlefield as could feasibly have any effect on the enemy – and limbered up ready to flee.

It was quickly decided to move up to Hangard Wood where there was a better chance of standing up to and even counter-attacking the enemy than in the open country.

Maxwell and his Australians were in high spirits as they moved to their new positions, encouraged by the fact that they were now supported by close-up Australian guns rather than the distant British ones. Also, shamelessly, they looted Villers-Bretonneux. 'Bottles of champagne, fowls, rabbits and underclothing of every kind had come into their net. Men changed underclothes that were alive with vermin for dainty undies that had been left by their owners when the village had been evacuated.' At one point, the lavish village provisions were also supplemented by two Germans who had lost their way in the mud and darkness. One of them carried an urn of hot coffee and the other was bowed down under a bag of boiled potatoes.

The Germans had positions in Hangard Cemetery and a nearby coppice. Maxwell and the Australians met up with the French along a sunken road by Hangard Wood. Before either side went into the attack, there was a chance for the French and Australians to get to know each other.

There was a language problem which was nearly the death of an Australian Lance-Corporal called Doherty. The French had a pass-word, 'Dijon'.

'*Halte là!*'

'Demijohn!'

The Frenchman fired.

'Hey! Strike you flamin' purple!' (The Frenchman had missed) 'Can't you frog-eatin', bone-headed gazobs comprez your own *** language. Allez tout sweet, yer flamin' mugs.'

The French had doubts about the Australians' guts. They considered them British and, after all, the British Fifth Army had just collapsed.

'Don't you worry about us, Manure. We're a flamin' très bon mob when it comes to the rough 'ouse stuff. Comprez?'

'*Oui, oui, Monsieur.*' (An uncomprehending French captain poured Doherty another glass of wine and received a kiss on each cheek; it rather startled him.)

'Oh yes, when we get on the warpath the Allemande promenade très *** tout sweet' (Doherty went through the actions of tearing a man in two). 'Yes we eat the flamin' Germans alive and without salt too.'

The Frenchman strummed some gentle chords on his guitar. Doherty sung lustily 'Mademoiselle from Armentières' (which he thought was the French National Anthem).

After a few days the order came to attack the cemetery and the coppice. The cemetery was deserted but the coppice had hidden infantry from two German battalions preparing to resume their offensive.

'From the coppice burst a murderous hail of rifle and machine-gun fire. Men tumbled everywhere. It was a sharp and grim struggle. The remnant charged fiercely and in a quarter of an hour it was all over. We were flung back before a raking fire.'

Over the next week, the Germans attacked the weakened French and Australian positions by Hangard Wood without success. These

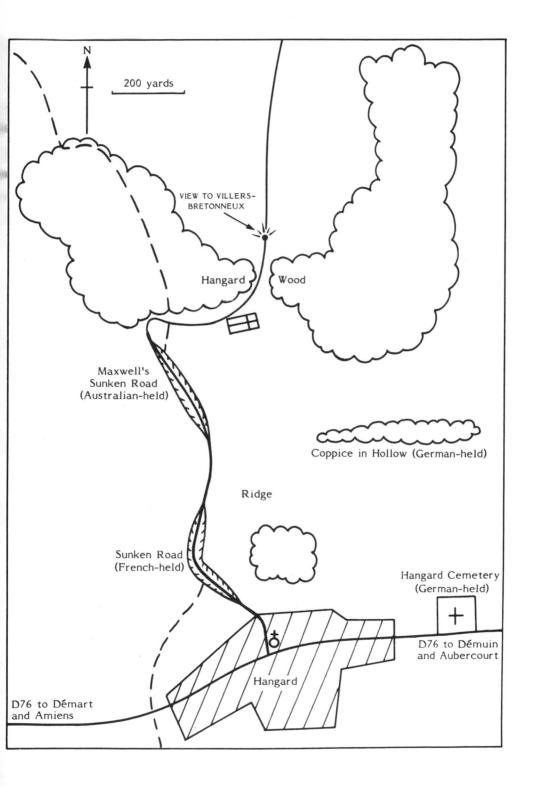

N

200 yards

VIEW TO VILLERS-
BRETONNEUX

Hangard   Wood

Maxwell's
Sunken Road
(Australian-held)

Coppice in Hollow (German-held)

Ridge

Sunken Road
(French-held)

Hangard Cemetery
(German-held)

D76 to Démuin
and Aubercourt

Hangard

D76 to Démart
and Amiens

failures and the rain and mud which set in eventually sapped German morale. The offensive ground to a standstill. The heroic stand by the Australians and French in Hangard Wood had been crucial.

Source
J. Maxwell, *Hell's Bells and Mademoiselles*

German Spring Offensive, 1918

Tank versus Tank for the First Time Ever: 24 April 1918

The Tank Corps had left some of its heavy Mark IV machines in the Bois de Blangy, a wood from which Moroccans and Algerians of the French Army had just been driven by mustard gas and tear gas from German shells. Some lighter Whippet tanks were hidden near Cachy. The advancing German army meanwhile threatened to capture the city of Amiens.

By 24 April 1918, the German Spring Offensive seemed to have its second wind, and Villers-Bretonneux fell to them with many casualties and masses of prisoners. All the high ground dominating Amiens was under immediate threat. The tanks were ordered into battle.

The commander of one of the tanks in the Bois de Blangy was Lieutenant F. Mitchell. His and two other tanks made their way towards the front, as far as Bois d'Aquenne: 'The wood was drenched with gas, and had been evacuated by the infantry. Dead horses, swollen to enormous size, and birds with bulging eyes and stiffened claws lay everywhere. In the tree-tops the half-stifled crows were hoarsely croaking. The gas hung about the bushes and undergrowth, and clung to the tarpaulins . . . the crews had worn their masks during the greater part of the day, and their eyes were sore, their throats dry.'

'My mouthpiece is broken!'

'Run like mad for the open!'

A gasp – and a man crashed away through the undergrowth like a hunted beast.

Another man forgot to fit his nose clamp and collapsed. 'We put him up against a tree, gave him some tablets of ammonia to sniff, and then, as he did not seem to be coming round, we left him, for time was pressing.'

Mitchell's tank blundered forward at 8.30 in the morning of 24 April towards the new hastily dug front line near Cachy, which was still, just, in British hands. The tank survived the continuous German barrage.

Just as Mitchell reached the front-line trench, he saw that the two tanks which had come up with him had been knocked out by shells. Mitchell and his crew were on their own. At the same moment he also sighted German tanks about 300 yards away, followed by waves of infantry. 'We had met our rivals at last! For the first time in history, tank was encountering tank!'

Mitchell ordered a sighting shot for range and direction. Fired. Way out. No reply. Fired again. Closer. No reply. Fired again . . .

'Suddenly a hurricane of hail pattered against our steel walls, filling the interior with myriads of sparks and flying splinters! Something rattled against the steel helmet of the driver sitting next to me and my face was stung with minute fragments of steel. The crew flung themselves flat on the floor. The driver ducked his head and drove straight on.

'Above the roar of our engines sounded the staccato rat-tat-tat-tat of machine-guns, and another furious jet of bullets sprayed out steel side, the splinters clanging against the engine cover. The Jerry tank had treated us to a broadside of armour-piercing bullets!'

Mitchell took advantage of a dip in the ground to get out of sight so he could manoeuvre to get the left gun on to their moving targets, as the right gun had been knocked out. The gunner shifted painfully across the tank, his right eye swollen with gas; he would aim with his left.

The infantry on both sides tensely watched the duel, like spectators at an amphitheatre.

For Mitchell and crew, the drama was immediate. The deafening engines and guns and the stifling cordite and petrol fumes nearly overwhelmed them. But their lives depended on keeping their concentration despite this fierce assault on their senses. Mitchell calmly ordered the tank to stop, a terrific risk, but it would give the gunner a chance for one really accurate shot.

'I took a risk and stopped the tank for a moment. The pause was justified; a well-aimed shot hit the enemy's conning tower, bringing him to a standstill. Another roar and yet another white puff at the front of the tank denoted a second hit. Peering with swollen eyes through his narrow slit, the gunner shouted words of triumph that were drowned by the roar of the engines. Then once more he aimed

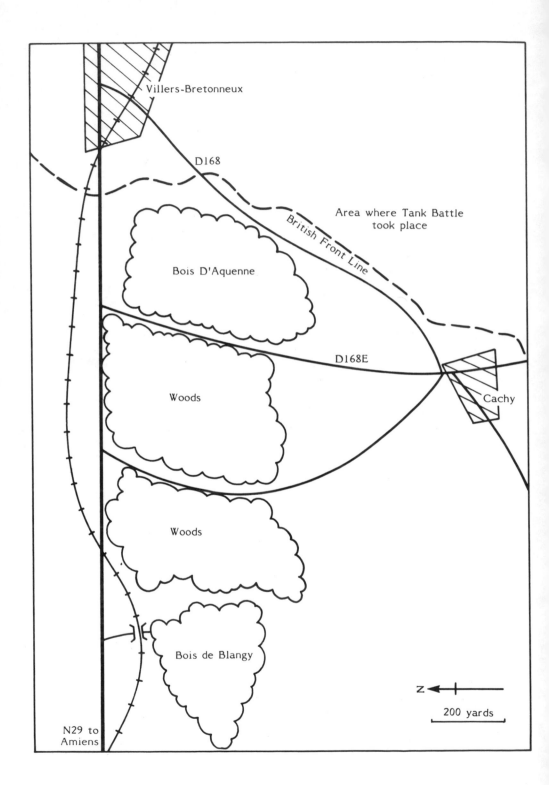

Villers-Bretonneux

D168

Area where Tank Battle
took place

British Front Line

Bois D'Aquenne

D168E

Woods

Cachy

Woods

Bois de Blangy

N29 to
Amiens

Z

200 yards

with great deliberation and hit for the third time. Through a loophole I saw the tank keel over to one side; then a door opened, and out ran the crew. We had knocked the monster out.'

At this point, the Germans made a serious miscalculation. They withdrew their other tanks from the battlefield and relied on a massive artillery barrage to eliminate Mitchell's tank and the smaller, faster Whippet tanks which were now being brought up from Cachy to support him. The artillery did have a serious effect, eventually knocking out four of the seven Whippet tanks and crippling Mitchell's tank by blowing up one of the caterpillar tracks, but it did not stop Mitchell and the Whippets from first having the destructive run of the battlefield.

The German infantry scattered in all directions, 'fleeing terror-stricken from this whirlwind of death. The Whippets flung into the midst of them, ran over them, spitting fire into their retreating ranks'.

A handful of tanks overran some 1,200 German infantry, stopping their attack. Those that came back from the fight dripped with German blood. Four were left burning out in the field. Their crews could not hope to be made prisoners after such slaughter, and only one crew-member from the crippled Whippets escaped to another tank.

Mitchell's tank was hit only a few yards from British trenches so its crew was luckier. They all escaped. Later, they got medals for their brave, unique and highly successful morning's work. Mitchell got the Military Cross.

Source
F. Mitchell, *Tank Warfare*

Rossignol Wood, 1918

A Sniper is Sniped and the British Army Takes Revenge: July and August 1918

The British were starting to treat the Germans like dirt. The great Spring Offensive of 1918 which had hammered the British Third and Fifth Armies had petered out. The German Home Front was collapsing, while the British, supported by a continuing high pitch of jingoism at home and by the Americans, were in a position to pile on the pressure. There was a prevailing mood of optimism which got through to the ordinary soldier in the front line. Optimism could, however, breed over-confidence, and it did so in British ranks on the static front line around Rossignol Wood.

Captain Ernst Junger of the 75th Hanoverian Fusiliers was angry. The crater to the right of his trench was bombarded every now and again with 'black balls as big as pound weights' which whistled over from the British side; they were rifle-grenades. They were more of an annoyance than a serious threat, blowing up, for example, the soup dixies and burning a greatcoat hanging out to dry. Occasionally, though, they did cause serious injuries, and the men had to keep alert all the time. Their nerves were on edge. They flung themselves to the ground if a bird flew over the trench or a distant shot was fired anywhere along the front.

Junger decided that action was needed. An old communication trench, now weathered to a mere furrow, ran between the British and German lines. If only he could get a few yards up the remains of that trench, he might be able to see the post where the rifle-grenades tormenting his men were fired. He might snipe the man who was firing. A previous night expedition had failed and the officer had been killed. Junger decided to go himself, and by day – at noon, 'because the posts are then at their drowsiest and no superior officers are likely to come along'.

It was a hot summer's day. Junger had waited in the coolness of his dug-out. Then he was off and in no time found himself in the remains of the old trench. He wriggled along on his belly through the spirals of barbed wire protecting his own front line and into the open, with little more than flowering grasses for cover.

'It is difficult to describe this feeling of being without cover. In modern war it is always uncomfortable to feel oneself bereft of armour plate or earth work. Every spot of one's body becomes painfully sensitive from a consciousness that one may be hit anywhere at any moment.' He crept forward between long pauses. The ground was parched and cracked, and so hot it almost burned his hand. 'The acrid scent of the earth was mingled with the aromatic essences of a thousand flowers. It is a smell one notices only when, on hot days like these, one lies like an animal with one's nose to the ground.'

At last Junger reached the top of the rise. There was a shell-hole he could creep into – a very lucky find. Just in front grew a mass of thistles with huge purple blooms typical of farmland unploughed for years.

'I could see nothing at first, and had to get out my knife and cut a thistle stem to make a window. I had to do it with caution and noiselessly, for the enemy might just as well be two or two hundred metres away. For the same reason the plant, after the stem had been severed, had to vanish slowly inch by inch. This done, I had a view. I saw little, but all I wanted.'

A trench extended to right and left, well kept but deserted. What he saw straight ahead made Junger start, then smile.

At right angles to the British front line, he could see a continuation in good condition of the trench he had been following. About thirty yards away was a sentry post surrounded by 'hedgehogs' of barbed wire. It was exactly where Junger calculated the rifle-grenades had come from. He was in no doubt that it was the hostile post.

The sentry at the post was totally hidden from view. The tormentor of Junger's men could laugh and smoke in peace and confidence. He could not be sniped.

Junger looked up and down the sniper's trench and saw his chance. Just a yard of two of trench was exposed. He pushed the muzzle of his carbine rifle through the thistles. Everything was ready. He settled down for a long wait.

'There was not a movement. Once a grasshopper began to chirp and then, as though alarmed by the noise he made, was still again. Then a swarm of small sky-blue butterflies appeared and played about the thistle heads. I almost believed I could hear the beat of their wings. I heard the ticking of my watch and the sound of the heat as it broke away a crumb of earth from the edge of the shell-hole.' Junger could see the heat rising in waves. 'It beat on the skull and made the lock and butt-plate of the rifle burning hot, and it glowed on the shell-hole till it was like the hot-plate of a stove. All power of thought began to melt away like wax. But though one's thoughts wandered as they do on the edge of sleep and lost themselves in strange by-paths, yet the will was alert like a wild beast.'

Two hours went by.

'Suddenly a sound rang out – a sound foreign to this noontide scene, an ominous clinking as of a helmet or a bayonet striking against the side of a trench.'

A khaki figure passed in an instant. It was the relief. Now it could only be a matter of seconds till the man he relieved passed across the same spot. Junger sighted his rifle sharply on the short stretch of visible trench.

There were some light-hearted exchanges at the post. Then there was a puff of smoke from a cigarette. The time seemed endless. Then a figure. A shot.

All in an instant.

'I saw him fall, and having seen many fall before this, I knew that he would never get up again. He fell first against the side of the trench and then collapsed into a heap that obeyed the force of life no longer but only the force of gravity.'

Junger ducked and wriggled backwards as fast as he could. He heard a whistle go in the British trench and a machine-gun started up. A rifle-grenade was fired at him so perpendicularly that it exploded before reaching the ground. He was soon well down the German side of the rise, back in the trench and back in his dug-out.

What would the British do now?

The British were sure the Germans were outnumbered and exhausted. Why should they put up with these incidents? But there was no point in charging over the hill to Junger's trench. They knew from bitter experience where that was likely to lead. They waited nearly two weeks. More incidents. The odd shell. The odd bit of sniping. Then the British let rip with the artillery on nearby Rossignol Wood.

Alarm! Red lights over Rossignol Wood!

The massive British artillery attack had already wiped out the German advanced posts and threatened the front line in the wood.

Junger and his men had started to relax after a week in which they had been taken out of the front line and in the support trench. Now they were up once again in the middle of the night and on their way to the front in the wood. 'It is the eeriest feeling one can imagine – a night like this with its vast array of fiery apparitions over the dark earth, and its tumult of noises that now distractedly lose themselves and rage afar, now leap forward . . . The point of danger is utterly indistinguishable. Danger is on every side, blind and furious as an element.'

Up Puisieux Alley, the winding communication trench leading to the front line in the wood. As quickly as possible up the alley because the British were bombing it heavily, knowing that reinforcements had to use it.

They cursed their way through the bombardment, up the exploding and disintegrating trench to the crossroads. Rossignol Wood lay straight ahead. It was barely distinguishable amidst the smoke of explosions. What could be seen of it was broken tree trunks and branches strewn on the ground and bare remnants of trees standing lifeless. There was also a smell of gas which had been used earlier in the bombardment.

As he was deciding what to do next, 'a loud rushing sound plunges with incredible swiftness down upon us from above, as though a flying griffin swooped to rend us. No time is left to prepare for the burst by throwing ourselves flat. Already it has hit the slope of the trench with irresistible fury and hurled us to the ground. Fortunately it

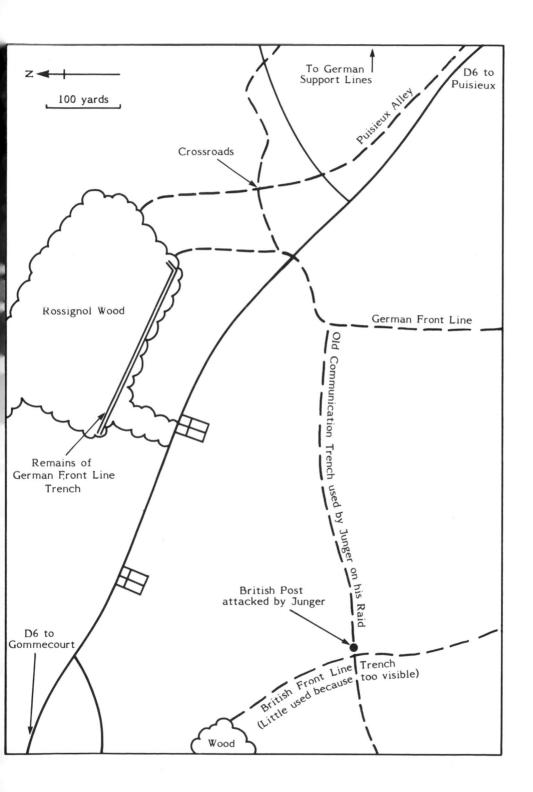

Z ⟵|⟶

100 yards

To German
Support Lines

D6 to
Puisieux

Puisieux Alley

Crossroads

Rossignol Wood

German Front Line

Remains of
German Front Line
Trench

Old Communication Trench used by Junger on his Raid

D6 to
Gommecourt

British Post
attacked by Junger

British Front Line Trench
(Little used because too visible)

Wood

explodes straight upwards.' The shell blew Junger over but he was un-hurt. He picked himself up slowly and brushed himself down, a hair's-breadth escape. Only one man lost, shrapnel in the back of his head.

The attack made Junger's company more warlike. They charged into the wood. No ducking or falling behind. Each man took his chance. In a moment they were in the wood.

The bombardment was less severe in the wood. The British reckoned that most of the Germans were cleared from there, and they were concentrating on the trenches like Puisieux Alley.

Where precisely were the British? Junger and his men held the wood and realized that there was no British infantry attack. In fact, there were no British to be seen anywhere. Only when they accidentally came out of the wood into the open did they encounter an enemy patrol, which even then didn't stop to fight but slunk away as quickly as possible. The whole bombardment was preparation for nothing! It was a softener, a tester, a bit of revenge.

The bombardment ceased as suddenly as it had started a few hours earlier. Junger's company was keyed up to fight. Now it was in a dreary blown-up wood, surrounded by destruction, gas and corpses. It was quiet now – just the occasional distant shell. 'Their spirits, wrought up by the excitements of the past night, are in sharp discord with the frightful dreariness of the surroundings. They remind one of a band of drunken men in the grey light of dawn. It is, however, intelligible. Everyone rejoices to find himself alive, and is incapable of changing himself at a blow from a creature led by wild instinct into a calm, and rational human being. Veiled by all the resources of up-to-date battle, the emotions of last night are the same as they always were and will always be.'

At first light, a machine-gun started up and took two casualties. Junger quickly got his men back together. He was ordered back to the support trench.

'They can't have blazed away half a war-loan for fun.'

'We don't talk of fun here nowadays.'

'Yes, but they must have had some purpose in it.'

'Purpose? Listen to me. There's a fresh regiment every fourteen days over there. As they can get no change out of a big offensive, they are trying to crumble us down like stale cake, and that in the end comes to the same thing. I don't deny they're practical, and if they smoke us out it spares men. Last night it was only a small detach-ment – to see if we had crumbled yet.'

It would not be long now before the German army crumbled.

Source
E. Junger, *Copse 125*

Battle of Amiens, 1918

Priest in Battle: 8 August 1918

The eight-mile advance in a single battle in a single day on 8 August 1918 by the 16th Canadian Battalion was a wonder for the First World War. The Reverend Canon Scott was the chaplain, the Padre, with honorary officer status. He went along with the battalion.

In all the elaborate preparations for the attack, Scott found himself rather superfluous to requirements. A thousand tanks were getting ready. The movement of troops was being conducted with unprecedented secrecy – so much so that Scott found it exceedingly difficult even to find his own battalion.

The jumping-off trenches for the front-line troops were temporary affairs. Even the colonel of the battalion had a hole so small that Scott had to crawl in backwards. It was soon made clear to him that there was no room for a visitor, so he crawled back out again, to spend the rest of the night chatting with the men, who were waiting tensely till 4.20 a.m. when they would have to climb out and charge across the valley to take the German front line in Hangard Wood.

When the barrage started up at 4.20 to support the attack by destroying as much as possible of the opposition, Scott found it a religiously moving experience: 'The long barrage burst in all its fury. The hissing rain of shells through the air on a twenty-mile front made a continuous accompaniment to the savage roar of the thousands of guns along the line. Those guns sent their wild music round the globe, and sounded that note of victory which only ceased when the bells of the churches in all the civilized world rang out their joyful peals at the signing of the Armistice. The noise was earth-shaking . . . I was so carried away by my feelings that I could not help shouting out, "Glory be to God for this barrage!"'

Scott went over with the troops in the front line and earned their respect by doing so. But he soon got behind because now he was no longer superfluous but very much needed, to care for the needs of the wounded and dying. First, he would do what he could physically, giving them water and staunching wounds. Then he would say prayers with them and give them his crucifix to hold. Even unbelievers found comfort in Scott's ministering on the battlefield.

The enemy ran. Their reply was weak. Many of the dead and wounded were German, and Scott refused to discriminate:

'Poor men, I was sorry for them, for I knew it would be long before they could receive medical attention. I made my way to each in turn and gave him a drink from some of the water bottles which I carried round my belt. As they happened to be Roman Catholic, I took off the crucifix which I wore round my neck and gave it to them. They would put up their trembling hands and clasp it lovingly, and kiss it, while I began the Lord's Prayer in German. This happened many times that day. One man who had a hideous wound in his abdomen was most grateful, and when he handed me back the crucifix he took my hand and kissed it. It was strange to think that an hour before, had we met we should have been deadly enemies.'

Not all the Germans Scott encountered were wounded or dead. Some just pretended to be. He came across three Germans lying in a shell-hole and was puzzling how they had been killed – shell-shock, he concluded, for they were not messed about – when one hand moved. Scott remembered one important German word, the one used for 'Surrender!' '*Kamerad?*' '*Kamerad!* Mercy!' They pleaded with Scott for their lives. Scott handed them over to a sergeant, who had offered him, long ago, $25 for any prisoner he took. The idea of the Padre taking prisoners had seemed so ridiculous that till now he had felt his money was safe.

Scott followed the quick advance as well as he could. He hitched a lift on a tank, he walked for miles, he stole a horse (the owner reclaimed it on the way and he had to hand it back – 'The War had not entirely extinguished the light of conscience in my soul'). He rested briefly at a mill on the Gentelles-Caix road and filled up his water-bottles, in the dirty millstream, for it was all there was, and Scott needed the water for relieving the wounded and baptizing the dying.

By nightfall, he was in Caix, eight miles from where he had started, much further by the route he had taken. Caix was the new front line. A weak German force was in Rosières, and some shells were falling in Caix. He visited the church, which had been a casualty clearing station but had been shelled, and he visited the colonel, to whom he handed a letter a young officer had dictated to his wife while he died on the battlefield.

Once again, there was no room in the colonel's quarters, and so Scott slept with the runners, who welcomed him as the Padre who went over the top with their front-line comrades. The runners did not have physical comforts. The accommodation was a brewery cellar well below ground and vaulted in brick: 'The floor was simply earth and very damp. Two candles were burning in a box where a corporal was making out a ration-list for the men. I got two empty sandbags to put on the floor to keep me from getting rheumatism, and lying on them, and using my steel helmet as a pillow, I prepared for sleep.

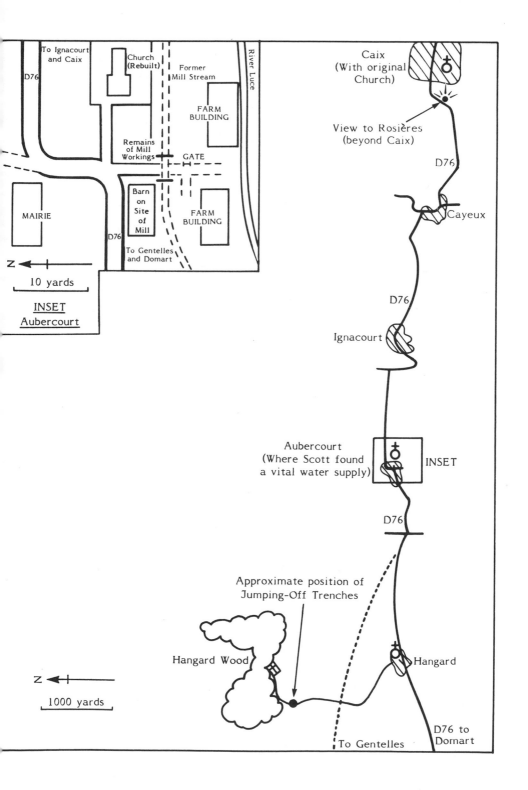

INSET
Aubercourt

10 yards

To Ignacourt and Caix

D76

Church (Rebuilt)

Former Mill Stream

River Luce

FARM BUILDING

Remains of Mill Workings

GATE

MAIRIE

D76

Barn on Site of Mill

FARM BUILDING

To Gentelles and Domart

Caix
(With original Church)

View to Rosières
(beyond Caix)

D76

Cayeux

D76

Ignacourt

Aubercourt
(Where Scott found
a vital water supply)

INSET

D76

Approximate position of
Jumping-Off Trenches

Hangard Wood

Hangard

D76 to Domart

To Gentelles

1000 yards

The runners, except those on duty, did the same. Our feet met in the centre of the room and our bodies branches off like the spokes of a wheel. When anyone turned and put his feet on one side we all had to turn and put our feet in the same direction.' Never mind that it was uncomfortable, the shells outside could never reach them.

The Padre was where he liked to be most, and where he was most appreciated, among the ordinary men of the battalion.

Source
F. Scott, *The Great War as I Saw It*

HINDENBURG LINE

Introduction

German strategy on the Western Front after 1914 was defensive. Attacks were launched only to secure tactical features which would improve the German army's defensive position.

By spring 1917 the Allied offensive on the Somme had left the German front line an awkward shape and also longer than it had been before. There had also been a great loss of manpower. So during winter 1916–17 the Germans constructed a new defence line back from the front line between Arras and Soissons. In perfect safety, the Germans constructed the most formidable set of defences yet seen. Using all the best natural features, it consisted of three lines each made up of a double set of deep trenches, and there were also additional fortifications, such as dug-outs and pillboxes. At the end of February 1917 the Germans began to retire to what they called the Siegfried Line and the British (as a result of an Intelligence error) the Hindenburg Line.

The area they left behind they destroyed. The villages were all razed, the woods cut down, roads and bridges blown up and even the water supplies were poisoned. The Allied response was slow and, when the pursuit did begin, haphazard; the British army of 1917 had very little experience of the open warfare in which the 1914 British Expeditionary Force excelled. Indeed, there was a great deal of confusion which from time to time proved disastrous.

The Hindenburg Line was defence in depth for the Germans. An enemy who attacked would meet an increased line of resistance with each line he crossed – line after line, each one with more strongpoints than the one before. And, even before the first line was reached, there were effective and flexible outposts.

Apart from the battles in the Arras sector which ran up against the northern end of the Hindenburg Line, no serious attempt was made to attack it until the Battle of Cambrai in November 1917.

The Battle of Cambrai was dramatic and innovatory. Its strategic importance was insignificant. It started as a British attempt to try out new tanks in massed formation. The tactic worked. Most generals had not expected it to work and so there were inadequate plans and insufficient troops to take advantage of the tanks' success in crossing the Hindenburg Line and punching a significant hole in the German front. The battle ended after a few weeks with the Germans trying out their own new tactics, infantry infiltration which involved highly concentrated artillery barrages and the use of élite troops on the weaker points of the British lines with the aim of infiltrating deep behind the front line – which would thus be reduced to a number of isolated strongpoints – and causing as much destruction and panic as possible behind the front. These German infantry tactics worked as well as the British tank tactics, and as much land was recaptured as had been lost.

The stalemate of trench warfare returned. The winter was severe. The troops on either side became less and less willing to engage and suffer more.

In 1918 German strategy changed. Russia had collapsed and more than half a million men were transferred to the Western Front. There was to be one last attempt to win before the Americans could really tip the balance.

In the early hours of 21 March 1918 the British troops facing the Hindenburg Line were suddenly subjected to a five-hour hurricane bombardment from 6,500 massed artillery pieces firing a mixture of high explosives, shrapnel and mustard gas. Then came the Storm-troopers using the infantry infiltration tactics carried out at the Battle of Cambrai and penetrating deep beyond the British front line. The front crumbled and the British were in full retreat. There were some rearguard actions but they were unco-ordinated. Only when the Germans had reached the old Somme battlefields were they stopped.

The whole offensive cost the British and Germans over half a million casualties between them.

By September 1918 the British were back at the Hindenburg Line facing an exhausted German army. It was successfully assaulted on 27 September, and the Hindenburg Line stayed in Allied hands until the Armistice.

German Withdrawal, 1917

Rumours of Cavalry: 28 and 29 March 1917

One of the worst experiences of war is to be fired on by your own side. That is what happened on 28 March 1917 on the hill between Capron Copse and the village of Villers Faucon to Lieutenant Charles Edmonds's platoon of the Royal Warwickshire Regiment. There was a rumour that 30,000 fierce German Uhlan cavalry were about to attack. Everyone was on edge. Everyone was ready to fire at anything that moved.

The Germans made a tactical withdrawal in March 1917. Villers Faucon was captured by British cavalry only two days before Edmonds arrived. It was the last village in British hands. The next villages, Ste. Emilie and Epéhy were both in German-held territory.

The Germans intended to retire no further. Their artillery was hitting back, and they had brought across cavalry from the Eastern Front. The accepted view among the British soldiers around Villers Faucon was that there were thousands of Uhlans waiting in the vicinity of Capron Copse to attack, waiting for the order to charge the stretched British lines.

Edmonds was sent out with a few men to search the copse to see if there really were any Uhlans. If it was clear, they would occupy it. If it was occupied and they were fired on, they were to retire. It was not thought necessary to tell other regiments about this minor exercise.

Edmonds and his men reached the copse by nightfall and had the dangerous job of searching it in total darkness. They crept for an hour through brittle undergrowth in the dark wood which, supposedly, concealed the fiercest of the enemy. The only way they could ever have found out if the wood had contained Uhlans would have been through the sudden pain of a lance through the chest.

There were no Uhlans in Capron Copse.

Edmonds and his platoon dug in with great relief amongst some old gun pits on the eastern edge of the copse. They thoroughly enjoyed a meal of cold, congealed stew; it was, after all, a meal they had not expected to survive to taste.

A still and freezing night was followed by a cold, dull dawn. Enemy patrols came close and the platoon hardly dared to breathe. Eventually they summoned up the courage to boil tea over a tiny fire in one of the gun pits. There was no breakfast and the prospect of a dreary long day. They should be safe, Edmonds reckoned, if they stayed quite still.

At about eleven o'clock in the morning, a gunner officer called Williams, obviously unaware of the delicacy of the situation, strode noisily through the copse to the gun pits. The Germans now knew exactly where Edmonds and his platoon were hiding.

Williams then returned to Villers Faucon and called out a battery of guns. It was a splendid sight. A team of horses galloped just west of the copse; the guns fired and scattered some Germans near Epéhy; and they galloped back to Villers Faucon; Edmonds and his platoon were left behind to wait for German revenge.

Every hour, at twenty past the hour, for the rest of the day, the

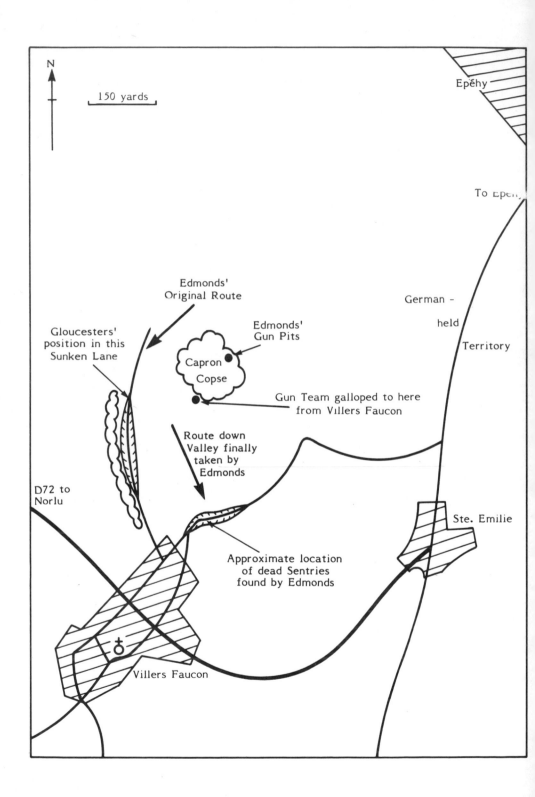

Germans shelled Capron Copse. They missed the gun pits by just fifty yards.

Night fell and Edmonds and his men were relieved by another platoon. By now, icy rain was being swept by a gale from the west. As they left the north of the copse, they found themselves exposed in pitch-black open country.

A few yards and there came a burst of fire a short distance ahead of them. The Gloucestershires were edgy about German patrols!

'Cease fire, confound you! We are the Warwicks,' Edmonds tried to yell above the gale.

'Give 'em another burst with a Lewis gun, and the rest of you at the same time five rounds rapid!'

The bullets cracked and whistled around them. Edmonds tried to go in close but was forced down into the mud by a solid burst of fire. They tried shouting all together but still failed to make themselves heard above the rain and wind. They belly-crawled to a nearby hollow and then crawled and slid back to the northern edge of Capron Copse.

By incredible luck the gale had made accurate firing by night difficult, and the only injury was one man wounded in the hand. However, Edmonds had risked the lives of his men, and he was stuck with them high on a hill in a freezing wet gale and without food for twenty-four hours, and he had no idea of the way back.

He decided to look for the way to Villers Faucon by himself and slipped off alone, telling his men to stay put by the side of the copse. He managed to steer clear of the Gloucestershires and at last found the winding sunken lane from British-held Villers Faucon to German-held St. Emilie. Which way to go? He chose. At last he came to some sleeping sentries. He crept near with his revolver drawn and cocked. With a surge of joy, he realized the sentries were British.

Edmonds rushed up to one and tapped him on the shoulder, turned him over impatiently and saw that half his face had been blown away by a shell. The other 'sentry' was the corpse of a friend.

Still, the way back had been found.

Edmonds returned to his men, who were chafing at their further delay. After a long, dreary and fearful march, they found Villers Faucon again. There they found their camp, where, still in the gale and still with no food, they bivouacked without blankets.

Source
C. Edmonds (C. E. Carrington), *A Martial Medley*

Riqueval, 1917

Germans against Indians: 12–19 June 1917

In front of the Siegfried Line was the dangerous outpost zone. It was at one of these outposts that the 73rd Hanoverian Fusiliers learned to respect the 1st Haryana Lancers. Lieutenant Ernst Junger, inspired by Nietzsche, said of his Indian enemy, 'I hate them but do not despise them; I am proud of my enemy, essential for a fighting man.'

Junger and his fellow officer, Oskar Kuis, held the British artillery in scorn. They lay sunbathing by the outpost hut.

'That you, Ernst.'

'Hm.'

'They're shooting, aren't they?'

'Well, let's lie where we are a little longer. I think those were the last ones.'

After a quarter of an hour, 'That you, Oskar?'

'Yes?'

'They're not going to stop today. I think that was a shrapnel bullet that came through the wall just now. We'd better get up. That artillery observer fellow cleared out long ago.'

On 12 June Junger had to occupy the outpost with twenty men. If there had been no war, the situation would have been idyllic. The outpost was a hut in a flower-covered meadow half way up a steep bank looking across to two hills opposite. The British lines were in the hills.

The night was silent until about midnight. Then Junger thought he heard a rustling sound.

'Sir, there are seventy Englishmen advancing to the edge of the wood.'

A body of men could be seen gliding across the meadow behind the outpost. Junger and his section were disastrously outnumbered. What could they do next? Junger decided to form a defensive line across the meadow from the outpost to the edge of the wood. But as soon as they left the outpost, the British opened fire and advanced on them.

The Germans fled to the edge of the wood, where they crouched elbow to elbow in a ditch.

Silence. What would the British do next?

Minutes passed. Some men were coming across the meadow.

'Password.'

No reply. Nearer.

'Who goes there?'

Nearer.

'Fire!'

For a minute the rifles rattled. Sparks showered up whenever the storm of bullets encountered weapons or steel helmets.

'Look out on the left!'

Another party of British attacked along the edge of the wood from the left, but they were massacred in a minute. The Germans were well entrenched.

By the morning Junger had enough confidence to order that the hut should be retaken.

Prisoners were taken. Indians!

'Quelle nation?'

'Pauvre Rajput! Anglais pas bon!'

Junger sat down to a breakfast of poached eggs. This was just bravado. Any chance of enjoyment was ruined by the screams of wounded Indian Haryana Lancers and, as the sun rose, the spreading smell of corruption. This got worse. Junger led a patrol later in the day through the wood. 'As I was working my way alone through a thicket I heard a peculiar hissing and murmuring sound. I went nearer and came upon two corpses in which the heat had awakened a ghastly life.'

The Indians were obviously not deterred by the drubbing they had received on the 12th. On the 17th they attacked again, and this time they were successful. Junger tried to organize a withdrawal but again the Germans were heavily outnumbered and this time there was a rout.

The Indians took only one prisoner. They tortured him by flogging his face with a wire whip.

The Indians did not attempt to occupy the outpost for long.

Junger and his men returned and tried to regain the initiative by climbing up the hill to the Indian lines by night and attacking a stronghold on a sunken road which cut through the hill.

'Suddenly came the sharp rattle of a rifle-bolt. We sank into the ground. Every old hand knows the series of feelings that occupy the next seconds. For the moment one has lost the initiative and must wait and see what the enemy does next.

'A shot broke the oppressive stillness. I lay behind a broom-bush and waited. On my right someone threw bombs into the sunken road.'

At once all the Indian guns started to fire. It was obvious they were only a few yards away. Junger ordered flight. 'We all sprang up and

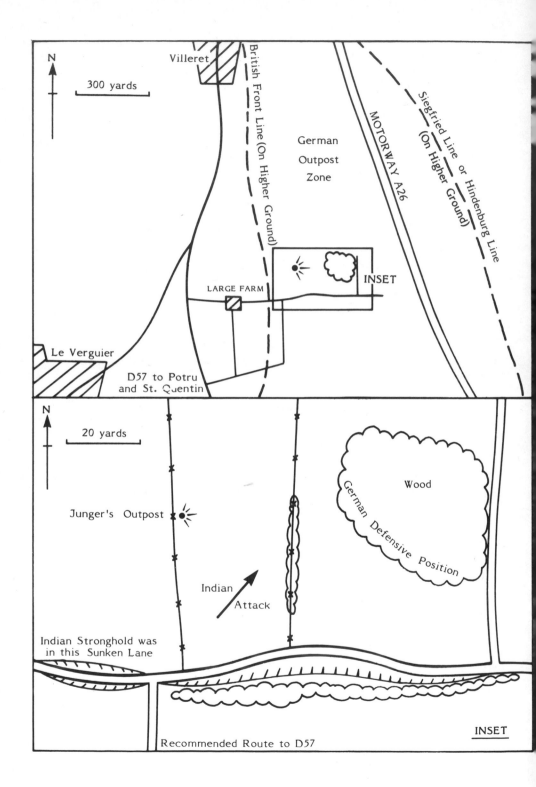

sprinted for all we were worth, while rifle-fire was opened on us from our left as well. I gave up all hope of a safe return when I heard this unholy clatter. Unconsciously, I was in constant expectation of being hit. Death was out hunting.

'Somewhere near us a detachment advanced to the attack with a shrill Hurrah. Little Schultz confessed to me afterwards that he imagined a lean Indian behind him wielding a knife and already clutching him tight by the neck.

'I tumbled once and brought down the NCO, Teilengerdes, over on top of me. I lost my steel helmet, revolver, and bombs. Anything to get on! At last we reached the protecting bank and tore down it.'

Only one serious injury and a machine-gun lost.

A half-hearted attempt to retrieve the machine-gun failed. Junger's men were now unreliable. Their 'covering fire' went between Junger's legs – 'a very unpleasant experience!'

Junger and his men left on 20 June. The outpost fell to the Indians on the 21st.

Source
E. Junger, *The Storm of Steel*

Battle of Cambrai, 1917

Unstoppable Tanks Cross the Hindenburg Line: 20 November 1917

Tanks.

Forward. Tearing through shattered remains of a corner of France. Through woods and copses, farmyards, fields, always driving on. Thundering along the main road, sparks flying. A long time since this stretch of countryside was crossed. No more trenches! No more mud! Forwards, across the Hindenburg Line like a country ditch. Forward, until sheer exhaustion ends a glorious day.

The special train carrying some of the 400 tanks on their way south stopped at the Somme battlefield. No corpses, just wooden crosses and the silence of death.

Many hours later the tanks detrained in Havrincourt Wood, where they were loaded up silently with petrol, ammunition and stores. The scene was quite tranquil. The occasional swish of a long-distance shell far overhead could not disturb the peaceful scene, woods, fields and trees disguising unhurried preparations for the great tank attack.

The British artillery opened up at 6.20 in the morning of 20 November. At 6.30 the tanks started rolling. The infantry followed behind.

As the tanks left Havrincourt Wood, German machine-guns started. They had no effect. They had no idea what to aim at. The tanks kept on coming, and eventually the machine-guns were withdrawn. Knife-edged entanglements defending the British lines were broken in seconds. Everything that was in the path of the tanks, dead or living, was crushed into the earth.

Driver Bacon's tank moved, slowly and steadily, heavily and noisily, past Yorkshire Bank and Wigan Copse and up to the famous 'impregnable' Hindenburg Line.

The first part of the Hindenburg Line to fall was the barbed wire. Deep and vicious, the failure to get through the German barbed wire had been the end of many British attacks in the war. This time, it was flattened in a few minutes by a whole row of tanks together on full throttle.

Once the other side of the wire, the tanks had to take the whole firepower of the Hindenburg Line's machine-gunners and riflemen, including those who had withdrawn earlier from the front line. The resistance was furious. Bullets rained on the tanks 'like 50 hailstorms on one corrugated iron shed'. Defending riflemen climbed on top of the tanks to engage in hand-to-hand fighting or be shot by the crew.

To cross the colossal main trench of the Hindenburg Line, each tank had on its roof bundles of sticks bound together to form a bridge. The tanks were soon across. The enemy had fled or surrendered.

Bacon found that his tank's engine was getting very hot. It was time for him and the crew to rest.

Lunch was a shared bottle of whisky.

Before long, the Germans brought up reserves. 'Whilst we had been resting, the shrapnel fire had become more intense and there were several nasty punctures in our exhaust pipe on top of the bus. When we moved forward again a fusillade of bullets rattled on the front armour-plating, telling of a gun crew waiting for a duel. I quickly closed the window and drove by means of a pinhole aperture. The firing got hotter and there was obviously more than one gun concentrated on us. No matter how I zigzagged the bus, they stuck to it, and very soon white-hot sparks were flying into my face as I peered out.' The tank's periscope was blown away. A sponson gunner only slightly exposed had got a bullet-rip from his right palm

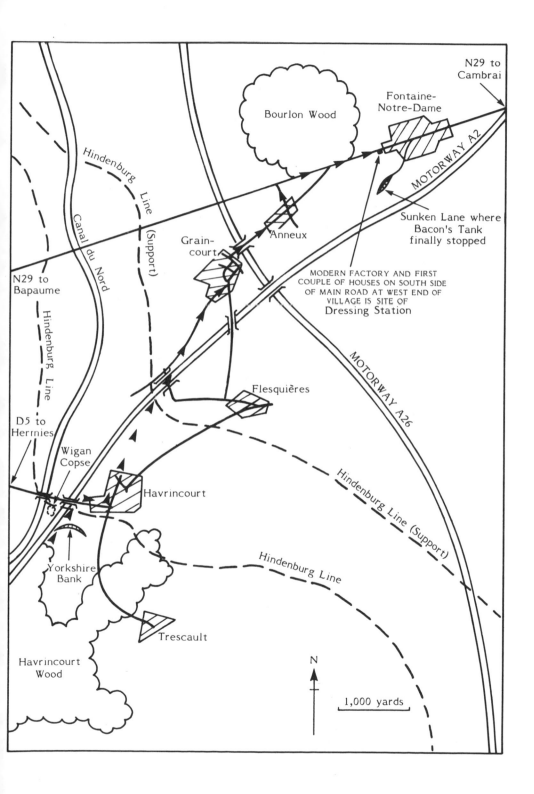

N29 to
Cambrai

Fontaine-
Notre-Dame

Bourlon Wood

MOTORWAY A2

Sunken Lane where
Bacon's Tank
finally stopped

Hindenburg Line (Support)

Canal du Nord

Anneux

Grain-
court

MODERN FACTORY AND FIRST
COUPLE OF HOUSES ON SOUTH SIDE
OF MAIN ROAD AT WEST END OF
VILLAGE IS SITE OF
Dressing Station

N29 to
Bapaume

MOTORWAY A26

Hindenburg Line

Flesquières

D5 to
Hermies

Wigan
Copse

Hindenburg Line (Support)

Havrincourt

Hindenburg Line

Yorkshire
Bank

Havrincourt
Wood

Trescault

N

1,000 yards

to his elbow. Another gunner reached up to shut the roof-hatch, and his trigger finger was blown away. Even so, although the Germans stood up to 400 thirty-ton tanks defiantly, they could inflict only peripheral damage. In the end, they had to run away or surrender.

On through the remains of the villages of Graincourt and Anneux to the Bapaume-Cambrai road. Occasionally they 'mopped up' pockets of resistance, but there was little more that could be achieved that day. Dusk was falling, and Bacon finally rested his tank for the night in the shadow of a brick factory, now being used as a field dressing station.

Bacon and all the tank crew were exhilarated but weary. They soon found a luxurious German dug-out (checked carefully for booby-traps). Inside, they sat on comfortable mattresses on the officers' bunk-beds and ate a tasty meal of roasted German pork with 'brownish' bread and distilled water. They finished up with mugs of German coffee and went gratefully to sleep.

It was a good way to end the Tank Corps' most glorious day. The tanks which had been abused at Ypres had shown their mettle at Cambrai.

Source
J. Hammerton, ed., *I Was There!*

Battle of Cambrai, 1917

Following Tanks: 20 November 1917

Four hundred tanks were assembled into a great battering-ram to break down German defences around Cambrai. In anticipation of the attack the Germans had withdrawn most of their men and guns from the area, so in terms of enemy dead and wounded any victory at Cambrai was bound to be rather hollow. But in terms of territory it was spectacular. The first day's four-mile advance seemed to the British a turning-point. The tanks, 'these new-fangled Wellsian monsters', Corporal George Coppard of the Machine Gun Corps called them, were an overwhelmingly effective weapon. Morale soared all along the front – and on the Home Front, where church bells rang for the first time in the war.

Corporal Coppard, along with four thousand other men, was ordered out to an open field just after midnight on 20 November 1917. After many months of hiding in dug-outs and trenches, they felt extremely vulnerable. At every stray bullet they flung themselves to the ground. Along with thousands more men on a front stretching from Gonnelieu north for eight miles, they were waiting for the beginning of the Battle of Cambrai.

The men had to wait in the bitter cold in silence and without smoking for over six hours. So serious was the risk of being observed that officers were ordered to shoot dead anyone caught smoking, and there were many who found six-and-a-half hours without a Woodbine very hard indeed. Some porridge and tea relieved the tense misery of that night in the open. There was also some relief for many of the men, like Coppard, who felt that the Germans would now at last get their comeuppance from the tank: 'I felt they were really going to settle, on behalf of all of us, the countless miseries and privations that we poor blighters had suffered at Jerry's hands. This was to be the reckoning, and the entire Third Army was at the ready, summoned to arms for the great assault.'

The tanks were at the front, ready to take the brunt of the attack for once instead of the infantry. Behind them the infantry were ready to advance. Behind the infantry were an incredible 2,000 pieces of artillery.

Just before Zero Hour the tanks started to warm up their engines. At 6.30 a.m. precisely, the artillery lit the black November morning sky with fierce flashes of light, and over an eight-mile front shells roared, whined and exploded away to the east. The noise was deafening as innumerable shells exploded with the utmost violence over enemy positions for as far as the eye could see.

The tanks rumbled in their hundreds over the top of the slight slope which marked the German front line. There was no effective resistance to them. Soon the artillery stopped firing. The tanks were now in close contact with the enemy, and it was time for the infantry advance. It was one of the easiest infantry advances of the war. In four miles, Coppard was stopped only once, at a crossroads between his path and a sunken road. A German machine-gun had been hidden by the road embankments from the first line of tanks and was taking its toll of British infantry. Seeing what was happening, Coppard managed to attract a second-line tank crew's attention. The tank lumbered to the sunken road and turned up it. The crew spotted the machine-gun post, and the machine-gunners with the terror of death realized the tank was coming for them. They fired in panic. The bullets bounced off the steel of the tank. The tank's light cannon ponderously and unstoppably turned on the machine-gunners and killed them. Then the tank crushed them.

The way was clear now.

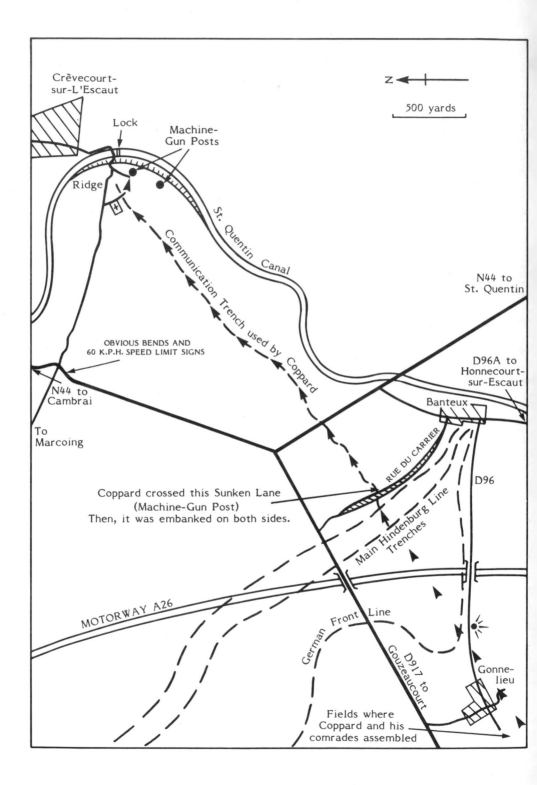

Crèvecourt-
sur-L'Escaut

Lock

Machine-
Gun Posts

Ridge

St. Quentin Canal

Communication Trench used by Coppard

Z ←

500 yards

N44 to
St. Quentin

OBVIOUS BENDS AND
60 K.P.H. SPEED LIMIT SIGNS

N44 to
Cambrai

To
Marcoing

Banteux

D96A to
Honnecourt-
sur-Escaut

RUE DU CARRIER

Coppard crossed this Sunken Lane
(Machine-Gun Post)
Then, it was embanked on both sides.

Main Hindenburg Line Trenches

D96

MOTORWAY A26

German Front Line

D917 to Gouzeaucourt

Gonne-
lieu

Fields where
Coppard and his
comrades assembled

Coppard was in charge of twelve men carrying two machine-guns. They were not needed, as they marched forward up the right flank of the Gonnelieu section of the attack, up a former communication trench and over no man's land to the small rise where the St. Quentin canal turns westward.

At first, Coppard thought the tanks had won a massive victory, wiping out all the Germans. Then it dawned on him that there were only a few dead Germans and no destroyed artillery pieces. Of course, it would have been impossible for 400 tanks and an army of artillery and infantry to be gathered without the Germans knowing anything of what was happening. The great tank battle of Cambrai had been an important and exhilarating advance, leaving the British army only just short of Cambrai itself, but it was not a hard-won victory on the day.

Coppard set up his guns overlooking the bend in the St. Quentin Canal. The other side of the canal was German-held territory, but little was going on. Nearly everyone stayed where they were the following day, 21 November.

'It was a clear day, and several Jerries were popping about close to the canal, but there were no targets big enough for using the guns. I made a nuisance of myself with a Mauser rifle tormenting stray Jerries. One dropped and didn't get up. The day passed with nothing of importance happening . . .'

There was still mopping up to be done behind the new British front line. When a tank was in the area, it could be relied on to finish off some previously hidden machine-gun emplacement, but if not, Coppard was in for a nasty shock. He took a bullet through his femoral artery. Somehow the machine-gun failed to finish him off.

Some German prisoners carried him on a duckboard back to the dressing station and he survived. Victory at Cambrai was certainly not the reckoning that Coppard had expected when the battle began.

Source
G. Coppard, *With a Machine-gun to Cambrai*

Battle of Cambrai, 1917

A 'Good Show' Wasted: 29 November to 3 December 1917

More troops were needed after the brilliant start of the Battle of Cambrai: troops to clear the area of German outposts and stragglers, troops to consolidate the gains, troops to make more gains. They brought in new men by rail (for which the British paid the French railway-owners handsomely for every man carried) and by old London buses. Among those arriving by bus was Frank Dunham, medic and stretcher-bearer with the 7th Londons.

Kangaroo Trench was Frank Dunham's destination. He was rather surprised to see the village of Graincourt practically intact to his right since villages anywhere near the front were usually smashed to smithereens – this was a new front indeed. He was rather pleased to be in a support trench and not in the immediate firing line. Supplies were good, and he was in the middle of a hearty breakfast at eight o'clock on the morning of 30 November when the Germans opened up. Dunham's mates rushed to join him in the shelter of a dug-out but there was very little room and most of them had to stay outside in the trench and take their chance.

Soon the call went out for stretcher-bearers. Private Ward was groaning. A piece of shrapnel was in his heart and he died before Dunham could do anything.

The Germans advanced. Everyone had to grab a rifle and defend Kangaroo Trench, even the elderly labourers who had been improving the trench and who had never used a rifle before. The Germans advanced down the slope towards them. The front line must have been hell as the Germans got near, but they kept the enemy at bay. Dunham's support line meanwhile fired at the Germans on the slope and were strafed in turn by a machine-gun in a German aeroplane flying over them. Soon they also received heavy German artillery fire directed to them by signals from the aeroplane.

In occasional quieter spells, Dunham tried to tend some of the wounded. There was usually little he could do. Seriously wounded men could sometimes be dragged into the dug-outs, where they would have to wait in agony until they could be evacuated after the battle.

Eventually the Germans withdrew over the hill in disorder, but the shelling carried on almost as heavily as before. Dunham and another stretcher-bearer were instructed to take a wounded man a mile back to an ambulance station: 'This proved a very tiring and nerve-racking journey. The trench was full of troops moving up to the line as reinforcements, consequently we had to get out of the trench and get along in the open. Fritz was shelling all along the area of this trench, and several times we had to drop the stretcher and lie flat to escape pieces of flying shells.' Dunham reckoned that the wounded man (he had a bullet in his stomach) would always remember that journey, 'for he did get some bumps, and was almost shot off the stretcher on occasions, but he stuck it very well and never once complained'.

When they got back to Kangaroo Trench, it was empty except for the labourers. No one there knew where the 7th Londons had gone.

For two days and nights, Dunham and a small group of stretcher-bearers wandered around a maze of dangerous narrow trenches asking in vain for the 7th Londons. They were lost and scared. They were freezing cold. They had no rations: 'Our breakfast consisted of scraps found in the bottom of the trench, and a cooked potato which I found jammed into the mud proved a treasure indeed.' Nor did they have permission to be away and Dunham was frightened he might lose his leave as a punishment.

At last they came upon the remains of a sugar factory with shell-proof cellars. There they found the brigade signallers, who could tell them where to find their mates.

They were told to head twenty minutes uphill to a certain gun pit to find their HQ. They set off, forgetting that this was newly gained ground and there were still pockets of German resistance.

'After going some distance, we were just about topping the ridge, when we noticed a derelict tank well ahead, and almost immediately a bullet whistled close by us. We at once dropped flat to the ground, but bullets still continued to drop around us, and it was obvious that a Fritz was sniping at us from the tank. Close by, we noticed the bodies of four dead Britishers, who had apparently been killed by this sniper earlier in the day.'

They had no wish to share their fate and started to crawl back down the slope. 'The crawling method seemed a slow process of getting out of range of this sniper, but none of us dared get up to run for fear of offering him a better target. However, a short way down the slope, when we were lost to view from the tank, we made for the shelter of the nearest bunker.' They waited till nightfall before trying again. This time they went very cautiously and got through.

Back with their company, they got a telling-off but nothing worse. Gratefully they settled to a good meal.

At 8.15 p.m. they took part in an attack on German trenches. The

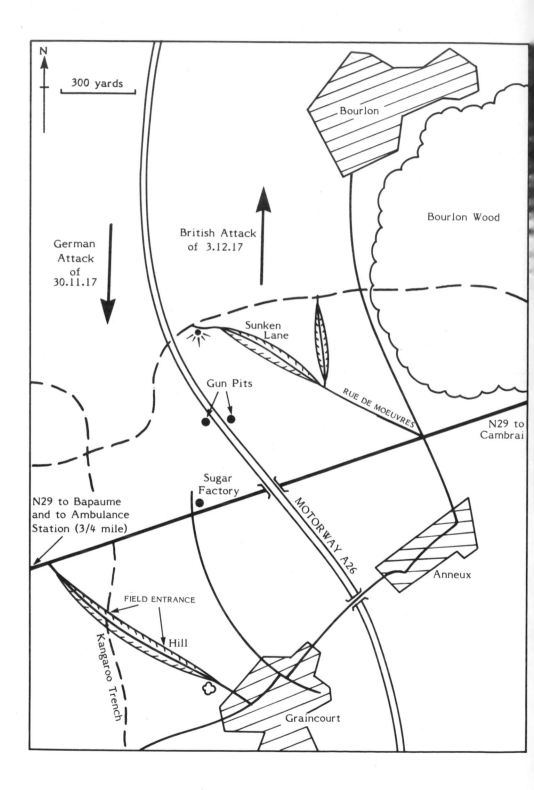

N

300 yards

Bourlon

Bourlon Wood

German
Attack
of
30.11.17

British Attack
of 3.12.17

Sunken
Lane

Gun Pits

RUE DE MOEUVRES

N29 to
Cambrai

Sugar
Factory

N29 to Bapaume
and to Ambulance
Station (3/4 mile)

MOTORWAY A26

Anneux

FIELD ENTRANCE

Hill

Kangaroo Trench

Graincourt

casualties were terrible. Dunham was amazed at his own escape carrying stretchers up and down the banks of a sunken lane on the way back across the battlefield. Bullets whistled all around him, and many of his friends died that night.

Dunham wondered if they died in vain. The Londons were told two days later to evacuate the trenches they had just won, for there were not enough British troops in the Cambrai area to hold the new lines. 'Our attack was described as a "good show" and we learned it had been made with the idea of proving to Fritz that we still had plenty of sting left,' Dunham faithfully recorded in his diary.

Counter-attack at the Battle of Cambrai, *1917*

The German Art of Trench Warfare: 1 December 1917

The storm-troop technique for trench warfare started with a grenade attack, using grenades passed down to the front from hand to hand. A light machine-gun was quickly mounted where there was a good field of fire. Snipers took up positions in the traverses, and platoon commanders kept an eye over the top of the trench to get some warning if possible of any counter-attack. Lieutenant Ernst Junger of the 73rd Hanoverian Fusiliers and his platoon of eighty men had perfected the storm-troop technique. He was a formidable opponent in the Siegfried Line trenches.

The enthusiasm which Ernst Junger felt about going back into battle was tempered with some concern about his men. They were exhausted after dreary years in Flanders. They were getting careless – one dropped a grenade which seriously injured himself and a friend while they were getting on a lorry. Some were getting desperate – one of his men feigned madness. Still, orders were orders and now he was leading his company up to the front line after the Battle of Cambrai where the British had used tanks to puncture a hole in the German defences. The bulge was to be excised; the line was to be straightened again.

Junger's first sight of the Cambrai battlefield was encouraging: a British observation balloon was tumbling to the earth in flames, and the occupant was parachuting to certain capture. The platoon had good luck when, to get to the front line, they had to run up a section of the bed of the dry Canal du Nord, which was almost continuously shelled by the British; many German lives had been lost in those few hundred yards but Junger's platoon received only one big shell – it exploded well in front of them and helped them to see where they were going. It was now the night of 30 November 1917.

It was a freezing cold night but they still got a few hours' sleep out in the open before going to battalion headquarters for their orders.

The chaotic atmosphere of headquarters was thick with cigar smoke. To the left and right, from high on triple-bunks and down the dark steps below, orders were barked and suggestions shouted. It was some hours before Junger got his orders, and then they were wrong and had to be changed. 'Fighting experience', Junger remarked bitterly 'can often, in cases like this, spare unnecessary bloodshed.'

Junger's platoon was detached from the rest of its regiment and, as they feared, they were not destined to be 'pampered' under another command. They were to start their part of the counter-attack at Cambrai from a dangerous sunken road leading out of a communication trench called Dragon Alley; no one could remember where Dragon Alley was, and there were no maps to spare. The company spent some hours crawling up and down muddy and dangerous trenches before coming across a scarcely legible sign to show them they had arrived. A little way up the alley they heard voices, English voices!

'I was very much astonished to find the enemy so close and, indeed, almost in our own lines, without having come upon any measures of defence; and I at once posted a section to block the trench.'

The platoon was certainly not being pampered. Junger sent most of the men back a few hundred yards until it was time for an attack at 7 a.m. If they stayed where they were, there was a pretty good chance of accidentally giving their position away and being shelled.

7 a.m. came and went. The attack started. Junger's platoon made its way right up Dragon Alley to the sunken road. Where the British had been before, there was nothing. They advanced up the road until it was no longer sunken and emerged in the open. The company then slipped back quietly into a Siegfried Line trench leading off to the right.

They were now far out in unknown territory and never knew what to expect at the next corner. They explored the trench which they had just entered, using the full drill of the storm-troop technique. They need hardly have worried. All the occupants were British dead.

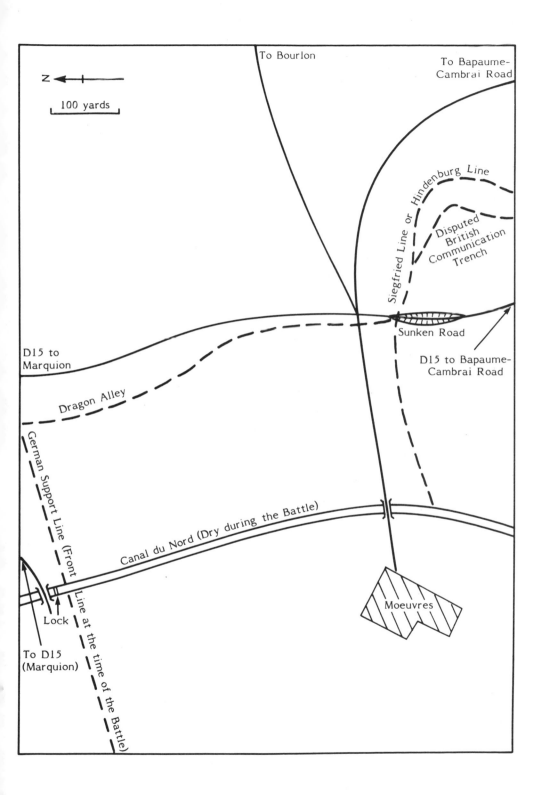

Z ← 100 yards

To Bourlon

To Bapaume-
Cambrai Road

Siegfried Line or Hindenburg Line

Disputed
British
Communication
Trench

Sunken Road

D15 to
Marquion

Dragon Alley

D15 to Bapaume-
Cambrai Road

German Support Line (Front Line at the time of the Battle)

Canal du Nord (Dry during the Battle)

Lock

To D15
(Marquion)

Moeuvres

Then they turned a corner and the real fight started. The storm-troop technique was used in earnest. It was very effective.

'We heard agitated voices from the other side, and before we understood what was happening the first Englishmen came towards us with their hands up. One after another turned the corner of the traverse and unbuckled his belt, while our rifles and revolvers were threateningly levelled. They were all young, well-set-up fellows in new uniforms. I let them pass with the command "hands down" and detailed a squad to take them to the rear. Most of them showed by their confiding smiles that they trusted in us as human beings. Others held out cigarettes and chocolates in order to conciliate us. My enthusiasm and delight when I saw what a bag we had made were unbounded. The procession had no end.'

Two hundred surrendered to Junger's platoon of eighty.

Along with the prisoners came booty. Like an old soldier of fortune, Junger allowed an interval for plunder. Machine-guns, mortars, grenades, water-bottles, mackintosh capes, groundsheets, bully-beef, jam, coffee, cocoa, tobacco, rum, tools, revolvers, pistols, gloves. Junger himself enjoyed a pipe of 'Navy Cut' and a full English breakfast.

Fire from the pillbox which blew a soldier's brains out of his head spoiled the end of Junger's breakfast. Another shot pierced the crown of a soldier's helmet and tore a long groove in his skull. Junger proudly recorded, 'His brain could be seen throbbing with each beat of his heart, and yet he was able to make his way back alone.'

The British decided to evacuate by way of their own communications trench which ran parallel with the trench Junger's company had just taken. They were ambushed. Junger described it: 'Now began an indescribable carnage. Grenades flew through the air like snowballs till the whole scene was veiled in white smoke. Two men handed me grenades ready to throw without a moment's pause. Grenades flashed and exploded among the mob of English, throwing them aloft in fragments with their helmets. Cries of rage and terror were mingled. With the fire in our eyes we sprang with a shout over the top.' They crossed over and took the communication trench.

The German victory cost Junger's platoon forty casualties out of eighty men. They had inflicted at least 150 casualties on the British. The 'bloodthirsty nerves of these princes of the trenches, brave to madness', were rewarded with a great many promotions and decorations, including at least one Iron Cross First Class.

Source
E. Junger, *The Storm of Steel*

La Vacquerie, 1918

Fraternizing with the Enemy: January 1918

The entrance to Newport Trench was deceptive: '. . . only a gesture of goodwill to all who entered, for the floor upon which we trod was not the true floor of the trench which bore the name of Newport. We slid down a gentle slope and felt the chill icy water half way to our knees, and the gluey grip of mud around our ankles. Here was the general level of the trench, and for the remainder of its length it varied from ankle to thigh deep in its composition of mud and water'.

It took Able Seaman W. A. Downe and his friends in the Anson Battalion of the Royal Marines about an hour to get along Newport Trench to their slimy quarters in the mud. Their job was to be carrying rations up to the front line and later, if they lived that long, relieving the front line. The only consolation was knowing that things were bound to be just as bad for the enemy.

It poured. The trenches all around flooded. An ancient pump, brought in to help, clogged, and the walls of the trenches started to cave in.

The journey up Cornwall Avenue, a communication trench which was now a river, to the front line carrying heavy rations was a nightmare. If Downe and the others went up the trench, they risked being sucked into the mud and drowned. A particular terror was the frequency of hidden entrances to dug-outs; the man in front of Downe slipped into one of these, and it took four men an hour to pull him out – he left his boots in the mud and carried on the journey in a piteous condition with his feet and legs encased in sandbags roughly tied with string.

At last the sergeant-major who was leading the expedition decided they would have to chance German machine-guns and walk in the open. They clambered out of the trench half expecting that the first man to stand up would at once be mown down. Not so. In fact, Downe could make out, dimly in the twilight, grey figures bent double under their own loads beyond the enemy front line. No shots were fired by either side, but by now, after several hours of carrying rations through mud, Downe was in such an exhausted state that he hardly noticed anything as he clambered across disused trenches (into one of which the sergeant-major fell but managed to save both himself and the rum ration he was carrying) to the front line.

Half an hour later they were on their way back, still keeping out of the trenches, once again fearing German machine-guns which surely must now have been expecting them. They could also see the enemy ration party trudging back from its own front line – unbelievably, one of the enemy party waved.

Downe and the ration party got back hours later, unharmed, to their shelter, which was flooded and exposed to the January wind. They huddled together for warmth and tried to get some sleep, but the roof started to cave in and they had to escape quickly into the rain and flood outside. In the end, they had hardly any rest before setting off again up to the front line, this time to stay there. They were now the relief and not the ration party.

The man who lost his boots earlier dropped out on the way to the front. He wanted to carry on but couldn't. His feet were swollen to three times their normal size, great shapeless pink lumps. Almost certainly both feet would be amputated. The relief party carried on, minus one.

Once again no firing. Why? It was one thing not to shoot a ration party and quite another not to fire at the relieving party. After all, the aims of the relieving party were hardly humanitarian!

Downe took up his post with another Able Seaman called Williams at a high sandbagged barricade in an old communication trench which now led from the British front line into German-held territory.

They spent the night trying to stay alert, creeping round the barricade. At dawn they slipped behind the barricade with a feeling of despair at the hopeless day before them. There was no shelter. There was no possibility of carving out some sort of seat in the side of a trench which was made of soft mud and was starting to cave in. There was no chance even of standing still without being sucked through twelve inches of water into the mud; they had to shift their weight from foot to foot constantly, and they knew all about the risk of trench feet – their luckless friend who lost his boots was at that moment probably losing his feet.

Suddenly Downe's companion, Williams, seemed to be taking leave of his senses: 'He raised himself above the top of the barricade and waved towards the German line. Standing up beside him I peered ahead, and saw a German with his head crowned like a hood in his coal-scuttle helmet, standing partially exposed in the trench opposite. The figure rocked as he stood on alternate feet, and staring straight at us, waved his arm with a friendly gesture. The nearness of the man was unexpected, I could distinctly see his features . . .'

Downe looked to his right where the rest of his company were and saw two Germans walking slowly and unarmed towards the barrier of wire between the opposing front lines. They stopped at the wire,

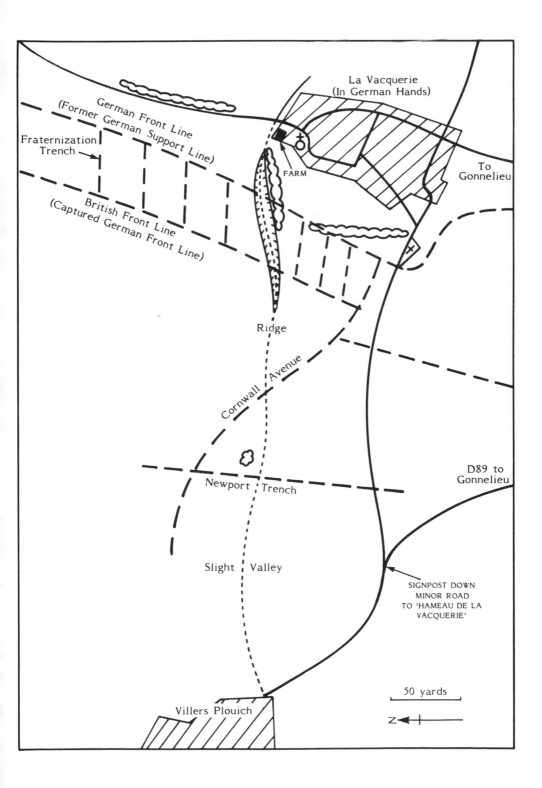

La Vacquerie
(In German Hands)

German Front Line
(Former German Support Line)

Fraternization
Trench

British Front Line
(Captured German Front Line)

FARM

To
Gonnelieu

Ridge

Cornwall Avenue

Newport Trench

D89 to
Gonnelieu

Slight Valley

SIGNPOST DOWN
MINOR ROAD
TO 'HAMEAU DE LA
VACQUERIE'

Villers Plouich

50 yards

Z

while all along the front the heads and shoulders of the occupants of the trenches started to show. A few seconds later, British and Germans clambered on to their parapets and began to converge on the figures by the wire.

Two German officers were seen to be hurriedly discussing the situation, and they ordered a machine-gun team to turn their weapons towards the advancing unarmed British, but its crew had other ideas and left it where it was, pointing up towards the sky. Before a few moments were up, the two sides were all mixed together, and British and Germans, including Downe, shook hands and chatted. British and German officers shrugged and made themselves scarce.

All morning the two enemies mingled, exchanged souvenirs and had a good time. The Germans had plenty of brandy and coffee. The British had (for once) plenty of bread. The dead, who had been left out in no man's land for too long, were buried. Downe buried an old friend and also received from the enemy numerous cigars and a mouth-organ which he couldn't play.

As the day wore on, the euphoria started to wear off. These two armies had fought each other bitterly for 3½ years and in the most terrible circumstances; it would take more than a few hours to patch things up.

Downe was in the midst of the breakdown of the truce.

He saw a souvenir he had always wanted, a German brass buckle inscribed '*Gott mit Uns*'. Bending down to take the buckle off a dead body, he became aware of a shadow on the ground alongside and looking up saw a tall, thin German in spectacles, who spoke some English. Downe gave up trying to detach the buckle and listened instead to a ticking-off followed by a lecture on how the British had started the war and would lose it. He could take only so much and walked quickly away to avoid a more serious incident, noticing as he went that German NCOs were now taking advantage of the truce to mend their barbed wire defences.

Evening came and both sides withdrew to their trenches. One German tried to desert but was rebuffed – to what fate nobody knew. A few shots were fired that night. The next morning, much earlier than scheduled, a fresh battalion of the Marines came and relieved Downe and the Anson Battalion. No more fraternizing.

Source
Great War Adventures

German Spring Offensive, 1918

The First Outpost Falls: 21 March 1918

In the low-lying mists of the morning of 21 March 1918, seventy-four German divisions were massed for a great attack on the British Third and Fifth Armies on a forty-mile line south of Arras. The attack had been expected for some weeks but the British were still unprepared. Despite brave fighting, defences like the Brown Quarry Redoubt on Manchester Hill were quickly surrounded. Brave men, such as the former Prime Minister's son, Lieutenant Herbert Asquith, were lucky to escape with their lives and without being taken prisoner.

The town below was silent. St. Quentin had been a thriving industrial city but now it was in the German front line.

Asquith and his fellow officers in the Royal Field Artillery needed to range their guns. They climbed up their concrete observation post on Manchester Hill: '. . . after a short discussion as to which was the ugliest house in view, we chose a new and garish villa as our target, and succeeded in hitting it with the third round. After we had ranged six guns on this villa, the roof was blown to pieces, and a pathetic piece of furniture that looked like a four-poster bed protruded through a jagged gap between the shattered windows'.

Asquith's battery was right in the front line on top of Manchester Hill, looking out over no man's land and St. Quentin beyond. There was little doubt in Asquith's mind that the battery and the whole network of defences on Manchester Hill and Brown Quarry behind would be swept over in no time by the mass of the German attack. He fully expected to be killed or captured.

It was one o'clock in the morning of 20 March. Asquith knew a huge attack was expected, and 21 March was the likely starting date. A German officer had admitted to his interrogator that 21 March was the date, and all the signs were there: the rumbling of traffic through St. Quentin by night and silence by day, many times the usual number of wireless messages between St. Quentin and German headquarters behind the lines, and, most recently, small blue balloons which floated over no man's land, apparently to test the direction of the wind for gas. On 20 March the German artillery ranged their guns; in the early hours of the morning the gunners on Manchester Hill heard the low whistle of gas-shells coming down through the darkness; they burst in great numbers on either side of the quarry, with soft, spluttering sounds, disgusting to the ear, and they were swiftly followed by a half-hour's heavy bombardment with high explosive. Then silence.

The silence and calm were interrupted by a raid in which the Germans took prisoners from several units for interrogation. This alarmed Asquith and other officers. They quickly decided to burn all their secret documents. Asquith recalled 'the delightful sense of burning cherry-wood mingled with the acrid aroma of the divisional defence scheme, which was now crumpling up and dissolving in ashes before our eyes'.

At 4.40 in the morning of the 21st, the Germans suddenly opened the bombardment with terrific violence. Five hours later, the German army was on the move.

Early in the bombardment all the telephone wires were blown to pieces. The mist and smoke-shells made signalling by flag imposs- ible. The only other method of communication in the forward area was by runners, but gas still hung over the field; runners were often killed, and their progress through the gas was, at best, slow and precarious.

Conditions deteriorated.

'The noise was so great and varied, so many different chords of sound being mingled in this vast tornado, that an order could barely be heard even when it was shouted through a megaphone at a range of a few yards. Hundreds of heavy shells were exploding just behind us; mingled with their explosions we could hear now and then the crash of a falling tree, while high above our heads huge projectiles from long range guns passed through the sky with a metallic roar on their way to targets far behind the battlefield.'

The major in charge finally drove up through the mist in a mule-cart, bringing with him several wagons of ammunition. He had come up through a hail of German shells, looking as though he was out for a cool afternoon ride: 'His arrival at that moment was an incident that I shall not forget, and it had a very cheering effect on the men, who were greatly amused by the equipage in which he was riding and the demure appearance of his mule, which was perfectly groomed, and showed no signs of disturbance at the shattered trees or the thunder of the bombardment.'

The major made quickly for the main dug-out. He was soon in conference with Asquith and the other officers commanding batter- ies on Manchester Hill. They had all had doses of tear-gas and were affected by the smoke, so they all had bloodshot, streaming eyes and found concentration difficult. They heard that Manchester Hill and Brown Quarry were almost surrounded by the mass of German infantry. If they were to get out at all, they had to limber up the

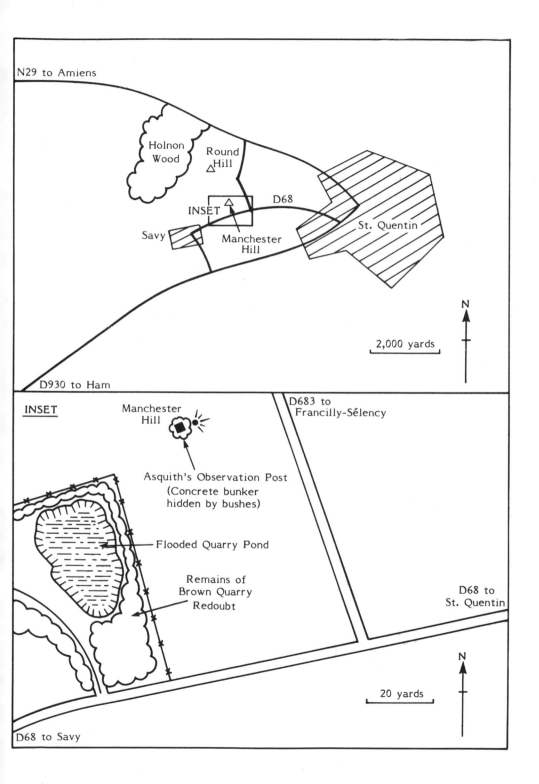

N29 to Amiens

Holnon Wood

Round △Hill

INSET △

D68

Savy

Manchester Hill

St. Quentin

N

2,000 yards

D930 to Ham

INSET

Manchester Hill

D683 to Francilly-Sélency

Asquith's Observation Post (Concrete bunker hidden by bushes)

Flooded Quarry Pond

Remains of Brown Quarry Redoubt

D68 to St. Quentin

N

20 yards

D68 to Savy

battery and get out now. The only possible route was over Round Hill and from there back to Holnon Wood.

They just managed to get out in time.

The Germans rolled over Manchester Hill, and German aeroplanes harried the retreating battery. 'The scene at this moment was one of great grandeur: the German aeroplanes came on, dipping and swerving in front of the grey lines of infantry and firing with their machine-guns at the advanced sections of the British field artillery, who replied to their fire with rifles and light machine-guns; the German artillery, whose numbers like those of their infantry, vastly exceeded our own, were pouring their fire on the battle zone behind, and there was a continuous background of thunder which seemed to extend for many miles on either side of us beneath the dun-coloured sky in which the smoke of battle was mingled with the remains of the mist.'

The timely arrival of the major had enabled Asquith and the batteries on Manchester Hill to retreat in good order – always keeping one gun-team firing to cover them.

They were exceptional. All down the front, the British Third and Fifth Armies were starting to crumble, routed, with heavy losses.

Source
H. Asquith, *Moments of Memory*

German Spring Offensive, 1918

The Artillery Flees: 21 March 1918

Of all the people who knew the attack was coming, Arthur Behrend was probably the best informed. He had interviewed personally a number of German prisoners and, as adjutant in the 90th Brigade of the Royal Garrison Artillery, he received messages from air reconnaissance about German troop movements and German artillery. He would work out from the messages he received exactly where the enemy was massing and then order the six batteries under his command to range their guns and fire accordingly. But Behrend did not grasp the scale of what was going on. It was a great shock to him when, after five months of relative peace at his Beugny headquarters, giant shells started falling around him, blowing up the shacks he, his colonel and his staff had been living in, blowing up all the telephone wires he had not yet got round to burying, and killing his friends. It was five in the morning on 21 March 1918.

It was Behrend's job to stay at his headquarters and to give and receive information and orders. He was in touch with corps head-quarters by an unreliable wireless and, as most of the lines were blown down, with his batteries by runner or pigeon. An exception was Battery Toc 1 to which the cable incredibly survived the first German artillery onslaught. Toc 1 was connected by one of the very few underground cables to Tusculum, an advance look-out post.

The attack unfolded quickly.

Phone message from Tusculum: 'SOS on Left Division Front. All our batteries seem to have opened out.'

Runner from Toc 1: 'Lines still down. Enemy fire persistent . . .'

Phone message from Tusculum: 'Enemy advancing on Lagnicourt at 11.30. Numbers of infantry and cavalry and tanks on right of Pronville.'

Runner from Toc 3: 'Officer commanding Battery wounded; two Other Ranks killed.'

Phone message from Toc 1: '. . . numerous Huns in Leech Avenue and Lynx Support. Pretty heavy fire would be appreciated.' And later, just before pulling out, Toc 1's frantic message: 'Large bodies of Boche advancing up valley . . . am engaging. Juice running short.'

All day, Behrend tried his best to keep in touch. He was able to get hold of information from brigade headquarters, and originally from air reconnaissance, about where important enemy concentrations were, and he was in touch with look-out posts as well. The trouble was that the attack was advancing so quickly that information was usually out of date when Behrend received it, let alone when a runner had survived a gauntlet of shells and machine-guns to reach one of the batteries. His artillery was nevertheless very important in slow-ing down the enemy on that crucial day, consistently strafing German communication trenches and vital supply lines such as the road from Quéant to Lagnicourt.

Brigade headquarters sent Behrend a message to pull out. It was now 4.30 p.m. and possibly too late. Behrend decided to go and see for himself if there were any chance of getting Toc 1, Toc 4 and, most dangerously, Toc 3, out of the battle intact. Amazingly, his official car had not been hit and he set out chauffeur-driven through the village of Beugny, towards the front.

The damage around his headquarters had not been too bad after the initial barrage, and Behrend was shocked but not really

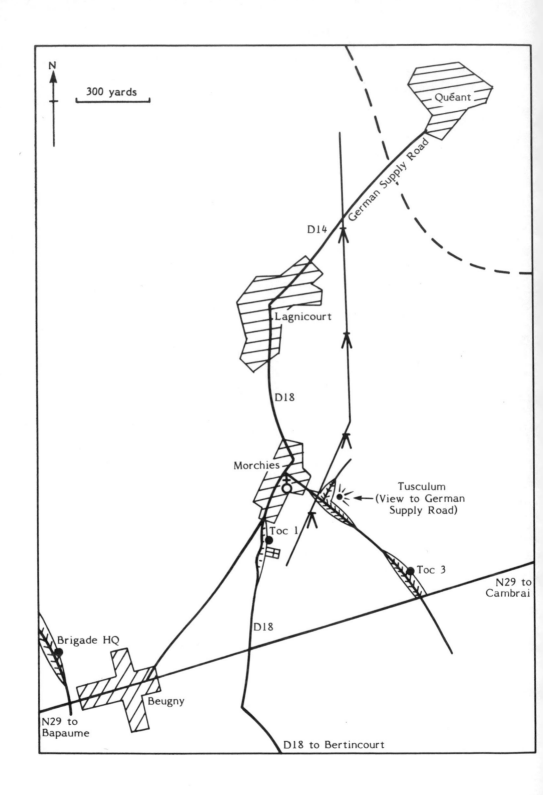

N

300 yards

Quéant

German Supply Road

D14

Lagnicourt

D18

Morchies

Tusculum
(View to German
Supply Road)

Toc 1

Toc 3

N29 to
Cambrai

Brigade HQ

D18

Beugny

N29 to
Bapaume

D18 to Bertincourt

surprised by the devastation of Beugny. Nearer the front, the devastation got worse. What was left of the batteries would have to be either dismantled and extracted or abandoned.

By the time he reached Toc 1, the dismantling process was nearly complete. Toc 4 would have to hurry if they were to avoid simply blowing everything up and running.

Toc 3's position turned out to be 150 yards from the enemy, but when Behrend crept up to the position, leaving the car behind, torch in one hand and revolver in the other, he found that they had already managed to escape – in record time. So he crept back to the car where restarting the motor had a predictable effect:

'Thompson gave the starting-handle a turn; the noise of the engine vibrated through the cold stillness with startling loudness. A burst of fire from a machine-gun which sounded less than a hundred yards away startled me out of my wits – it was so totally unexpected and hitherto everything had been so quiet. The bullets seemed to swish all round us. Thompson let in the clutch with an even bigger jerk than usual, the Vauxhall leapt away, and for the next mile he drove like a man possessed. Before the War he had driven a Landaulette belonging to an old lady who lived near Manchester, and the Colonel often used to grumble because he drove so slowly. I wondered what the old lady would have said had she been with us now.'

Behrend drove back to his headquarters, where everything was now packed up. He picked up the colonel and they drove away. To fight another day.

Source
A. Behrend, *As from Kemmel Hill*

German Spring Offensive, 1918

Rearguard Action: 22 and 23 March 1918

'Come on, man; you'll be killed if you stop here!'

'Och awa' wi' ye. I'm aff duty!'

'You'd better come. It's not safe here, mind.'

'I'm aff duty, I tell ye!'

There was not much time to waste on a lunatic like that. Any minute Signaller Aubrey Wade expected the grey uniforms and coal-scuttle helmets of the German army to come round the corner.

Wade was halfway back to his heavy artillery battery when a shell shrieked into the hut where the Scotsman had been resting. The Germans were advancing, and the retreat was on.

The Germans nearly cut off Wade and his battery, which had retired through Jussy up the long hill south to Faillouël. In the field where they stopped at last late on 21 March, they could get little sleep and little food but they prepared to make a stand. The morning revealed that no one else was making a stand. In the icy dawn Wade saw routed infantry everywhere running away from the advancing mass of Germans.

The major in charge decided to harry the Germans from the field where the battery had stopped for the night. They fired all day and kept firing. An aeroplane flew overhead and signalled to the German artillery, which got more accurate but still had little effect.

The German advance faltered.

Wade's battery was the only one on the British side firing for miles around, and it was effective. For twenty-four hours the Germans stopped advancing up the Jussy valley and waited for their artillery to get near enough to give decent support to an advance uphill to take Wade's battery.

That night there was little sleep. By midday on the 23rd, the Germans, now with full artillery support, were on the move again and on the move uphill to the battery. 'Limber up!' The guns kept firing even while the gun-teams were attached.

Everyone rushed and sweated, pulled and pushed to get the guns ready to move out of the field. The first gun made it and moved along to the sunken lane. The second followed. Then the third. Now there was only one gun in the field. 'Over-eagerness and the psychological effect on the drivers of being last out had resulted in their trying to take the gate with them. The Major was there, directing the efforts of sweating gunners and steadying the frantic horses.' Then on top of everything else came the whining scream of shells, one after the other, pounding the fields around them and making the horses snort with fright.

'Who are you and where are you going?' Wade turned round, startled, to find out who was sliding down the bank of the sunken lane towards him from the side where the Germans were now very close.

It was a young infantry officer. He had obviously been having a rough time. His face was dirty and bloodstained, his uniform nearly in tatters. Wade realized with a shock that he was mad.

Wade identified his battery and said they were retiring.

'Retire? Retire? RETIRE?!' crescendoed the officer. Then he

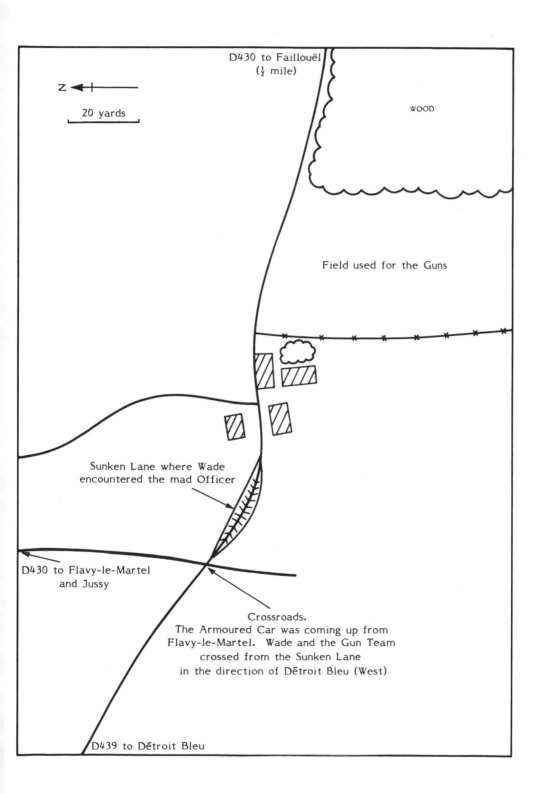

Z ←

20 yards

D430 to Faillouël
(½ mile)

WOOD

Field used for the Guns

Sunken Lane where Wade
encountered the mad Officer

D430 to Flavy-le-Martel
and Jussy

Crossroads.
The Armoured Car was coming up from
Flavy-le-Martel. Wade and the Gun Team
crossed from the Sunken Lane
in the direction of Détroit Bleu (West)

D439 to Détroit Bleu

added dreamily: '. . . but you can't retire. Don't you know the German army is advancing up this slope?'

'Yes, sir.'

'Well, damn you, you most stop them! Now, come along all of you. Get those rifles off the guns and climb up on the bank and hold the enemy. Get a move on, damn you!'

Wade hesitated.

The officer raised his rifle and prepared to shoot him.

Meanwhile the last gun in the field was freed. The major gave the order to advance. Nothing happened. He came rushing up frantically to Wade's team to see what was going on. The infantry officer slunk back over the side of the sunken road to face the Germans alone.

The battery hurried down the sunken lane where they were well protected by the embankments. Then they moved out towards the dangerously exposed crossroads.

'At a fast trot that threatened to break into a gallop we rode into full view of a German armoured car that was stuck there on the road up from Flavy with its machine-gun spitting and cracking at the unexpected target that had so suddenly presented itself. Faster and faster grew the pace; the noise of the guns and vehicles behind us increased to a sustained roar, and round we went with our heads down alongside the necks of our horses and the air full of eerie whistlings.'

A mad scramble for four more days, sometimes just minutes ahead of the German advance, brought Wade and his battery to safety. They were not destined to stay out of the fighting for long.

Source
A. Wade, *The War of the Guns*

Epilogue

No one could deny that for most people at the beginning of the century life was drudgery, life was boring. Long hours at the same work for low pay were typical. So the war for many offered a way out into adventure and perhaps glory too. Most soldiers were not casualties; many had great stories to tell when they got home. For them the First World War created a sense of belonging and purpose, despite all the tedium and discipline of the day-to-day life of a soldier and the mental and physical scars some carried for the rest of their lives. This was a new experience, an escape from routine and a chance to participate in a victory.

One crucial reason why the front line experiences were new was the gulf between the battlefields and society as a whole. The population at home and behind the lines all participated in a great modern industrial state at war. The soldier at the front, however, participated in a primitive struggle with rifles, bayonets and sharpened spades. The industrial state enabled the biggest fighting force in history to be put in the field but once there, the type of battle encountered by the infantrymen was often basic.

After four years, from August 1918 victory was inevitable. Although the British Army bore the major brunt of these last few months of the War, some of the positive adventure of soldiering, lost in the mud of the Somme and Ypres, returned. The bad moments were soon forgotten. Final victory came on 11 November 1918 at 11 a.m., although when the Armistice was signed, many soldiers greeted it with scepticism rather than elation.

By the words of the men themselves, by the sight and feel of the ground itself, this book has uncovered something new. Its study of man in his First World War environment has uncovered the sheer exhilaration of soldiering at the time. It looks beyond the casualty figures and the mud and the horror, and thus it provides new insights. Sometimes the war was terrible in the suffering it caused and sometimes it was rather aimless; but this combined study of personal record and terrain over the whole of the war reveals a soldiery committed to a cause, for the most part competently generalled in conditions of very quickly changing technology.

Above all, men in the front line experienced the very extremes of the emotions of fear, comradeship, hate, pity – far beyond nearly every experience of ordinary life. It is these emotional extremes which are the very essence of life in battle. It is these emotional extremes which this book puts into context, providing an insight into man at his worst and his best.

Bibliography

Asquith, H., *Moments of Memory: recollections and impressions* (Hutchinson, 1937)

Bairnsfather, B., *Bullets and Billets* (Richards, 1917)

Baker, H. A., *History of the 7th Field Company Royal Engineers, 1914–1918* (Institute of Royal Engineers, 1931)

Becton, J., and E. L. Odell, *Hunting the Hun* (Appleton, 1918)

Behrend, A., *As from Kemmel Hill* (Eyre & Spottiswoode, 1963)

Blunden, E., *Undertones of War* (Cobden-Sanderson, 1928)

Clapham, H. S., *Mud and Khaki: the memoirs of an incomplete soldier* (Hutchinson, 1930)

Clark, A., *The Donkeys* (Hutchinson, 1961)

Coppard, G., *With a Machine-gun to Cambrai: the tale of a young Tommy in Kitchener's Army* (HMSO, 1969)

Craster, J. M., ed., *Fifteen Rounds a Minute: the Grenadiers at war, August to December 1914* (Macmillan, 1976)

Edmonds, C. (pseudonym of C. E. Carrington), *A Subaltern at War: being a memoir of the Great War from the point of view of a romantic young man* (Peter Davies, 1929) *A Martial Medley* (Eric Partridge, 1931)

Fox, C. L., *Narrative of the 502 (Wessex) Field Company, Royal Engineers, 1915–1919* (Rees, 1920)

Graves, R., *Goodbye to All That* (revised edition; Cassell, 1957)

Great War Adventures (afterwards *War Adventures*): *true stories by ex-fighting men by land, sea and air* (Heinemann, various editions 1932 to 1942)

Grieve, W. G. and B. Newman, *Tunnellers* (Jenkins, 1936)

Haigh, R. H. and P. W. Turner, eds., *The Long Carry: the journal of stretcher-bearer Frank Dunham* (Pergamon, 1970)

Hammerton, J., ed., *I Was There! The human story of the Great War, 1914–1918* (Amalgamated Press, 1938)

Hitchcock, F. C., *Stand To: a diary of the trenches 1915–18* (Hurst & Blackett, 1937)

Hutchison, G. S., *Warrior* (Hutchinson, 1932)

Junger, E., *The Storm of Steel* (Chatto & Windus, 1929) *Copse 125: a chronicle from the trench warfare of 1918* (Chatto & Windus, 1930)

Kelly, D. V., *Thirty-nine Months with the 'Tigers' (the 110th Infantry Brigade) 1915–1918* (Hollis & Carter, 1930)

Macdonald, L., *They Called It Passchendaele* (Michael Joseph, 1978)

Macgill, P., *The Great Push: an episode of the Great War* (Jenkins, 1916)

Malins, G., *How I Filmed the War* (Jenkins, 1919)

Maxwell, J., *Hell's Bells and Mademoiselles* (Angus & Robertson, 1932)

Mellersh, H. E. L., *Schoolboy into War* (Kimber, 1978)

Middlebrook, M., *First Day on the Somme* (Lane, 1971)

Mitchell, F., *Tank Warfare: the story of the tanks of the Great War* (Nelson, 1933)
Morris, A., *The Balloonatics* (Jarrolds, 1970)
Pedley, J. H., *Only This* (Graphic, 1927)
Purdon, P., ed., *Everyman at War* (Dent, 1930)
Richards, F., *Old Soldiers Never Die* (Faber & Faber, 1933)
Rogerson, S., *Twelve Days* (Barker, 1933)
Sassoon, S., *Memoirs of an Infantry Officer* (Faber & Faber, 1930)
Scott, F., *The Great War as I Saw It* (Clarke & Stuart, 1934)
Toland, J., *No Man's Land: the story of 1918* (Methuen, 1982)
Vaughan, E. C., *Some Desperate Glory* (Warne, 1981)
Wade, A., *The War of the Guns: Western Front 1917 and 1918* (Batsford, 1936)
Westmann, S. K., *Surgeon in the Kaiser's Army* (Kimber, 1968)

Index